One-Armed Mac

The story of
Squadron Leader James MacLachlan
DSO, DFC and 2 Bars,
Czech War Cross
based upon his diaries and letters

BRIAN CULL
and
ROLAND SYMONS

GRUB STREET · LONDON

Published by
Grub Street
The Basement
10 Chivalry Road
London SW11 1HT

British Library Cataloguing in Publication Data
Cull, Brian
    One-armed Mac: the story of Squadron Leader James
    MacLachlan DSO, DFC and 2 Bars, Czech War Cross
    1. MacLachlan, James Archibald Finlay 2. Air pilots,
    Military – Great Britain – Biography 3. Amputees –
    Great Britain – Biography 4. World War, 1939-1945 –
    Aerial operations, British
    I. Title II. Symons, Roland
    940.5'44941'092

ISBN 1 904010 46 6

Typeset by Pearl Graphics, Hemel Hempstead

Printed and bound in Great Britain by
Biddles Ltd, Guildford and King's Lynn

BRIAN CULL is the author of the following Grub Street titles:

AIR WAR FOR YUGOSLAVIA, GREECE and CRETE 1940-41 with
    Christopher Shores and Nicola Malizia
MALTA: THE HURRICANE YEARS 1940-41 with Christopher Shores
    and Nicola Malizia
MALTA: THE SPITFIRE YEAR 1942 with Christopher Shores and Nicola Malizia
BLOODY SHAMBLES Volume 1 with Christopher Shores and Yasuho Izawa
BLOODY SHAMBLES Volume 2 with Christopher Shores and Yasuho Izawa
SPITFIRES OVER ISRAEL with Shlomo Aloni and David Nicolle
TWELVE DAYS IN MAY with Bruce Lander and Heinrich Weiss
WINGS OVER SUEZ with David Nicolle and Shlomo Aloni
249 AT WAR
THE DESERT HAWKS with Leo Nomis
HURRICANES OVER TOBRUK with Don Minterne
SPITFIRES OVER SICILY with Nicola Malizia and Frederick Galea
WITH THE YANKS IN KOREA Volume 1 with Dennis Newton
HURRICANES OVER MALTA with Frederick Galea
BUFFALOES OVER SINGAPORE with Mark Haselden & Paul Sortehaug

CONTENTS

4

INTRODUCTION &
ACKNOWLEDGEMENTS

**This book is dedicated to the memories of
Sqn Ldr James MacLachlan DSO, DFC & 2 Bars,
Czech Military Cross – died of wounds 31 July 1943 and
Flt Lt Gordon MacLachlan – killed in action 16 April 1943**

This is the Happy Warrior; this is He
That every man in arms should wish to be.

William Wordsworth

This is the story of a hero, as far as possible in his own words. The main part of James MacLachlan's story is taken from his diaries, letters, logbooks and official operation reports to which we have added an explanatory commentary where necessary. The main sources of information for this book have come from James MacLachlan's sister, Mrs Elizabeth Scratton. She has kindly allowed us access to her brother's logbooks, correspondence and a copy of the diary that her husband Mike transcribed from the original. Many of the photographs used within have been made available to us by Liz, whom we warmly thank for her and Mike's hospitality and encouragement on the occasions of our visits to their charming home.

We would like to thank all those who have provided information concerning James MacLachlan. They have ranged from school friends and relations to flying crew who served with or flew with him. For their help, information and advice, we are very grateful; these include John Orr-Erwing (a cousin), F.E. White, Wg Cdr David Annand, Sqn Ldr Leslie Davies DFM, Wg Cdr David Prichard DSO, Sqn Ldr H.W. Bennett DFC, Alan Thomsett, Sqn Ldr Bam Bamberger DFC & Bar, Flt Lt Jim Pickering AFC, and Sqn Ldr Colin Downes. We also appreciate the assistance of our German friends Heinrich Weiss and

Gerhard Stemmer; and the information provided by Joss Leclercq; and, as ever, Brian's gratitude is extended to Jack Lee, gentleman and scholar.

We acknowledge the help received from the staffs of the RAF Museum, Air Historical Branch, Imperial War Museum and the Public Record Office. Books consulted include *The Flying Sailor* by André Jubelin, *Shot Down in Flames* by Geoffrey Page, *Valiant Wings* by Norman Franks, *Number One in War and Peace* by Norman Franks and Mike O'Connor, *History of 73 Squadron* by Don Minterne, *The Mouchotte Diaries* edited by André Dezarrois, *Night Hawk* by Roger Darlington, *The Big Show* by Pierre Clostermann, *Malta: The Hurricane Years 1940-41* by Christopher Shores and Brian Cull with Nicola Malizia, *Hurricanes over Tobruk* by Brian Cull and Don Minterne, and *Hurricanes over Malta* by Brian Cull and Frederick Galea.

In a letter home in 1942, James MacLachlan mentioned he hoped that his diary had found a publisher. Unfortunately, it never did. Perhaps 61 years later it is time that it saw the light of day.

* * *

Brian Cull thanks his wife Val for her continuing support and encouragement in helping him to complete this book, his sixteenth for Grub Street, none of which would have come to fruition without her at his side and steering him through difficult times.

Roland Symons similarly thanks his wife Penny for her understanding of his obsession in documenting the life of James MacLachlan, an 'old boy' of his school.

Brian Cull and Roland Symons, 2003

FOREWORD

Liz Scratton (née MacLachlan)

I have been very interested to read the edited and expanded diaries of my brother James (Jay). I realise that I saw him from a very different point of view to his contemporaries. Perhaps it would be of interest to say something here about James and his family background before the war.

He had a dramatic change in circumstances when father died in 1928. After his death, father's business was declared bankrupt and almost everything of value had to be sold to repay creditors. He had had a very good offer from Unilever to take over the business, and for my father to be Managing Director, but his mother – our grandmother – would not allow the business to be sold. From a relatively carefree life in the country, James and the family – there were six of us children – moved to Southampton to live in very straitened circumstances.

I remember him as an older brother, to be respected, obeyed and stood up for when away. He was full of ideas, always making different things and gathering an odd selection of wildlife and pets in our town garden. I remember an owl, a squirrel, and a magpie, which shared our summer holiday on a farm. We also had canaries, the aviary made by Jay, guinea pigs, chickens, bantams, rabbits with a warren dug under poor Hugh's vegetable garden, white mice in 'flats' made by Jay, which Archie and I rented from him, rent rarely collected, and a kitten. He was always very careful of money. One Christmas, Archie, the youngest, received a huge parcel. After unwrapping many layers, a sugar mouse with obvious teeth marks underneath, was all it contained. Jay said he had had to pay to have the carving done. On another occasion he made a papier-mâché boat, fitted it with a steam engine and we sailed it across a local pond until it sunk.

At Monkton Combe School he appears to have been thought of as a 'loner'. This may have occurred because we were a large, pretty close family, and did not feel much need to make outside friends. He did make friends with whom he kept in close contact. During his short stay at home between leaving school and starting his Short Service Commission he made fireworks for Archie and me. He made an aerial railway on mother's washing line, and a marvellous 'nest' high in an old lime tree. Unseen, from there we could drop water-bombs on other children. A lot of winter evenings were spent playing card games, not with playing cards, but with cards of four different colours, totalling 14, and when we were given Monopoly we seemed to play that endlessly, gaining our first knowledge of London and property values. Mother read aloud to us a great deal, and we all absorbed my brother's holiday tasks. Just prewar, I remember during a prayer meeting being held in our old nursery, a pistol parted the curtains on the garden door, and Jay appeared! Life was always exciting when he was around. He used to bring friends home. As our home was in Southampton, mother and Archie and I spent most holidays with relatives, until the latter part of the war when we really enjoyed the freedom of working on a small farm in the New Forest. Sadly, I didn't see much of him during the war, he was always busy or away, and I was at boarding school.

Liz Scratton

MAC REMEMBERED

I was posted from RAF Cranwell Electrical and Wireless School to No.88 Squadron at Boscombe Down in March 1938. At that time WOp/AGs were in a 'pool' and pilots just put down the name of any one they wanted. When crews were formed, Mac asked me to be his WOp/AG. I was delighted. Mac was considered to be a very good pilot but a bit wild!

Whatever Mac planned to do always ended up with us doing, or starting every trip, low-level. Low-level was his life and I was delighted to take part. With Mac I felt just as happy and safe at zero feet as I was at 10,000 feet, but our observers thought otherwise and kept changing. One thought Mac was a bloody idiot who would soon kill everyone. Something similar was reported to his brother Gordon in June 1941 when he met someone who knew Mac at Boscombe. He said he never knew if he was a 'reckless sod or a damn fine pilot' until the war started, and then he knew he was all of the latter and a bit of the first.

He treated the Battle like a Hurricane – I am sure it saved our lives – and aerobatics were tried at all heights. He taught me to fly the Battle and was quite impressed. As a result of this he recommended me for a pilot's course. After returning from France – and another tour, on 2 Group Blenheims – I did qualify as a pilot. Mac kept an eye on my flying career. The last time we met was at RAF West Malling when I was flying night fighter Mosquitoes. Mac arrived in his black and dark green Mustang and asked me to join him and Flt Lt Geoffrey Page in a low-flying unit. I said I would be delighted but Mac was killed shortly after.

He will always be remembered.

Sqn Ldr Leslie Davies DFM
WOp/AG No.88 Squadron 1938-40

My first meeting with (then) Flt Lt James MacLachlan was on the King George V Dock in Glasgow, where he was responsible for twelve Hurricane fighters being loaded on to the very old aircraft carrier HMS *Argus*. I was a sergeant pilot. The *Argus* was en route to the Mediterranean and the Hurricanes, with Mac in the lead, were to fly off at dawn on 17 November 1940, to reinforce Malta's air defences. The operation was a disaster and eight Hurricanes were lost; only Mac and three other pilots reached Malta safely and one other was rescued by a Sunderland flying boat. Indirectly, Mac probably saved my life, for he excluded me from flying off the *Argus* as I had only one hour flying experience on the Hurricane.

Mac was a cheerful, friendly, extrovert character whose aggression and leadership as a fighter pilot were to come to the fore when the Luftwaffe moved in force to airfields in Sicily in January 1941, followed by major assaults against Malta. Our Hurricanes were well out-numbered by the German fighters (and bombers), but Mac frequently led the fight to the enemy with unbounded enthusiasm and with little thought of self-preservation. Though the Messerschmitts always had height and speed advantage, whenever I flew with Mac he always attempted to press home attacks whatever the adverse situation. Flying together in such combat circumstances or sharing the doubtful protection of an old bus when being ground strafed, built up a close bond between pilots and Mac was no exception. When Mac was shot down on 16 February 1941 and lost his arm, his enthusiasm and leadership were greatly missed, but Mac himself was in good spirits when I eventually visited him in hospital, and he still retained his passion for flying. He achieved his objective by being fitted with an artificial arm, which allowed him once again to fly in combat.

In late 1942, Mac visited me in Northern Ireland were I was then based. His surprise arrival, flying a Hurricane using his artificial arm, was to try to persuade the Northern Ireland RAFHQ to release me from duties so I could join his new squadron. Unfortunately, it was not to be, so we discussed over lunch the merits of an artificial arm and that was the last time I had the privilege of his companionship. Mac gave his life for his country in July 1943.

Sqn Ldr C.S. 'Bam' Bamberger DFC & Bar
Sergeant Pilot No.261 Squadron 1940-41

I first met Mac when he arrived on Malta on 17 November 1940. The fighter defence of Malta was 261 Squadron, with half a dozen serviceable Hurricanes and occasionally a Gladiator. The opposing enemy in Sicily was more than 200 aircraft of the Regia Aeronautica. This was a 'no-win' situation. The best that 261 Squadron could do was to shoot down, in chance encounters, Italian bombers and avoid combat with Italian fighters. The loss of our fighters would have left the island without an air force. The AOC had grounded one RAF pilot for engaging an Italian fighter.

On joining 261 Squadron, Mac became officer commanding A Flight. I was in B Flight. Operating a four-watch system, we only met the pilots of the other two flights at change-over time. There were differences of opinion in the tactics to be used, and Mac favoured an aggressive attitude to all enemy aircraft. In January, about twenty pilots with Hurricanes joined 261 Squadron from the Middle East, where the fighter squadrons had been successful against Italian aircraft in Cyrenaica. It was hoped by the AOC that the RAF pilots from the desert would be beneficial to Malta, though by January 1941, the problem was German fighters.

Mac devised a plan whereby a flight of Hurricanes would fly in a conventional formation below a flight of Messerschmitt 109s. When they attacked the Hurricanes from above, the Hurricanes would change their formation to a defensive circle until opportune targets crossed the path of the Hurricanes. When this tactic was tried by A Flight, it was my day off. Some of us had clubbed together to rent a flat in Valetta, and I had gone there. When the air raid warning was given, I went onto the balcony of the flat and could see a Hurricane chasing a 109, and a 109 behind the Hurricane. There was a short burst of gunfire and the rear 109 overtook the Hurricane, whose engine had obviously stopped. After what seemed a long time, I saw the pilot leave the aircraft and his parachute open. This was Mac, although I did not know who it was until I returned to the Squadron. Two more Hurricanes of A Flight were also badly damaged.

There could have been a big loss of confidence in the squadron, but the reports on Mac's injuries at first gave some hopes of recovery. When he flew the Magister solo two weeks after his arm was amputated it proved to be a necessary boost to morale. That he intended to continue flying after his experiences in France, the Battle of Britain, the *Argus* losses and now this personal injury, showed that determination could overcome difficulties. Mac went to Cairo some weeks after this. I followed in April. He was waiting for a passage to the UK. We celebrated our meeting. I did not meet him again.

Flt Lt James Pickering AFC
Sergeant Pilot No.261 Squadron 1940-41

Of all single-minded men Mac seemed to me the purest and loftiest I had ever met . . . Slender, with an obstinate expression in his triangular countenance, he exhibited a broad black line round the irises of his luminous eyes and wore a slight reddish moustache under a sharply pointed nose. Mac was a born leader. In a branch of the Service where, one may as well admit it, true discipline did not exist except in battle, Mac introduced it with ease into the smallest details of squadron life.

Mac was already a legendary figure. Other cripples gravitated to him as to one who had been the subject of a miracle. They gained new strength when they saw him spring in triumph from the cockpit of his black aircraft.

Rear-Admiral André Jubelin, Free French Navy
Fighter Pilot No.1 Squadron 1942

Extracted from *The Flying Sailor* by André Jubelin.

In a letter Rear-Admiral Jubelin wrote to Mac's youngest sister Liz in 1955, he added:

"There is no better way to tell you than what I wrote in my book, all the friendship and the deep admiration I had for your brother. Amongst all of the heroes it was my privilege to encounter he stood out as the perfect incarnation of what constitutes a hero.

I do not know if sometimes you have occasion to come to France. I would like you to know that it would always be a great happiness for us to welcome you here. We would enjoy, I think – you and I – talking about one whom we both loved, and believe me, it is from the bottom of my heart that my wife and I would welcome you."

One of Mac's visits while in the USA in 1943 was to the US Army Air Corps base at Clewiston where I was one of many embryonic RAF and Commonwealth pilots receiving flying training. He thrilled us with his stories of air fighting.

He was certainly a colourful character and he put on an impressive display of aerobatics in his P-40 Tomahawk while operating the throttle, the propeller and other controls with an artificial left arm. He dramatically described his combat over Malta. Recounting this to me, he said – 'You know, they say that when you are dying your life passes before you in a flash. Well, I can tell you, old boy, that's a load of crap!

If I thought of anything at the time it was of the girls I'd had with a sense of regret there had not been more!'

A short list of unforgettable characters I met while flying in the RAF would certainly include James MacLachlan.

Sqn Ldr Colin Downes, US Air Medal
RAF Cadet Pilot USAAC Base Clewiston 1943

Once qualified, Colin Downes returned to the UK and joined 65 Squadron flying Mustangs during the closing stages of World War II. He remained in the RAF postwar and in 1953 was posted to Korea where he flew F-86s in action with the USAF, for which he was awarded the US Air Medal.

CHAPTER I

EARLY LIFE

James Archibald Findlay MacLachlan arrived in this world on 1 April
1919 at Styal in Cheshire, the second of six children to be born to
Helen and Hugh MacLachlan. The MacLachlans, with their strong
Christian beliefs, lived in middle-class comfort at the family home at
Styal, where Hugh was an oil and chemical manufacturer, but
following her husband's premature death from peritonitis in 1928,
Helen moved her large family to Southampton to be near her parents.
It was probably her connection with the mission-field – her father,
Archibald Orr-Ewing, was with the China Inland Mission, and her
father-in-law was a member of the Plymouth Brethren – that led to
James being boarded at Monkton Combe School just south of Bath in
September 1931, when he was twelve years old. He initially attended
the Junior School, having first completed two years at King Edward's
School in Southampton. Monkton Combe had, as it still has, strong
evangelical and missionary associations. James's brothers Hugh,
Gordon and Archie would follow in his footsteps.

At Monkton, James proved to be no great academic, although he had
a talent for poetry and would make up libellous rhymes about his
contemporaries and members of staff. He was not a star on the games
field either, though he rowed and played rugby; he was never a very
'clubbable' person with lots of friends, but maintained his individuality
as best he could in the hothouse atmosphere of a boarding school. He
did, however, have a great love of the countryside and wild animals,
which allowed him to go off on lone expeditions. He had his own
menagerie of jackdaws, red squirrels and a sparrowhawk, but
entrepreneurial skills were also seen when he supplied the biology lab
with the rabbits they needed for dissection, and various boys with
hedgehogs and grass snakes as pets!

He was never a prefect and never rose to any high rank in the
school's Officers' Training Corps. To his masters he seemed devoid of

all ambition. So, wherein lies the origin of the highly decorated fighter pilot and wartime commander? A contemporary of his at Monkton, F.E. White, provides a possible answer:

> "Perhaps it arose from a desire to prove himself to himself and to preserve his very marked individuality and independence. He did not want to put himself in a position where authority could compromise or dilute these traits; neither did he want them restricted by commitments to binding friendships. So he went to considerable lengths to keep himself free of school trammels and serious dependence on, and involvement with friends."

He did have a practical side to his nature. He spent a lot of time in the carpentry shop using his hands and ingenuity to considerable effect. With only scrap pieces of wood and metal and the use of the then limited equipment available, he manufactured in secret a .22 pistol complete in every detail. F.E. White continues:

> "When it was ready for a test firing those of us who were to be involved wisely decided that certain safety precautions needed to be taken. The pistol was firmly attached to a stake near a cowshed and pointed at the trunk of a large elm tree. Lookouts were posted and about four of us then went into shelter in the cowshed from where Jay pulled at a long piece of string attached to the trigger. The pistol certainly fired, but as we were unable to locate a bullet mark on the trunk of the elm tree, it was not possible to ascertain the range and accuracy of the pistol."

James had intended to use the pistol against stray cats that persecuted his tame birds, but after the test firing it was hidden away, to be taken home at a later date. A similar experiment in 1939, with a genuine service revolver, led to a self-inflicted wound through the hand! That he was brave and fearless was demonstrated on many occasions. He was a boarder at a house situated a mile away from the school up a long, steep lane. James soon gained the reputation of being able to cycle from Combe Ridge to school faster than anybody else and when he found there was no challenge to this claim, he decided to go one better and do the journey on roller skates towed behind a bicycle. He accomplished this in such a dramatic fashion that by the time he reached Monkton Combe, the bearings on the rollers of the skates had burned out. A ban was imposed immediately on any further attempt to undertake this feat!

Inevitably, he had to think of the future and of what to do with his life. He wrote, when aged fourteen, in a religious vein about this to mother:

"I don't know really what I am to do when I am grown up. I don't think I have had any definite call to the mission field, but I am willing to go if God wants me to, so please pray."

In 1936 the MacLachlan family holiday took them to Comrie near Crief and back to their roots in Scotland. While there, James and his brother Gordon spent two weeks with their cousins at St Andrews, and it was while staying with the cousins that James went up for a five shilling pleasure flight at the RAF Leuchars Open Day. It was that experience which settled his future. In May, he wrote to mother:

"Last Wednesday Captain Pullein-Thompson, the careers specialist came. He said that if I wanted to go in for flying and could not afford Cranwell, the best thing I could do was to join the Short Service Commission. Please pray about it because I do want to do what God wants me to do . . . Captain Pullein-Thompson said that to be good at rowing and games was better than being good at work, but of course I must do my best at everything."

James eventually secured his School Certificate and, with the blessing of mother, gained entry into the RAF. He was one month short of his eighteenth birthday.

CHAPTER II

TRAINING BEGINS

On 1 March 1937, Mac – as he was to become known in the RAF – arrived at No.10 Elementary and Reserve Flying Training School at RAF Yatesbury in Wiltshire, which was run by the Bristol Aeroplane Company, to begin his training for the Royal Air Force. The RAF Year Book for 1937 outlines the training programme for potential pilots:

> 'The training period is now divided into three stages. For the first stage the pupil goes to a civil school, which is operated on a commercial basis under an Air Ministry contract. The pupil is under strict discipline, although he lives in civilian conditions and does not wear uniform. Here he learns to handle a light aeroplane properly and has elementary instruction in instrument flying and simple cross-country flying. This course lasts eight weeks.'

Mac was obviously thrilled to be at Yatesbury. His first letter to mother on the day he arrived fairly bubbles with enthusiasm and the legacy of Monktonian Puritanism:

> "It is simply super here. I have made friends with an awfully decent chap called Alistair. He lives near Dunoon. He does not drink and is 20. I am sleeping next to a very decent Canadian who came over here to play ice hockey. There are about 25 planes here. I am in B Flight. We go up tomorrow. I have been issued with my flying kit. A great, fur-lined thing with zip-fasteners. This afternoon we had a lecture on parachutes and I was fitted with one.
>
> Most people here seem very nice – they mostly seem to smoke – I have been offered six fags so far, but of course have not accepted. As no women are allowed in the club I have no fears. There is not the slightest need to drink or smoke, in fact most people seem to envy me not smoking as it is so expensive. There is a billiard table, full size and 3d a game. Tennis and squash are free. When we play snooker, at which I am getting quite good, we usually play for beers

i.e., the pair who lose give the winners $1/2$ pint each. I have ginger beer if I win which costs 1d less, so of course they are glad I don't drink beer. I have not lost a game yet! Almost all the chaps here are very decent. Most have filthy minds but that is only natural I suppose. Do pray that I can keep from swearing because everyone does it and I find I do it without thinking. They all say 'Christ' or 'Jesus' – it sounds awful. Mess bills are £2 10s a week and laundry is about 5s, so that is where all the money goes. I get paid on Friday and pay my mess bill on Saturday.

There is a very nice lounge with a wireless, where I am writing. None of the other chaps know hardly anything about the books I have been reading, so I am one up on them. Some people say we do not have to dress for dinner tonight, but I am not sure. Alistair says he will help me with mine and teach me to dance if it is necessary. There is one chap with a Crusader badge, but I have not had a chance to speak to him yet. I am longing to go up. My instructor's name is Mr Sharp. I go up at 9am tomorrow. My room (we have one each) has hot and cold water laid on. I am not very struck with the food I have seen so far, but all is clean and plain."

As with thousands of other would-be pilots, Mac's first flight was in a Tiger Moth – 45 minutes of straight and level flight in G-ADOA on the day following his arrival. He was obviously very proud of his achievement and was determined to impress mother. He wrote home later that day:

"I went up twice this morning. First of all I got in and Mr Sharp told me how to start the engine. You switch on the petrol, put the ignition switch off, close the throttle and tell the mechanic to put the prop in the 'suck-in position'. When he has done that he says 'Contact' and you switch on the ignition and open the throttle about half an inch. He swings the prop, takes the chocks away and then you taxi across to the take-off place. Mr Sharp took off and we climbed to about 1,000 feet, then he let me take control of the rudder. After I had got that all right I took all the controls and just kept the plane in straight and level flight. We flew about ten miles to Netheravon. After coffee I took off all by myself. It is very easy. I climbed to 3,000 feet (right above the clouds which look like a sea of mist) and Mr Sharp taught me how to stall. Then he landed and I took off and landed almost completely by myself. I felt quite OK except when we dived, that was really OK but I wasn't ready for it. I got in an air pocket and with the sudden drop I pushed the control column forward. However, I got out of it OK. My maximum speed was 95 mph. Mr Sharp says I have got the natural instinct of a good pilot."

From here on it was a matter of constant practice in the twenty-seven skills needed to pass the *Ab Initio* test. On 9 March came his first solo flight and another proud letter home:

> "You will be glad to hear that I went up solo to-day. I am the first person of those who did not fly before they came here to go solo. I can do spinning superbly now and to-day Mr Sharp did a slow roll. It was pretty grim when we were upside down with nothing but 6,000 feet of air between us and the ground."

If that was not enough to frighten mother, he went on:

> "Did I tell you that I am easily the youngest here? I should think the average age is about twenty-one . . . Alistair and I walked to the churchyard at Yatesbury. There are about ten graves of pilots who crashed during the War. One was only nineteen and two or three only twenty. It seems very sad."

But there was no hiding his own enthusiasm for this dangerous activity:

> "I simply love flying. The feeling that you are way above the world. You see the clouds fade into a hazy mist on the horizon and away below you are little fields, towns, rivers and railways – it's grand. Then the feeling that the bus is yours; one gentle touch on the controls and she does just what you want. I am beginning to fly much more instinctively now. I do not have to think which controls to move for any manoeuvre, but it is beginning to come naturally . . . I always ask God to help me before I go up and realise I am completely in his hands, then I never think of danger. Provided you keep your wits about you, and keep a good look out for all the other planes, you're as safe as sitting in a chair."

After 23 hours solo and 28 hours dual, Mac took and passed the *Ab Initio* test as an 'Average' pilot on 27 April. When the results of the course became known, it transpired that he had come second. The next stage of his training was to take place at RAF Uxbridge. From Uxbridge, he wrote:

> "We spend most of the day doing drill – more or less the same as OTC, except we had no rifles. Then the rest of the time we had lectures on various subjects such as hygiene, mess etiquette, Air Force law, and customs of the RAF etc. This afternoon we went into town to get measured for our uniform. I went to Moss Brothers. PS: I am an acting pilot officer."

And so, on 18 May 1937, 39639 Acting Pilot Officer James Archibald Findlay MacLachlan entered the RAF, on probation, with a Short

Service Commission lasting four years. He was posted to No.3 Flying Training School at Grantham in Lincolnshire. The school was equipped with Hawker Harts, a two-seater advanced trainer, and Hawker Audaxes, another two-seater used for army co-operation and which could reach 180 mph – twice as fast as the Tiger Moth! Mac was excited by the prospects of the course and he enjoyed his first Guest Night in the mess:

"I went up for my first solo in a Hart [K5043] yesterday (20 May). They are simply marvellous to fly. I always run to the hangar and get into flying kit so my instructor, Sgt Reddick, takes me up first, then if there is any time to spare after he has taken the other chap up, he takes me up again. Last Tuesday was our Guest Night . . . we had a fight with the senior term. They made us have a tug-of-war, and then they threw buckets full of water over us. I managed to get out in time with only a bleeding nose and a cut lip! Tables were smashed and chairs flung around the room. Then we found two chaps had gone to bed, so they were dragged into the anteroom and buckets of water, mud and orange were flung at them. They were then stripped and chased up to bed naked! Another thing we did was to blindfold two people, then put down two trails of pepper on the floor. At the end of the pepper there was a glass of beer – they said. By the time the winner reached the beer, he was coughing and spluttering from the pepper. Then he took a huge gulp of beer and it was ink! It was great fun and I enjoyed myself no end. We do PT at 6.45 every morning now."

He also bought his first motorcar at this time:

"Surprise, surprise! I went to Nottingham today looking for a car. I saw quite a nice Austin 7 Saloon (1931) for £16. I got it down to £14 7s in the end. It seems to run very well and is in good condition. I would have bought it but I had great difficulty in getting insurance. You see, no company wants to insure Air Force officers for some reason or other! Then, I am a learner and under 21, which makes it all the worse.

PS: I have decided to buy the Austin 7. I have found an insurance company who will insure it Third Party for £5 6s per annum."

As happened at all training stations there were many accidents and Mac's letter home on 21 June must have cheered up mother no end!

"Last Friday we had the worst day of flying accidents I have ever known. One chap hit a tree at the forced landing ground and tore his wings off. Another chap piled up on night flying. Two people got lost on cross-country flights and force-landed. Lennie got lost and came home an hour late with only two gallons of petrol left. I mistook the wind indicator when landing at Peterborough and landed down wind at 94 mph. I only just pulled up about 20 yards from the hangars. So, altogether it was a pretty bad day. Still we are not as bad as Netheravon. They have had fifteen crashes in seven weeks."

And then, one day, he got lost and had his first encounter with 'gremlins':

"I have had one of the worst experiences of my life this afternoon. I was sent up to do aerobatics for 45 minutes [in Hart K4927]. There were lots of cumulus clouds at about 300 feet, but plenty of holes through, so I climbed above. After doing aerobatics for about 15 minutes I thought I had better come down and look where I was, so I dived down through the clouds, but could see no sign of Grantham or the aerodrome, or any other landmark that I recognised. I felt for my map but it was not there. I think it is the first time I have ever been up without it and I was lost! I thought if I flew due north I would either hit Grantham or the railway going to Lincoln, so I tried to set north on my compass and found that the range ring of the compass was jammed. That meant I had no map and my compass was very little use to me. I flew around in circles for about five minutes hoping to find a landmark but it was no use. The only thing left for me was to fly east, as far as I could with a jammed range ring and get to the coast, then fly up or down hill until I found Boscombe and then fly west for 20 minutes. That should have brought me over Grantham. I flew east for 45 minutes and still no coast, so I came to the conclusion that I was in Norfolk. I then flew and hit the coast.

I followed the coast to Boscombe and tried to fly west, but the wind blew me off my course and the compass was not much use. I flew for what seemed ages and the clouds were so low I could only see about three miles. I had almost given up hope of getting home by myself, so started praying for some landmark that I knew. I only had about half an hour's more petrol and not a penny on me if I force-landed. I opened my eyes and looked over the side and there was Peterborough about a mile in front! I could have danced for joy if I hadn't been strapped down. There is a railway running almost straight from Peterborough to Grantham, so I followed it. Then I came to a fork. I did not know which to follow, so, of course, took the wrong one! I got to Stamford, so I had to go back to the junction again and follow the other line. I switched over onto my gravity fuel tank and just managed to fly her home OK. I must have been about 150 miles at least. I'll never go up without a map again!"

Despite these adventures, he qualified from the course on 31 July. He had been graded as 'Above the Average' as a pilot and was awarded his wings. He had also made his choice as to the type of squadron he wanted to fly with, and put his name down for medium or light bombers. Now came the third stage of training, and he was posted to No.3 Advanced Flying Training School at South Cerney near Cirencester in Gloucestershire, where he continued to fly Harts and Audaxes, but more realism was creeping into the training. In his letters home during September, October and November, he records the following incidents:

> "We have started bombing today. It's awful! You have to lie on your belly and look through a trapdoor in the bottom of the plane. All the hot oily air from the radiator blows straight into your face. It makes me feel quite sick. Then you have to set the bombsight for height, air speed, wind-speed and direction, terminal velocity of the bomb and heaven knows what else! Then you fly over the camera obscura and fuse a flashbulb when you would normally release the bomb. Then they can tell by plotting the path of the aircraft where the bomb would have hit. It's a really marvellous idea. I have been doing air-to-air gunnery with the front guns today. It is super! One aeroplane tows a drogue and you fly over the plane and dive on the drogue. The only trouble is that you get unpleasantly near to the drogue if you don't look out. Then we do air to ground firing. Oh, by the way, we don't fire bullets – we take photos with camera guns and then you can tell if you would have hit or not."

The real thing came when the course went to No.5 Armament Training Camp at RAF Penrose, near Pwllheli in North Wales:

> "I have done a terrific lot of flying since I have been here. The first day, Wednesday, I did four hours' bombing. Each bomb costs £1 1s and I dropped sixteen of them. It's super watching the bomb get smaller and smaller till it goes out of sight. Then there is a terrific splash and a cloud of white smoke."

On 26 November 1937, Mac passed out of No.3 Flying School as an 'Above Average' pilot. He found that he had been posted to No.88 (B) Squadron at RAF Boscombe Down. His logbook reveals a total of 92 flying hours to his credit.

CHAPTER III

A PEACETIME BOMBER SQUADRON

No.88 (Hong Kong) Squadron had been formed as a fighter-reconnaissance unit in July 1917. At the end of the First World War, having destroyed 164 enemy aircraft, it was disbanded. However, with the rise to power of Nazi Germany from 1933 onwards, the RAF was expanded in the hope that Britain might overtake the lead in air power that Germany had stolen earlier and thereby deter Germany from expansionist policies, which might threaten the security of the country. The plans failed on both counts, but expansion did provide Britain with an air force that was fit to go to war in 1939.

As part of the expansion scheme, in May 1935 the RAF was to increase its number of bombers in the hope of gaining parity with the Luftwaffe. No.88 Squadron was part of this scheme and was reformed at RAF Waddington as a light bomber squadron on 7 June 1937. It moved to Boscombe Down on 17 July and was stationed as part of No.4 Group with Nos.51 and 58 Squadrons. Mac was not too pleased to be joining this almost brand-new unit. His main complaint was the aircraft with which it was equipped – Hawker Hinds. In a letter to mother, he wrote:

> "You will probably be much more pleased than I am to hear that I have been posted to No.88 Bomber Squadron. They are only 35 miles from Southampton, so I shall be able to come home very often. It is a very small squadron – one squadron leader, four pilot officers and five acting pilot officers counting myself. I think they have got Hawker Hinds, which are very similar to the Audaxes we flew. It is a pity, but I may get to a Blenheim squadron later. Hinds can only do 200mph, whereas Blenheims cruise at 290mph and can do 310 flat out."

The Hind biplane – a development of the Hart – was a First World War type and typical of the equipment used by the RAF in its expansion schemes. It equipped thirty squadrons from 1935 onwards because there was little else available at this time. Numerically, the RAF was catching up with Germany, but it was way behind with regard to the quality of its equipment.

Mac joined his new squadron on 6 December 1937. What would have pleased him was the fact that he only had ten flights in Hinds before the squadron was re-equipped with the new Fairey Battle light bomber within weeks of his arrival. The pilots of No.88 Squadron were delighted with their new mount. However, when compared with the new Luftwaffe machines, the Battle was virtually obsolete. It had been ordered by the RAF in 1932, but did not make its first flight until March 1936 and was delivered to the RAF in March 1937. Although it could carry twice the bomb-load of the Hind, it was underpowered for its three-man crew, with just a single Rolls-Royce Merlin engine generating a maximum speed of 241 mph, and grossly under-armed with just one forward-firing .303 operated by the pilot and one Vickers rear-firing machine gun operated by the air gunner. It was almost as big as the twin-engined Blenheim but with no more engine power than the Hurricane. As early as December 1936, Sir Edward Ellington, Chief of the Air Staff, ordered that no more were to be built. "We are getting Fairey Battles," reported Mac on 11 December. ". . . apparently they are the hardest machines in the Air Force to fly."

Mac's first flight in a Battle (K7671) was on 30 December. Because of bad weather, Mac did not have an opportunity to get another flight until 10 January. He was assigned to B Flight. His logbook records 'Local Flying – Southampton, Shanklin, Christchurch'. In fact he had been 'visiting' home, as he wrote:

"Did any of you see me this morning? I circled round the house several times at about 10.30. I could even see the brown patch where Bug's [his brother Hugh] cabbages are. In fact, if I had looked in at the nursery windows I should probably have seen Liz [his younger sister] sucking her thumb! After I had circled over our house I went and had a look at the Queen Mary in dry dock. Then I flew down Southampton Water and saw three Empire Flying Boats. I chased someone in an Avro Cadet who was looping the loop. He must have thought his last day had come for as soon as he saw me coming his nose went vertically down and he did not come out of the dive till he was only 500 feet from the ground. After that I went past the Needles to Bournemouth. Here I ran into a hailstorm and had to come down to 300 feet. I followed the Avon up from Christchurch at this height, till at Ringwood I had to go down to 100 feet. I think my air gunner was quite scared. After hedge-hopping for the last five miles I just managed to reach the aerodrome. The whole flight only took 55 minutes. I was going at about 190-200mph all the way. I opened the engine flat out and did a very gentle dive this morning and the kite did 280mph."

Mac's logbook records a large number of cross-country flights and bombing practices – including the embarrassing entry for 19 January:

"Low level bombing at 250 feet and 100mph. I dropped a bomb in the middle of some sheep. There will be a Court of Inquiry."

In May the squadron went off to its annual air gunnery and practice-bombing camp at No.7 Armament Training Station at RAF Acklington in Northumberland:

"I was range safety officer yesterday. That means getting up at 5.30, but I get 4s a time, so it's not such a bad job as it sounds. You are responsible that there are no ships in the danger area before you give the 'all clear' signal to the bombing aircraft . . . By the way, I have got the highest air to ground firing scores in the whole squadron – 58 out of 100. It doesn't sound very good, but usually the score is about 15 and the highest anyone else has had so far is 34."

On returning to Boscombe, the squadron resumed its usual round of formation, cross-country and night flying, together with photographic, low-level and camera obscura bombing practices. Some of these practices were over towns such as Birmingham, Coventry, Manchester and Norwich. Sometimes, the practices had a touch of realism about them. On 6 August the whole of No.4 Group – five squadrons in all – carried out a formation attack on the Knightsbridge Barracks. On their return, they flew up the Thames to carry out a low level attack on RAF Hornchurch where they were 'attacked' by Hurricanes and Gauntlets. Sometimes such sorties ended in tragedy. A Home Defense exercise was scheduled for 7 August. Mac was flying with Aircraftman Clement as wireless operator and Corporal H.W. Bennett as observer in K7644. The latter remembered this flight vividly. The three Battles were to attack a viaduct at Burton-on-the-Water in Gloucestershire:

"The target was obscured by thick fog and the leader, although uncertain of his position, led the flight down through the fog. I was lying in the bomb aimer's position when to my horror I saw haystacks approaching with great rapidity. I yelled to Mac, 'Climb, climb, climb!', which he did. The other pilot saw the ground too late, overcorrected and stalled his aircraft at around 100 feet. His wireless operator managed to bale out, but the aircraft crashed into a tree, killing the observer. The pilot was unhurt."

With the Czechoslovak crisis and the Munich Conference of August and September 1938, No.88 Squadron went into a state of partial mobilisation on 27 September. They formed part of No.75 Wing with No.218 Squadron and had war markings painted on their aircraft. The CO decided that his crews should now stick together. Before this, Mac had flown with a different aircrew on almost every flight. Now he began to fly regularly with Aircraftman Leslie Davies as his air gunner.

He paints a revealing portrait of Mac at this stage of his career:

"Flying with Mac at Boscombe Down included cross-country, high and low-level circuses and practice raids at all levels on selected towns. Mac's specialities were low-level cross-countries – during day and night. A daylight cross-country at 5,000 feet meant 50 feet for Mac. On many occasions the CO used to get me into his office and ask, 'Davies, you were flying with MacLachlan and I have complaints from the police of an aircraft beating up Bournemouth at zero feet, and later Brighton. Was it you?' My reply usually was, 'Oh no, sir. My radio log shows we were having Direction/Finding bearings from Boscombe Down showing we were north of Worcester. Please ask the Ground Station for confirmation' – the latter had already been told what to say! One day he said let's go and look at part of Wales, so off we went to Carmarthen and to my home – at 0 feet! The village has never forgotten the visit!"

And so the daily round of flying went on, from exciting activities such as Empire Air Day formation flying over Kenley, Hanworth and Odiham, front and rear gun firing on sea markers, offensive and defensive formation practices, dive-bombing and low-level bombing practices on convoys, co-operation exercises with various fighter squadrons, regional bombing exercises and a Group mass formation raid on Tilbury Docks, to the more mundane engine tests, cross-country flights, forced-landing practice, local formation flying, night-flying, parachute flare dropping, refuelling and bombing-up demonstrations. The squadron was inspected by the new C-in-C Bomber Command, Air Vice-Marshal Sir Edgar Ludlow-Hewitt, and also by Marshal of the RAF Sir Edward Ellington.

By now there were ominous entries appearing in Mac's logbook which hinted of something rather nasty in the offing: 'Low level gas attack on troops and M/T at Goldenpot; [and] medium and low gas spray attacks on 2nd Division.' No.88 Squadron was one of sixteen squadrons that were part of a plan to spray mustard gas on an advancing army. The exercises involved using two practice tanks filled with a water-mixture, which smelled like aniseed, and special charts for height, airspeed and wind-direction to calculate the angle at which the liquid was to be released. However apart from the increasing number of exercises the squadron was carrying out, there was no hint in his letters home that war was approaching. But, on 2 September 1939, No.88 Squadron flew to Aubérive near Reims in France, its pre-arranged base in time of war.

CHAPTER IV

INTO BATTLE IN A BATTLE

No.88 Squadron, together with nine other Battle squadrons and two squadrons of Blenheims plus four squadrons of Hurricanes, went to France as the Advanced Air Striking Force (AASF) for operations anywhere along the Allied front. As well as this force, there was also the Air Component of the British Expeditionary Force (BEF) – thirteen squadrons of Lysanders, Blenheims and Hurricanes, which were in France purely in support of the BEF. The AASF could only function as a reaction force to any German initiative. The Germans were already battle-hardened through their operations in Spain and Poland.

The sixteen Battles from No.88 Squadron landed at Aubérive at 1630 hours on 2 September – the day after Germany had invaded Poland and a day before war was actually declared. From Aubérive the squadron carried out reconnaissance flights over the surrounding countryside. On 11 September, Mac undertook out his first operational flight (in K9248) – a low level reconnaissance up to the Franco-German frontier of the Siegfried Line. The same day, he wrote a heavily ironic letter to his sister Helen:

"How goes the war? I'm afraid I'm not allowed to tell you anything about our side of the show – not even what country I'm in (not that it would need a very vivid imagination to guess), so I shall have to confine myself to strictly unimportant and nonsensical chatter (not very difficult for me). Tomorrow we are moving for the third time since we reached this land of mystery (whose name I may not divulge), so I shall be a fully qualified 'packer' by the time this war is over . . ."

The place they moved to (on 12 September) was the French airfield at Mourmelon-le-Grand, 15 miles south-east of Reims. Mac was in B Flight and in charge of the armament section.

The war in earnest started early for No.88 Squadron when, on 20

September, three aircraft from the squadron's A Flight took off for a frontier reconnaissance. En route they were fired at by French anti-aircraft guns before encountering three Messerschmitt Bf109Ds from JG152 over Aachen. Two Battles were shot down at once by Hptm Karl Leesman and Oblt Hans Wiggers – K9294 flown by Flg Off Reg Graveley crash-landed in flames in Allied territory. The pilot was severely burned and was immediately flown to England for treatment, but his air gunner (Aircraftman David John, a 22-year-old from Cardiff) was killed and the observer (Londoner Sgt William Everett) died from his wounds. The other Battle – K9245 flown by Flt Sgt Douglas Page – crashed with the loss of all members of the crew (the other two were Sgt Alfred Eggington and Aircraftman Edward Radford). However, Sgt Frank Letchford, the observer aboard the remaining Battle (Flg Off L.H. Baker's K9243) reported shooting down one of the Messerschmitts – the first enemy aircraft to be claimed by the RAF in World War II, although in fact there were no enemy losses.

Battles from the various squadrons continued to carry out reconnaissance sorties. No.88 Squadron put up six aircraft on 26 September, with Flt Lt John Madge leading them to enemy territory east of Saarbrücken. On this occasion eight French fighters provided escort and no enemy aircraft were encountered. But, on the last day of the month, five Battles from 150 Squadron were intercepted by eight Bf109Es from 2/JG53 – four Battles were shot down, the fifth being written off, heavily damaged. As a result of this massacre, all offensive flying by the AASF Battle squadrons was halted. Pitted against the fast German fighter, the Battle had proved to be a disastrous mismatch:

> "If it had not been obvious to the Battle crews already that they were highly vulnerable when up against German fighters, it was now. Presumably the cessation of operational sorties ordered by AASF HQ also acknowledged this. Yet the aircraft could not be changed overnight, even if that course of action was considered. The AASF had a front-line strength, on paper, of 160 Battles. To take these from the Western Front would have caused concern not only to the British Government and the Air Council, but also our French allies. What was agreed was that the value of constant reconnaissance was obviously not worth the sending the Battles out over Germany."

With the Battle squadrons basically redundant, measures were taken to increase its defensive armament and a third Vickers K machine-gun was fitted on a moveable mounting in the bombing aperture, which gave an excellent field of fire both fore and aft. It was hoped that the additional gun would deter attacks from below. An observer with another Battle squadron recalled:

> "The powers that be decided in their doubtful wisdom to try the
> Battle out in many ways in order to get some usefulness out of that
> terrible, inadequate aeroplane. Even dive-bombing – a disaster, for
> over 60 degrees she went over on her back. Then there was the
> installation of two Vickers guns swivelled by the bombsight so that
> the poor bloody navigator could hang out and fire backwards
> underneath, to try to overcome the blind spot under the tail. The
> WOP/AG could easily, and did, shoot his tail off, our opposition
> knowing this fault."

No.88 Squadron's HQ was some two miles distant from the airfield, in
the village of Baçonne and the officers were billeted at the Café
Roubaix-Tourcoins. It was there that the squadron settled into winter
quarters. Mac celebrated his promotion to flying officer in October
with some exciting low-flying when he attacked machine-gun nests on
the 26th in K9321. Whilst doing so, a wingtip of his Battle hit a tree but
he was able to land safely. At this time, the squadron was constantly
receiving visits including one from Prime Minister Neville
Chamberlain. The squadron was also visited by General Alphonse
Georges, (commander of French Army Groups I and II, and NE
Command including the BEF and French 7th Army), as mentioned by
Mac in a letter to mother:

> "By the way, an old friend of mine was out here yesterday. The
> name's Georges. I don't know if you've met him? Anyway, he gave
> some of the chaps medals etc. for being shot down and being brave
> boys and all that. Personally I was bored stiff and frozen even stiffer
> – you've no idea what shocking weather these French people have to
> put up with. We've had fog, rain, snow and sunshine all in one day
> (not to mention a heavy shower of oil from a broken pipe in my
> engine)."

The weather during the first winter of the war was very severe. A fellow
pilot on No.88 Squadron, Plt Off David Prichard, remembered:

> "The countryside for miles around was snow-covered and I did not
> see the colour of French soil for almost three months. During this
> period, flying activities were severely restricted. There was very
> limited outdoor activity for all personnel. During this period I spent
> many pleasant evenings in the company of Mac, building a balsa
> wood model of a Spitfire. Mac designed and built his own balsa
> wood gliders, and very good they were, too."

Skating was an activity they enjoyed, but Mac told his sister Helen about one disaster in January 1940:

"Last week some of us went out to the Marne Canal, and I (trying to show off as usual) was skating backwards. Suddenly, long, spidery cracks appeared all round me, and before I could do anything about it, the major part of my anatomy was pervaded with an icy-cold, wet feeling. It took a moment for the full meaning of this sensation to dawn on my frozen mind, and it was not without misgivings, that I realised I was up to my waist in the cold, slimy waters of the canal. The others seemed to find the sight extremely amusing, but I, vainly trying to extricate myself from the ever-widening crater, was unable to see any cause for mirth. After all, there was I, soaked to the skin, five miles from the car, and, worst of all, wearing my best blue uniform, in which I was due to attend a cocktail party that evening.

During these last few snowy afternoons we have started what we call 'The 88th Armoured Car Squadron'. It consists of one of our Crossley lorries, manned by two 12-bore gunners in the front seat (for defence against an air attack by partridges, pigeons or pheasants), and in the back, one Lewis-gunner (for strafing rabbits, hares and coveys of partridges). This modern war machine is proving highly efficient. Yesterday we got eleven brace of partridges, five hares, six rabbits, three pigeons and a couple of Frenchmen! We did not actually pick up the Frenchmen, but assume them to have been killed during a Lewis-gun attack on a hare, with a French village in the background!"

Even by early March conditions in France and elsewhere in northern Europe were still wintry. Flying, however, continued whenever possible and with slightly improving weather the RAF decided to resume the offensive by bombing the enemy with leaflets! The first such raid was carried out, on the 18th, by Flt Lt Madge, his targets being Mannheim and Saarbrücken, the aircraft returning safely. Mac flew the next sortie by the squadron on the night of the 23rd, and was accompanied by Sgt Power and LAC Les Davies in L9321. Their target was Darmstadt, following which they carried out a reconnaissance of the Rhine from Worms to Wiesbaden. A second aircraft from 88 Squadron – P2247 flown by Flg Off David Halliday – became lost in heavy cloud, the crew eventually baling out.

On 1 April, Mac celebrated his twenty-first birthday. By then, the squadron had moved south to Perpignan on the south coast of France, for a week's live-bombing practice. He wrote to mother, noting:

"We are about 35 miles from the Spanish frontier and so far the weather has been simply perfect and I am quite sunburnt. On Saturday afternoon I went down to Spain by car. The guards let us

across the frontier and we went about a hundred yards into Spain.
There was a great heap of old rifles left by the refugees, and we
could see a town that had four air attacks made on it during the
Spanish War. The scenery is simply marvellous. From 8,000 feet
you can see right up the Pyrenees. The tops are all covered with
snow and look beautiful against the blue backdrop of the sky. I'm
certainly coming down here for a holiday when the war is over. I
can hardly believe it is my 21st birthday. I was up at five this
morning and have just had lunch after a wizard flight. I have got
the afternoon off and am going down to a little village on the coast
to sunbathe."

Back at Mourmelon, No.88 Squadron and all other Battle and
Blenheim units were put on the alert on 9 April when the Germans
invaded Denmark and Norway. Tension was heightened when German
bombers appeared over Berry-au-Bac airfield, although they were
engaged by French fighters and driven away. Mac had no illusions
about flying Battles:

"I would simply love to be posted to a fighter squadron – there is
nothing I want more . . . I am determined to get into one before the
war is over . . . You might pray about it – I have done so many times.
I want to have a crack at the Germans instead of sitting in a Battle
and being shot to pieces."

The Phoney War came to an end very abruptly on 10 May with the
German invasion of western Europe. Avoiding the heavily defended
French Maginot Line, the main weight of the German attack simply
went round its northern end and fell upon Holland and Belgium. The
first targets in Holland were its capital, The Hague, the main port at
Rotterdam, the military airfields, and the bridges across the Rhine at
Dordrecht and Moerdijk. In Belgium, the objectives were the two
Albert Canal bridges and Fort Eben Emael on the frontier. With 136
divisions, the Germans were outnumbered by the combined 149
divisions of the BEF, the French, Belgians and Dutch. But the
Luftwaffe was larger and more potent than the air forces the Allies
were able to muster. While the Dutch and Belgian air forces were being
knocked out, both the AASF and Air Component were hectically
embroiled in the air battle as the BEF moved forward to the River Dyle
in Belgium.

No.88 Squadron was not called into action on 10 May, which was
probably just as well, since thirty-two sorties were flown by the Battle
squadrons as they tried to stop the German advance through the Low
Countries during which thirteen Battles were shot down. It was to set
the pattern for the future. All the RAF airfields received raids.

Mourmelon was bombed twice, morning and evening. The second time, four Ju88s set a hangar on fire and destroyed two aircraft (K4956 and P2355) on the ground.

The airfield was bombed again the next day. Four aircraft led by Flt Lt Madge were sent to attack German columns. Three were shot down including Madge's P2251; he and his gunner were taken prisoner but the observer was killed. P2202 and P2261, flown by Plt Off A.W. Mungovern and Plt Off Bruce Skidmore respectively, also failed to return. All three were the victims of ground fire. Skidmore and his crew perished, as did Mungovern's observer. The remaining Battle, flown by Plt Off Norman Riddell, force-landed at Vassincourt. Not one of the four Battles from No.218 Squadron, which accompanied No.88 Squadron on this mission, returned; four crew members were killed and the remaining eight captured. One sympathetic fighter pilot commented: "Merely taking off in one [a Battle] would have been worthy of a DFC!"

By the end of 12 May, the AASF's bomber strength had been reduced to 72 aircraft from the original 135. On the 13th, the Germans found a crossing over the River Meuse and next day broke through the Allied defences at Sedan. Mac flew his first bombing raid on 14 May. He recorded in his logbook: 'K9321 – Dive-bombing attack on tanks on road north of Sedan. Aircraft hit five times by anti-aircraft fire.' LAC Les Davies, his gunner, remembers the briefing for that operation:

"Our war started on 14 May when 75 Battles took off to arrive over Sedan about the same time in loose formation. I remember the Intelligence briefing – 'fly at 9,000 feet where the 88mm guns are inaccurate and you are out of pom-pom gun range.' What nonsense! Mac went in much lower and attacked in a low dive and we got away again at very low level. When we got back [we found that] part of the controls had been shot away leaving $1/4$-inch metal to be effective."

All of the squadron's available aircraft – ten – participated in the operation, six attacking tank and troop columns and four attacking a bridge north of Villars. Only one aircraft – L9581 flown by Sgt William Ross – was lost together with its crew. However, the attacks by Blenheims and Battles that day on the pontoon bridges across the Meuse near Sedan resulted in the loss of almost fifty per cent of the aircraft involved. It was wisely decided that the light bombers should only be used at night in future.

On the 15th, the aerodrome at Mourmelon was bombed twice more and it was becoming obvious that it could no longer be held. After a night raid by eight aircraft on a wood supposedly concealing troops, north of Sedan, No.88 Squadron, along with the rest of the AASF, began pulling back to airfields further south and west. Luckily, these grass fields had been prepared during the period of the Phoney War. At 2315 the squadron began moving to Les Grandes Chapelles near Troyes. Mac just managed to get off a quick line home:

> "I was very ill about a week ago and had a temperature of 103°. However I am OK again now and have been flying. No one had time to find out what was wrong, for there were so many shocking cases in the casualty clearing station . . . I've just watched a wizard dogfight. One German bomber shot down and one of our aircraft in flames. There are aircraft here almost all the time . . . Keep praying for me more than ever, but don't worry. 'Underneath are the everlasting arms.' I don't get much time to write these days and I'm tired out, so please remember me to everyone and explain why I haven't written. By the way, I left a sort of will at Boscombe."

By 19 May the squadron was able to go into operation again with night raids. Mac carried out his first night operation (flying P2354, with Sgt Hardy and LAC Les Davies) on the 21st with a raid on the railway junction at Givet on the Belgian frontier. They encountered intense searchlight activity and some desultory anti-aircraft fire, but all aircraft returned safely. Next day, the squadron was forced back onto daylight operations, when a tank column north of the Somme at Arras was attacked. Mac (P2313, with Hardy and Davies) claimed to have hit one tank and to have registered near misses with his three remaining 250lb bombs. Mac's low level flying did not inspire confidence in his observer Sgt Hardy who told Les Davies:

> "I don't want to be killed by that f*****g MacLachlan – he does not care for his crew. I'm going to the CO and ask to be re-crewed."

The CO granted Hardy's request and on his second trip with his new crew he was shot down and posted missing.

Mac was operational again (in P2263) on the night of the 23rd, bombing a railway junction at Bingen, which could be seen clearly in the moonlight, but a second aircraft from the squadron, P2356 flown by New Zealander Plt Off Albert Wickham, failed to return. It was later reported to have crashed at Springen, north-west of Wiesbaden, with the loss of all the crew. During this period, Mac recorded a minor accident in his logbook on the 25th, when he landed P2263 at Rouen on one wheel while collecting new aircraft for the squadron. That night he experienced another scare when a flak burst damaged a fuel line during a raid on a road north of Sedan in P2313. Plt Off Prichard remembered the latter:

"Several of us who were not flying went down to the airfield to welcome the returning crews. Circling the airfield was a Battle giving a fairly good imitation of a 'crop sprayer'. It made a safe landing and we soon discovered it was Mac's aircraft, holed like a colander and losing fuel in a fine spray. Mac was unaware of the real situation and when he got out of the aircraft he was taken aback, to put it mildly. Several of the more senior pilots commented that Mac realised then that 'War Operations' could be highly dangerous and hazardous ones and that it was not a game as he seemed inclined to treat it!"

Mac and his crew were fortunate to get back, since a second aircraft (L5467) from No.88 Squadron was shot down at Harucourt south-east of Sedan, with the loss of Plt Off Colin Anderson and his crew. Mac carried out another night raid on the 28th, he and his crew (in P2313) bombing a railway junction at Libremont. They reported intense searchlight activity but little AA fire. Les Grandes Chapelles was now too close to the front line for comfort and further withdrawal became necessary. A new airfield was found at Moissy between Le Mans and Orleans. The unit moved there on 2 June. All this time, from 27 May to 4 June, the BEF was being evacuated from Dunkirk. The AASF – six squadrons of Battles and five of Hurricanes – was now wholly in support of the French and tried to help them by attacking the southern flank of the German forces, which had swept round like a scythe to cut off the BEF. On 31 May, the squadron was visited by Air Marshal Sir Arthur Barratt, AOC British Air Forces in France. He talked with the crews and tried to encourage them while explaining their new task. On the 28th, Mac had written home to re-assure the family of his own well being:

"Just a line to let you know I am still OK. We have just moved to another aerodrome so have been working pretty hard settling in etc. All the roads are full of refugees. They're the most pathetic sight I've ever seen – old women carrying babies; men driving cows, goats and even hens. Some of their horses died of fatigue and were lying by the roadside with no one to bury them. Heaven knows where they'll all go to. I'm sorry I can't tell you any more. For once there is something to write about, but it would be censored. I have been acting as flight commander for the last week. Until last night I had only six hours sleep for three days, so you can imagine how tired I was. I will close now as it is lunchtime. Keep praying and trusting – there's nothing to worry about. I think in a month's time, the situation will be quite different . . ."

After flights to reconnoitre the area around Moissy, operations were resumed on 6 June. However, the Luftwaffe had also found Moissy and began bombing it on the same day. Mac flew a bombing raid on the night of 8 June against troops in the forest of St Gobain in the Abbeville region. Flying P2354, they witnessed a French petrol dump blow up near Epernay – they were flying at such a low level that they were almost blown up themselves. There was heavy artillery fire from both French and German guns. Abbeville was the focus of operations on both the 9th and 10th. Mac raided a road junction near Fleury on the 10th, his bombs straddled the road. In doing so L5393's cockpit hoods were shot away, but they returned safely and there were no injuries. Les Davies recalled:

> "Our cockpit hoods were shot away but Mac kept up his attack with his four 250lb bombs, returning to fire away with his one Browning gun and I with my Vickers. He kept up the attack until all his ammo was used."

Next day the squadron lost Plt Off John Gillam and his observer when L5519 crashed near Perdreauville south-west of Nantes. Two more Battles were lost on the 12th, Flt Lt Alan Pitfield and his gunner being killed in L5334 near Beaurepaire, south-east of Beauvais, while a second aircraft, flown by Plt Off James Talmon, force-landed on a French airfield. They were part of a small force of Battles that attacked pontoon bridges at Verberie Pont Pointe, and both were victims of intense AA fire. A more dangerous raid was carried out on 13 June, as the Germans began a deeper penetration of France. The squadron was sent on a daylight raid to attack tanks in the Forêt du Goult. Mac records that they flew under a formation of twenty-five Ju87s and were then spotted by three Bf109s, which gave chase. According to his gunner, Les Davies: "Mac claimed that two of them were shot down by us, but this was not confirmed." In his logbook, Mac simply noted that while flying L5393 they managed to escape the fighters in cloud. The Messerschmitts did, however, shoot down Sgt Hayward's aircraft, although the two-man crew survived.

That same day (13 June) Mac flew to Châteaudun to pick up new aircraft for the squadron. However, the German advance was now gaining strength and speed as the French front crumbled once more. There was little the Battles could now do to help and it was therefore decided to pull the remainder of the AASF out of France. During the 13 days since Dunkirk, thirty-one Battles had been lost, bringing the grand total throughout the Battle of France to 137. But first, No.88 Squadron was called upon to undertake one final raid and, at dawn on the 14th, the Battles raided German troops south of Evreux, Mac and his crew participating in L5393. They returned to Houssay airfield instead of Moissy, from where, at noon, they took off for RAF Driffield in Yorkshire. It was an eventful flight, as recalled by Plt Off Prichard, whose aircraft had been shot down by French AA fire:

"... not having an aircraft of my own, my crew and I were allocated places on three different aircraft. The pilot of my aircraft was Mac. We were supposed to fly direct to RAF Abingdon, but Mac had other ideas and decided to carry out a fairly mild (for him!) 'beat up' of his old school, near Bath (Monkton Combe). With me huddled within the narrow confines of the Battle fuselage, plus miscellaneous bits and pieces and no secure strapping, I had a fairly rough ride. We eventually arrived at Abingdon, tired but happy, and, after a meal and a short rest, we continued our flight to what was to be our temporary base at RAF Driffield."

Mac's return was, unbeknown to him, witnessed by his brother Gordon, who was at school at Monkton. Gordon wrote to mother on 16 June:

"Three Battles came over yesterday, during dinner. They dived on the dining hall and missed it by about ten feet. The first time they dived, Ted [The Rev. E. Hayward, Headmaster] ducked in his chair!"

The unmistakable MacLachlan touch! One of the other Blenheims was flown by Mac's close friend Dudley Honor. It wasn't until the 21st that Mac was able to tell his family that he was home safely:

"I have arrived home OK. You will be glad to hear that I have got almost all my kit from France including my binoculars, cameras, films and flying logbook. We are moving from here soon, but have no idea (officially) where we are going."

Together with another Battle unit, No.88 Squadron flew on 23 June to RAF Sydenham, near Belfast. Mac had survived the Battle of France, but with the French signing an armistice, a new battle was just beginning and he was determined to be part of it.

CHAPTER V

FIGHTER PILOT

Throughout July and the first half of August 1940, Mac was based in Northern Ireland. He was put in charge of the Station Flight at RAF Sydenham. It was frustrating for him since his determination to transfer to an operational fighter squadron was uppermost in his mind. Nonetheless, he enjoyed the freedom his new command allowed, which was obvious in the letter he wrote to mother on 21 July:

"I've been made CO of the Station Fighter Flight (flying Hawker Demon biplanes!) – a job that I simply love. I expect I shall be made an acting flight lieutenant, but as long as I can fly fighters I don't mind what happens. I wonder if you've had any bombs dropped near you – I always think the whistle is the worst part, though getting covered in dirt isn't much fun either!"

But the big news the letter contained was that he had been awarded the Distinguished Flying Cross on 16 July:

"I expect you will have seen in the papers that I have got the DFC. It's rather a nuisance in some ways. I've now got about ten letters to answer."

On hearing the news, Gordon wrote home from school:

"Isn't it wizard about Jay? I would like to know whether he got the DFC for being a MacLachlan or what? 'Kitch' [A. F. Kitching, a member of staff] was the first to see it here, and came into the gym when we were doing an exam, and told old 'Puffles' [H.J. Powell], and then came over to me and said, 'Mac, your brother has got the DFC' and then went away smiling. All the other masters here came up to me and asked me to congratulate Jay. Morris said, 'I always knew he would do something like that.' The cutting out of the paper is still on the board with Jay's name underlined."

Without a shadow of doubt, it was the influence and example of his elder brother that led to Gordon joining the RAF in August. On 3 September, Mac was invested with his decoration at Buckingham Palace. Two months later newly-promoted Sergeant Leslie Davies, his former WOp/AG, was awarded the Distinguished Flying Medal for his 'gallantry and devotion to duty' during the Battle of France. He was later to be commissioned and went on to train as a pilot.

By August the Battle of Britain was reaching its climax but, so acute was the dearth of fighter pilots that Air Marshal Sir Hugh Dowding, C-in-C Fighter Command, had to ask the Air Ministry to lend him some Battle pilots. However, with so many casualties during the Battle of France, there were scarcely enough pilots left to fly the remaining Battles, which might well be needed to bomb a German invasion force. The Air Ministry compromised by calling for five volunteers from each of the Battle squadrons and three from the Lysander-flying Army Co-operation squadrons. On 18 August, Mac heard the news that he had been chosen as one of No.88 Squadron's five volunteers. His delight was tinged with just an element of regret:

> "At 9 o'clock this morning I was told that I had been posted to a fighter squadron and at 1 o'clock I left Belfast by air. I have just landed at Hendon, but am going on to an, at present, unknown destination. Now that I have achieved my ambition, I don't feel quite as happy as I thought I should be. I hated saying goodbye to 88 Squadron and all my old friends. Poor Davies is quite upset. Well, mother, our prayers have been answered so, 'Thank God and take courage.'"

Mac was posted to RAF Drem, west of Edinburgh, for training with No.145 Squadron equipped with Hurricanes. Over the next month he was to become familiar with the type of aircraft he was to fly for the next two years with such distinction. His first flight in a Hurricane (P3926) occurred on 22 August, and by the end of the month he had logged 18 hours on type. Mother appeared confused by all these changes. He wrote to her on 26 August:

> "You asked about my new crew – you don't have a crew in a fighter – you're all by yourself with eight machine-guns. That's one of the reasons why I like fighters. You've only got yourself to think of, and blame, if anything goes wrong. I have been doing lots of flying and am meant to be fully operational (after only five days and thirteen hours experience on Hurricanes). I never knew I could love flying so much – honestly, these Hurricanes are simply wizard to fly."

No.145 Squadron had been in the thick of the Battle of Britain, being based with No.11 Group at Croydon, Tangmere and then Westhampnett. During August it had suffered badly, losing ten pilots (half the squadron) in five days. As a result, it had been withdrawn to Scotland to train new pilots and be fitted with replacement aircraft and was classified as a C Squadron, meaning that one flight was operational in the defence of the east coast of Scotland, being based at Dyce (Aberdeen), while the other flight was at Montrose and non-operational, being charged with the task of training new pilots. Mac was inducted into fighter-pilot lore: operational take-offs, attacking positions, R/T practice, break-aways, and dogfights. To a pilot of Mac's temperament, aerobatics could not be resisted, nor could the firing of his guns, and on one occasion he shot down an unfortunate gannet, which had strayed into his gunsight! By 30 August, Mac began going out on patrols, in daylight and at night, over the Scottish coast, but making no interceptions. Training continued throughout September, with one mishap occurring on the 21st when he force-landed P3896 at Dyce owing to an oil leak.

On 27 September, there was a call for four experienced pilots to volunteer to join squadrons in the south that had suffered serious losses. Plt Off Jas Storrar DFC (already a seasoned campaigner with nine victories to his credit), Flg Off Peter Parrott, Flg Off Derek Forde and Mac answered the call. Mac and Storrar found themselves posted to No.73 Squadron, part of No.11 Group, based at RAF Debden in Essex. They arrived on the 29th:

> "As you can see, I have moved again and am now in 73 Squadron who were out in France with us. We are operating from a field right out in the wilds [Debden's satellite airfield at Castle Camps in Cambridgeshire] . . . Don't start worrying – it's not nearly as bad as France (I hope)."

Mac was posted to B Flight commanded by Flt Lt Mike Beytagh, who had been at Monkton Combe School five years before Mac. Mac joined the squadron in time for the closing stages of the Battle of Britain, and his first day in action (30 September) saw the last large daylight raid on London, by 200-plus bombers. It was a day of triumph for the RAF, forty-four of the raiders being shot down for the loss of only four pilots, although there were no interceptions for No.73 Squadron, which was scrambled twice to patrol over Maidstone. Mac flew P3398 on the first sortie, and V6677 on the second.

In October, while night attacks on London and industrial centres were constant, massed daylight attacks ceased. The Luftwaffe replaced these with 'snapper' raids by bomb-carrying Bf109s. The idea was to keep the RAF extended and to weaken it prior to resuming the offensive in the spring of 1941. Because of the ceiling at which the Messerschmitts flew, it was difficult for the Hurricanes to reach them. On 7 October, Mac intercepted one of these raids and carried out his first combat engagement as a fighter pilot. The day had dawned fine and sunny and, at 0950, No.73 Squadron was scrambled to patrol Chelmsford in company with No.257 Squadron. They then proceeded down to the south coast and returned over the Thames estuary. According to Mac's logbook, enemy aircraft were seen but not intercepted. At 1230 the two squadrons were scrambled again to patrol over Chelmsford at 20,000 feet. Mac (flying V6676) spotted two Bf109s:

"Flying as arse-end Charlie to the Debden Wing at 22,000 feet south of London, we were bounced by six Me109s. I saw two enemy aircraft break away below and followed, firing a three-second burst. Enemy aircraft dived, smoking."

The next time Mac (V7572) saw action was on 12 October, when his section from B Flight went in pursuit of a He111, which flew west over Castle Camps at 12,000 feet. He reported on this incident in a letter home:

"This afternoon, three of us went up after a lone He111, but it was too far away by the time we had climbed to its height [after 30 minutes they returned to base]. We've had very little actual fighting, as Jerry goes too high for us to get him. My hands froze the other day and it was absolute agony when I came down and the blood started to circulate again. Yesterday I saw one of our pilots [Sgt Bob Plenderleith in V6676] go down on fire. He managed to bale out and is only slightly burnt. It's the first kite we've lost since I've been down here, so it's not too bad, is it? My flight commander is a wizard chap and has just become a father. We have had a sweepstake to see who could guess the infant's weight. His name is Beytagh, so everyone was asked to invest their money in 'Beytagh's bigger, better, babies'."

At this time, Mac decided to maintain a diary of events, the first entry coinciding with the start of a new phase in his life:

17 October – Castle Camps: This morning came the news that two pilots from this squadron are wanted to volunteer for posting to the Middle East Command. Naturally, about fifty of the squadron put in their names; but after supplying the information that I was overdue for promotion to flight lieutenant, and would have to be posted anyway, I was put down as one of the names. Jas Storrar and 'Chubby' Eliot [Plt Off Hugh Eliot] had a hard fight for second place, but after we had convinced Murray [Sqn Ldr Alan Murray, CO of No.73 Squadron] that the squadron could not do without Storrar's car, Chubby's name went in with mine. Naturally there is great speculation as to where we are going, but the general opinion seems to be Egypt. I certainly hope so.

At lunchtime the CO got all the pilots together and said he had some bad news for us. As Jerry won't come below 35,000 feet to fight, Command have decided that we must catch him before he gets there. They are going to start fighter sweeps of the French aerodromes, and, as usual, the Hurricanes are the stooges. We are to cross the Channel at 20,000 feet just as Jerry starts to form up. The Hurricanes are then to scream down and take what shots they can, before going like hell for home. Jerry will then chase the wretched Hurricanes back to England (doubtless bringing them down like flies). In the meantime the Spitfire boys (who have been sitting up at 30,000 feet) will come down behind Jerry (who is supposed to be in a rabble by now) and do to him what he is doing to the Hurricanes. If I wasn't a Hurricane pilot I might think it was a damn good idea! Thank God I'm being posted!

19 October: After breakfast this morning the Adjutant produced the information that Chubby and I have to report to Uxbridge [HQ of No.11 Group] tonight . . . I've packed up my few belongings, and given my model Hurricane to the squadron. I've asked Scott [Plt Off Donald Scott] to finish it for me; I only wish I'd had time to do it myself.

No.73 Squadron was sorry to lose them, and the squadron's diarist recorded:

'F/O MacLachlan and P/O Eliot having volunteered earlier in the week to go overseas, have been ordered to report to Uxbridge. We shall miss them both very much indeed. They are both of the finest type, both as pilots as well as messmates and their going is a great loss to the squadron. We wish them the best of luck in their new sphere of activity.'

Mac's diary continued:

21 October – Uxbridge: I'm living in one of the wooden huts below the East Wing. This morning, after a late breakfast, I went down to Personnel Despatch Centre's office, where I discovered that I am in charge of a party of 12 pilots and 207 men going to Malta. We are going out with twelve Hurricanes in HMS *Argus* (the smallest aircraft carrier in the fleet). This afternoon I collected my tropical kit, visited the MO, and signed the leave book etc.

He informed his family by writing two letters that same day. The first was to his brother Hugh:

> "I am sailing for Malta in about ten days. I have been posted to 261 Fighter Squadron and as you can imagine, am pretty pleased about the whole thing. I'm longing to have a crack at those macaroni-sucking bastards! Malta will be my eleventh station in the last four months – there's nothing like a change, you know!"

Then, in another letter, he told his sister Helen about his imminent posting, adding:

> "By the way, my promotion to flight lieutenant is now overdue, so keep an eye on the London Gazette. I'm not going to let on that I'm a Flt Lt till I've been in Malta a week or two, in the hope that I shall be surplus to Squadron establishment and get posted on to Egypt or Palestine. Jerry has just dropped some bombs far too close for my liking. I've always maintained only bats and fools fly at night, and he's no bat!"

Diary:

24 October – Haywards Heath: At least the powers-that-be have decided that we can go on leave. I got away by 4pm and just reached Moss Bros before they closed. There I left a tunic to be altered, and have two stripes and a DFC [ribbon] sewn on – may as well create a good impression at my new squadron. The train to Haywards Heath was very slow and I did not get in until after eight. I got a taxi up to the house where I found mother and auntie just starting supper. I really enjoyed getting home and hearing all the family news. I am billeted in Miss Simpson's room, in one of the most comfortable beds I have ever slept in. Life seems more interesting than ever lately. I often think of John Madge [Flt Lt Madge of No.88 Squadron] and the other boys in prison camps, and thank God I'm still free. I'm sure I'll never be able to get used to normal life again after the war (perhaps I won't have to).

25 October – London: I arrived home in time for tea. There was a dogfight over the house and a 109 came tearing down to about 300 feet with a Hurricane on his tail. The 109, however, got away in cloud. A few minutes later, a Hurricane came down out of control and crashed. Mother and I walked up to the golf course and saw the burnt out remains of another Hurricane from No.145 Squadron that had crashed there that morning.

26 October – Abbotsinch, Glasgow: I left home at 7.30 last night and arrived in Town about three hours late. There was a huge fire somewhere in the docks and another at a gasworks north of Waterloo

Bridge. The AA guns were making a hell of a row and every so often a stick of bombs would go off. I got a bus from London Bridge to Piccadilly, but could get no further. I was feeling pretty bloody so spent the night at the Regent Palace. This morning I got the 1100 to Glasgow and finally arrived at Paisley at about 9.30pm. There I found that we should have sailed this afternoon, but for some reason or other it has been postponed. Boy, am I lucky! No one seems to have missed me.

28 October: Today I have been trying to borrow an aeroplane to go and visit the old squadron (73 Squadron). I am going down as far as Leicester with a squadron leader here, and then Chubby and I are taking the aircraft (a Swordfish) on to Castle Camps. Incidentally, we have been given five days more leave.

29 October – Church Fenton: Chubby and I are now at Church Fenton after one of the worst non-operational flights I have ever had. At 0900 this morning, the squadron leader informed me he was not going south after all, so we could not have the Swordfish. I then nearly got a Maggie [Miles Magister] but that went u/s. At last, after much wangling, we got permission to take the Group Captain's Tiger Moth [N9213]. Nothing daunted, we took off for Sealand near Chester, via Carlisle at 1300 hrs. I guessed a rough course, and, as it was too cold to look at a map, held the course, hoping to pick up our position on the south-west coast of Scotland. The clouds were down over the mountains, so we had to go above them. With a 40mph headwind at 4,000 feet above cloud, we crossed the mountains. I've never been so cold in all my life. My nose was streaming, but my hands were too cold to get out my soaking handkerchief and wipe it. Poor Chubby was even worse off in the back cockpit. After about an hour the cloud layer below us became 10/10ths, so we decided to go below it. When, at last, I found a hole and descended through, I could still see nothing but mountains. After another hour's flying, the mountains levelled off and sloped down to a coastal plain.

I landed at the first aerodrome I saw, and to my consternation, found it was Acklington on the Northumberland coast! We warmed ourselves up while the kite was refuelled and then set off south again and reached York at sunset. I had no maps of this area, so flew east hoping to find Driffield, which was the nearest aerodrome I knew. Eventually we found an aerodrome under construction, and landed on a road beside it. The locals, who rushed out to see us, said the place was called Pocklington and that Driffield was about 15 miles to the north-east. Chubby then said he knew the way to Church Fenton, so he took over, and after flying down the wrong railway for about four minutes eventually found his way to the right one, and so to Church Fenton. We pushed the Moth into a hangar and made our way to the mess as quickly as our frozen limbs would let us. Never have I been so thankful for a fire and a hot meal. After contemplating spending the night in some flea-infested haystack on a Yorkshire moor, the idea of a warm bed is too good to be true.

30 October – Debden: We got cracking straight after breakfast, Chubby doing the driving, and I sitting in the back with the hood up trying to keep warm. We landed at Peterborough to refuel, and got to Castle Camps in time for lunch. Naturally the boys were very surprised to see us, as they thought we were already on our way east. They are apparently being moved to Gravesend and used as night fighters. I certainly got posted at the right time! Mike Beytagh and Jas Storrar were reported to be over at Debden with [Sqn Ldr] Murray, so on we went to Debden. We found Murray there, but no sign of Mike or Jas. After tea we flew back to Castle Camps as we heard there was a chance of doing a dusk stand-by to catch lone raiders. I borrowed flying kit and to my surprise was ordered to patrol base. I screeched off midst a cloud of Very lights etc., but was immediately recalled by Kiwi Control. After stand-by was washed out, Chubby and I borrowed the CO's car and went over to Debden. As we came round a corner we saw Jas's car standing in the middle of the road and Mike Beytagh gesticulating frantically to a very dim member of the LDV. We pulled up and discovered that Mike had been driving with headlights full on during an air raid! Eventually we managed to convince the gentleman of the LDV that it was a good thing to use headlights, as it dazzles the Jerries!

31 October – Rannoch: After an early breakfast we drove back to Castle Camps to be greeted by the Adjutant with a telegram from Abbotsinch. I knew damn well what it was going to say, but read it just to make sure. I was right. 'Return here immediately'!

4 November – on board *Argus*: We are now at anchor in the Clyde, just off Greenock. We moved down here the day after the last lot of Hurricanes were loaded on, and it looks as if we shall be here for a day or two. My batman seems rather a good type. I asked this morning why my buttons had never been cleaned. He replied quite seriously, that it was no good cleaning them at sea as they only got dirty again. I refrained from asking him what happened when you cleaned them on land – working in his theory I don't suppose he'd ever experimented.

6 November: I had lunch with the Captain today and he tells me we are putting out at 0900 tomorrow. Simmonds, my batman, is quite a character. This morning when he came in I had a bad fit of toothache, and told him so. He mumbled something and left the cabin. In a few minutes he returned and told me to open my mouth. There was nothing for it but to do as I was told. 'Which tooth is it?' he demanded. I told him and after a moment's examination he said, 'OK, hold on.' Without any further warning he shoved something hard into the hole in my tooth. It hurt like hell, but I didn't let on. As soon as he took his hand out of my mouth I asked what the hell he though he was doing. 'Cloveing it,' he answered. 'It'll be OK in five minutes.' Apparently 'cloveing' consists of shoving a clove into the painful tooth and imagining that it doesn't hurt any more. I'm afraid my imagination isn't quite good enough!

7 November: We weighed anchor at 0930 this morning and at dusk this evening we were about ten miles north of Rathin Island. We are keeping an aircraft recognition watch on the bridge until we are out of range of enemy aircraft. I did the first one down the Clyde, and was very interested to see all my old haunts; Largs, Fairley, The Cumbraes, Bute and even Arran. In the evening we played poker. I am having rotten luck and am steadily going down.

CHAPTER VI

MALTA

With Italy's entry into the war in June 1940 and the collapse of France in the same month, it was obvious that the island of Malta would be at the heart of any campaign fought in the Mediterranean and North Africa. Such battles would hinge on supplies and on the capacity of both sides to reinforce. Malta lay across Axis supply lines to North Africa and was an ideal reconnaissance post to observe all their movements. Air defence was crucial, but in June 1940 there were no fighter aircraft on the island apart from a dozen or so crated Sea Gladiators, the property of the Royal Navy.

In August, Operation Hurry was launched during which twelve Hurricanes were flown off HMS *Argus* to Malta as reinforcements. The success of this operation led to a repeat performance being planned for November – codenamed Operation White. Another twelve Hurricanes were to be flown off *Argus* and it was these aircraft that Mac was in charge of. The need for these additional aircraft was urgent for the Axis air forces were already attempting to reduce Malta by aerial assault. One of the young pilots under his command was Sgt Bam Bamberger:

> "We, the NCO pilots, were accommodated in the bow of the ship, next to the anchor chain locker. A seaman was detailed to look after our meagre needs including meals, which we ate where we slept. I was allocated a hammock and eventually mastered the art of getting in it without damaging my head against the steel work of the *Argus*. The weather was a little rough as we headed south in the Atlantic, quite exciting when standing on deck with the seas breaking over the bow of such a large vessel, though not so wonderful when in our accommodation, the bow rising shuddering from the water, an apparent hover, then crashing back down into the sea."

Mac's diary continued:

10 November – *Argus* – We are now in the Bay of Biscay – or rather

800 miles out in the Atlantic somewhere off the Bay. There is a strong rumour that the German pocket battleship *Admiral Scheer* is trying to intercept us and everyone is slightly apprehensive. Our destroyer escort left us after we rounded the west coast of Ireland and now our only defence is HMS *Despatch*, one of the old 6-inch cruisers. Life is getting rather monotonous, as there is really very little to do except play poker and walk on the flight deck.

11 November: At about 1000 we saw two battlewagons on the horizon. Apparently they were British ships going north to catch the *Admiral Scheer*. I hear we are due in at Gib the day after tomorrow. I must say I shan't be sorry to see land again. This sea is all right for a week, but after that one wants a change!

14 November: We met the destroyers soon after dawn this morning and sighted land at about 1600 hrs. The lights of Tangiers were visible for miles. It must be wizard to have no blackout. How I long for the good old days of peace. We arrived in Gibraltar Bay shortly after 2200 and could see Morocco quite easily in the moonlight. We are not being allowed ashore as we are going on again as soon as we have refuelled.

Sgt Bamberger recalled:

"When in the area of Gibraltar, Flt Lt MacLachlan came to brief us in detail on the task which lay ahead. We discussed the technique to be used for flying the Hurricane off an aircraft carrier, for none of the pilots making up our group had previous experience of this form of take-off, and how and when the Hurricanes would be brought up from below deck and parked in a manner to facilitate the longest take-off run and getting airborne quickly. Additionally, considerable time was spent discussing speed, engine settings and height necessary to achieve maximum fuel economy/range. It was at the end of this briefing that Mac brought to our attention there were thirteen RAF pilots aboard but only twelve Hurricanes – we were aware of the latter. As the other Sergeant Pilots had considerably more flying hours on Hurricanes than my one-hour experience, it was inevitable Mac would decide I was to be the spare pilot. I was depressed and frustrated but the outcome saved me from a possible early watery grave."

Mac's diary:

16 November: We are now about due south of Sardinia, still sailing east. In our convoy are *Renown*, *Newcastle*, *Despatch* and *Ark Royal* (Force H), not to mention six destroyers. This afternoon I took some photos of aircraft landing and taking off from the *Ark*. This morning we took all the Hurricanes up on deck and ran them up. I have got one with wizard loose controls. Its number is V7474. We rather expected an Italian air attack this evening as we are now well within range of bombers operating from Cagliari (Sardinia). However it has not come off. We are going in two flights of six, with a Fleet Air Arm Skua leading each flight. Flights are going in sections of three, line astern. I am taking Chubby and P/O Hamilton with me, and the three Sgt Pilots [W.G. Cunnington, R.A. Spyer, and J.K. Norwell] are forming my second section. F/O Clarke is leading the second flight, which he is organising to suit himself [it comprised F/Os E.G. Bidgood, P.W. Horton, J.R. Walker and P/Os F.J. Boret and J.M. Horrox]. Sub Lts Gordon-Smith and Griffiths, Clarke and I had a conflab with the Captain. He wanted to send us off 400 miles from Malta, but we wouldn't play. My backside will be quite sore enough after 2³/₄ hours.

Reports from Malta indicated that an Italian force of one battleship, seven cruisers and a number of destroyers was concentrating south of Naples. This decided Admiral Somerville, commanding Force H, to fly the Hurricanes as far to the west as the safe operational range of the aircraft would permit.

17 November – Luqa, Malta: Today has been one of the most tragic in my life. Out of the twelve Hurricanes and two Skuas that flew off *Argus* this morning, only four Hurricanes and one Skua reached Malta. Nine [*sic*] chaps who were all alive and well twelve hours ago are dead, and I might easily have been one of them. We got up at 5am this morning and after having cocoa and sandwiches in the crew room, we went up to the flight deck. It was bright moonlight with not a cloud in the sky. The first flight of six Hurricanes was ranged up at the far end of the flight deck, and behind them the old Skua. Then Captain Rushbrook came up and said goodbye and we got into our kites. Mine started straight away and ran beautifully smoothly. It seemed very strange sitting up there in the moonlight waiting for the signal to take off. I could see Chubby and Hamilton out of the corner of my eye and was watching Chubby's spinner when I suddenly realised they were waving me to take off. I opened her up to 6lbs boost, and, in spite of a fuselage full of junk, she was off before I reached the accelerating fairing. I turned on my navigation lights while the others took off, and formed up. At last we were all together and I signalled to the Skua who set course for Galite Island where we were to meet a Sunderland. By this time it was nearly 0630 and just beginning to get light. We had a 20 mph tailwind and I felt quite happy about petrol.

It was quite light when we got to Galite and we spotted the

Sunderland without any difficulty. I exchanged the usual recognition signals with the Skua, and we all set off in the direction of Pantelleria Island. We had been flying for about an hour and a half when I checked up on my petrol, and was horrified to find I had already used about 45 gallons (leaving me about 50). The wind too, had backed slightly and was now almost full abeam, blowing at about 30mph. The Sunderland led us south of Pantelleria, thus adding about 15 miles to our trip, and completely foxing me. After flying about $2^{1}/_{2}$ hours I began to get extremely worried about my petrol. I formated on the Sunderland and asked for our estimated time of arrival (ETA) with my identification lights. They said, 'twenty minutes more' and as I then had about 15 gallons, I thought I could just about make it. The second section of Hurricanes was about half a mile behind and about 1,000 feet above us. I could only see two of them but did not worry as I thought the third was probably dead behind me. Five minutes later the Sunderland turned back and I realised that there was only one of the rear section still flying. There was still no sign of Malta and my fuel gauge was only showing 8 gallons. I don't think I've ever prayed so hard as I did then. The thought of drowning never occurred to me, but I imagined having to bail out and lose my logbooks, camera and binoculars (a fate far worse than death!). The visibility had deteriorated but I did not realise it was as poor as it proved to be. Suddenly the Skua turned to port and started waggling its wings. I turned to follow it and through the mist was just able to make out the brown cliffs of Gozo about a mile away. I wish I could describe the marvellous feeling of relief that came over me. I could have slow rolled and looped till I was dizzy – if I'd had enough gas, but I only had 6 gallons. I got my section to close in as we crossed the coast, and watched the Skua firing its recognition cartridge.

We circled the first aerodrome we came to (Takali), and having chosen a runway that was more or less into the wind, I landed. I had then four gallons left. Just as I was taxiing off the runway, I saw Hamilton doing an exceptionally split-ass approach from which he carried out a very spectacular crosswind landing. He had apparently run out of petrol while circling the aerodrome and landed with a dead motor. The Sgt Pilot, Norwell, had 3 gallons and Chubby had 14. It was 9.20am. We went off to a sort of mess place and had eggs and bacon. We had actually landed at Takali, so after refuelling we went on to Luqa – our original destination. There was no news of the second flight, but we heard that the Sunderland had picked up Sgt Spyer – the second of my flight to bale out. Sgt Cunnington was drowned.

The second flight was meant to be guided to Malta by a Maryland reconnaissance aircraft, but after waiting for about an hour, the crew saw no sign of the Hurricanes or the Skua. They had in fact all crashed into the sea and the pilots been drowned. They had been very unlucky. Their Sunderland escort had failed to take off from Gibraltar, they then missed their landfall at Galite Island, missed their guide from Malta and become hopelessly lost. The navigator of their Skua radioed for help, but his receiver was defective and he could not pick up any replies to his transmissions. One by one, the Hurricanes ran out of fuel and fell into the sea. Finally, the Skua crew spotted the south-western coast of Sicily, but before the pilot could land, it was fired on by Italian anti-aircraft guns and had to crash-land on a beach at Punta Palo on the Isola delle Correnti, near Syracuse. A Maryland sent out from Malta searched for five hours, but found no survivors of this second flight. In the meantime, the spare Hurricane pilot aboard *Argus*, Sgt Bamberger, returned to Gibraltar with the carrier, from where he was later transported to Malta aboard a destroyer. Of the tragic operation, Bamberger commented:

> "Flt Lt MacLachlan, whom I got to know well in Malta, would not have taken off from the *Argus* if he had anticipated a flight lasting three hours. On any long-distance flight, particularly if it were over the sea, it would be against the very nature of any fighter pilot not to economise on petrol. To my mind the Navy did not take them close enough."

Diary:

19 November – Imtarfa [M'tarfa] Hospital: Yesterday, Air Vice-Marshal Maynard (AOC Malta) came and asked me all sorts of questions about our flight from *Argus*. I felt very ill and in the afternoon was taken to Imtarfa Hospital. I had a temperature of 101° and have been too ill to eat or do anything and my throat is still too sore to talk much.

23 November: There was an air raid this morning but very little damage was done. A formation of Savoia-Marchetti 79 bombers came over at about 1,200 feet with a fighter escort of Fiat CR42 fighters. Our Hurricanes went up and I hear that one Wop was brought down. This evening we got a poker school going though not a very successful one. I feel very much better now and am hoping to leave soon.

24 November: This morning we had another air raid. Two CR42s came over at 0 feet and machine-gunned Sunderlands in St Paul's Bay, setting fire to one and destroying another. This afternoon they came over again and machine-gunned the Wimpies at Luqa, damaging three. I went out to Rabat this evening with four Army officers. We had tea there and then came back to the Imtarfa bar where we had some drinks. The patron there showed us his collection of army cap badges and old guns, rifles, pistols etc. He really has a very good collection. We bought some bottles of whisky and brandy and I took them back to hospital where we got a poker school going. Sister came in, so we put the drinks under the table. However, she smelt them and all but joined the party herself! I hear I have got to go to Gibraltar tomorrow for the Court of Inquiry about our trip from *Argus*.

25 November – HMS *Ramillies*: This morning I got up at 5 o'clock, packed my bag and at 6.30 am was taken down to the Customs House where I met Gordon-Smith (the navigator of the Skua) and an RAF despatching officer. We were taken out to HMS *Ramillies*, where we were given cabins. I am sharing with a Lt/Cdr who has to sleep in a gun turret. We put out at about 10 o'clock and at dusk were just out of sight of Gozo. In our convoy are *Ark Royal*, *Renown*, *Berwick*, *Sheffield*, *Newcastle*, *Gloucester* and about eight destroyers. Gordon-Smith and I spent most of the day looking at back numbers of Esquire and other mags in the far corner of the wardroom.

These ships formed part of Operation Collar which Admiral Cunningham had planned in order to pass ships both ways between Gibraltar, Malta and Alexandria. *Ramillies* and *Berwick* (Force D) had come from Alexandria to Malta with four merchant ships, Force H from Gibraltar sailed to Malta escorting three merchant ships for the island and Alexandria and two cruisers which would replace *Ramillies* and *Berwick*. Admiral Somerville with Force H was worried that the Italians might take advantage of their interior lines to attack this heterogeneous convoy operation. On the 26th, the Italian fleet did sail from Naples with two battleships, the *Vittorio Veneto* and *Giulio Cesare*, three cruisers and eleven destroyers. They were joined on the 27th by another force of three cruisers and three destroyers.

Diary:
27 November: At about 11 o'clock [midway between Cape Spartivento in southern Sardinia and the Tunisian coast] we sighted part of the Italian fleet on the horizon [one battleship, one cruiser and one destroyer]. We immediately gave chase, and by 12 noon were just within range. The *Renown*, who had steamed up to a position immediately abreast of us, opened fire and shortly afterwards we followed suit. The cruisers, which were of course much faster than us, were now about three miles ahead and firing at a terrific rate. I

could see salvoes of Wop shells landing all around them and was very thankful that old *Ramillies* was too slow to enter the real danger zone.

Ark Royal sent off relays of Swordfish to torpedo the Iti capital ships and try to slow down their retreat. We could see clouds of smoke on the horizon and later heard that one of the Italian 8-inch cruisers was on fire [in fact it was the destroyer *Lanciere*]. It really was most exciting. Gordon-Smith and I had quite a good view from the pom-pom deck, but were ready to beat a hasty retreat should any shells come our way. By about 1300 the Iti's were out of range and we were well within sight of land, so the chase was abandoned. Hardly had we got back to the wardroom when 'Action Stations' was sounded again. We started to make our way on deck, but just as I emerged from the hatch, the 4-inch AA guns opened fire just above me and scared me shitless. Standing in the corner of the hatch I saw a formation of about ten SM79s in squadron vic at about 10,000 feet. Their bombs fell about half a mile off our port bow and did no damage whatsoever. I heard later that one of the bombers was brought down by Fulmars from the *Ark*.

About twenty minutes later another wave of bombers came over and all the AA guns opened up. They made a hell of a row. Gordon-Smith and I tried several times to get up on deck but empty shell cases were being passed down all the hatches and it was impossible to get past. Suddenly there was a series of terrific crashes and we learned later that a salvo of about thirty bombs had been dropped all round the *Ark*. People who were on deck said that for a minute the *Ark* completely disappeared in spray and smoke. I wish to hell I'd been on deck as the *Ark* was only about 500 yards behind us and would have made a wizard photo. After the guns had ceased firing, we went up on deck and saw the tail of a Walrus flying boat sticking up out of the sea behind us. I don't know what happened, but apparently all the crew were picked up.

When *Berwick* dropped back into position beside us, we noticed that her upper front turret was jammed, with the guns pointing to port. Part of the bridge was also smashed. I hear that she stopped a couple of 6-inch shells, and that one officer and five ratings were killed. Two Fulmars that were sent to shadow the damaged Italian ships did not return. We were hoping that we would be sent to finish off the damaged Italian ships, but were not allowed to. I should have loved to have seen a bit of bullying on our side for a change.

In fact, Admiral Somerville had called off pursuit for a number of reasons – his prime task was to escort the convoy and his two capital ships lacked sufficient speed to catch the Italians. When Force H reached Gibraltar, Somerville was shocked to learn that he was to be the subject of a Court of Inquiry concerning his decision to discontinue the chase of the Italian Fleet.

Diary:

28 November – Gibraltar: The Italian official communiqué is wizard. It gives our losses as follows:- one cruiser of the *Berwick* class sunk; one aircraft carrier (they daren't say *Ark Royal* again) believed sunk, last seen listing badly with water over the flight deck; one battleship damaged. Actually the two hits on *Berwick* were the only damage to our ships. We got into Gib at about 1700 and tied up at the mole in the centre of the harbour. At about 7.30 pm we got a shore boat and were taken to the Rock Hotel. After dinner we met a Sqn Ldr Middleton of 200 Group who says we are to be at the Tower by about 10 o'clock tomorrow to attend the Court of Inquiry.

29 November: At 1030 we went to the Tower and there met Capts Rushbrook and Metcalf, also some other officers from *Argus* (which, incidentally, is still in Gib). We waited all morning and most of the afternoon for our turn to give the court our gen. When at last my turn came I was ushered into the room, and was somewhat taken aback to find an Admiral (Sir Dudley North), a Commodore, a Captain and a Group Captain facing me. Everything went to order till they asked me if I had any idea as to why eight of the planes failed to reach Malta. I said that the whole thing had been cut down too fine, but that had we all known to fly at 1,800 revs instead of 2,200 or above, we might have all reached Malta. Certainly all my flight would have done. I told them that Eliot, who flew at the lower revs, had 14 gallons left, whereas the rest of us who flew at 2,200 revs had only an average of two gallons each. This rather foxed the Admiral, who insisted that if Eliot flew at lower revs, he must have arrived later, and so been in the air longer than us – thus using up a correspondingly greater quantity of fuel. The Group Captain (Rogers) explained at great length that to fly at a given speed you can either employ a fine pitch and high revs, or a coarse pitch and low revs, but the Admiral still didn't get it. They asked me a few more questions and then said I could go. Just as I was leaving Admiral North said, 'That seems OK, but I still don't understand all this pitch business!'

The Court of Inquiry found that the loss of aircraft was attributable to errors of navigation and a failure by the pilots to keep to the most economical cruising speed, the distance being well within the endurance of the aircraft. Nonetheless, Admiral Somerville privately took some of the blame upon himself. He wrote on the day after the loss of the aircraft: "I feel now that in spite of the risk of meeting superior Italian surface forces it would have been better if I had proceeded 40 miles further east . . ."

However, it was subsequently tacitly agreed that the disaster was due to: (a) inadequate weather forecasting – the latest meteorological report received was 19 hours out of date; (b) a lack of liaison between Navy and Air Force as to the Hurricane's true range, with the pilots instructed to fly at 2,000 feet where the air is 'heavier' than at the height prescribed in the handling notes available to the Air Operations Officer aboard *Argus*. This stated the range of the Hurricane II (tropicalised) in still air, at 130 knots, was 521 miles – but only when flying at 10,000 feet; and (c) over-cautious handling of the fleet which had, in fact, played a much greater part in the tragedy than had aircrew error. The loss of so many operationally experienced pilots was particularly damaging. Much was learned from this tragic experience, which resulted in proper planning and preparation for future ferry flights. Prime Minister Churchill later wrote of this incident: "Never again were the margins cut so fine, and though many similar operations took place in the future, never did such a catastrophe recur."

Diary:

5 December: There is still no news of our return to Malta, so we are trying to get permission to go over to Tangier in Spanish Morocco for the weekend . . . The last few days have been spent in various excursions to such places as North Front aerodrome, Sandy Bay and the *Ark*. If we have to stay here very much longer I shall get decidedly browned off!

6 December – Tangier: We finally got leave to go to Tangier and spent the morning making last minute preparations. Yesterday we got our passport photos taken, got our provisional passports from the Colonial Secretary and our exit permits from the Defence Office. All we had to do this morning was to buy our tickets (costing £2 each) and change some money into Moroccan francs. I took £9 with me. I have borrowed a pair of grey flannel bags and a sports coat from Flt Lt Alexander of 200 Group, but feel rather naked in civvies. It is the first time I have worn them since war was declared. We put off at about 1400 hrs and went across the bay hugging the Spanish coast till we reached Tarifa. Here we turned south-west and headed for Tangier. We saw several schools of porpoises, some not ten yards from the boat. When we were about five miles off the Moroccan coast the Swordfish on evening patrol came and shot us up, much to the excitement of the Spanish passengers. Shortly after this it started to rain, but very fortunately for me (as I had no raincoat) it cleared up before we reached Tangier. As we entered the harbour we passed quite close to the two Italian submarines that had taken refuge there after being damaged by British destroyers. We dropped anchor about 200 yards from the quay and a motor lifeboat came up alongside. I was rather surprised to see it contained about five Arabs, complete with fezes and pantaloons. Somehow I had never realised there were Arabs so far west.

At last, after much shouting and gesticulating, one boatload of passengers was taken off, and soon the empty boat returned for the next lot. We were amongst them and eventually arrived at the quay. Alongside was a Spanish MTB very obviously of German design. I was tempted to take a photograph, but fortunately refrained from doing so. As we got out of the boat, we were besieged by about six Arabs, and I had great difficulty in hanging onto our parachute bag. One very toothy creature insisted that we gave our bag to a friend of his who would take us up to the El Minza Hotel where we had decided to stay. Short of a fight there was no way out of it, so we reluctantly handed over, or rather, loosened our grip on, the parachute bag. The Arab, whose name was Absolum, got our bag through customs, paid our passports, and bundled us into a taxi, all inside five minutes. I must say it was with a feeling of great relief that we shut ourselves into that taxi and drove out of the seething mass of shouting Arabs. At the hotel I tried to dispose of the Arab by tipping him, but it was no use. He refused the money and said he would be our guide and we could pay him when we left. I told him that we did not want a guide, but to everything I said, he replied, 'That's all right – you will see' – and we did!

8 December: It was a beautiful day, so we decided to go round the Moorish part of the town and take a few photos. It was really a very interesting walk. We ended up by coming through the old market and past the camel yard. At 2.30 we went to Legg's garage and got a car. Legg said he would not think of charging British officers and as long as we bought the petrol he would be honoured to lend us the car. Accordingly we filled up with ten litres and set off on our travels. First we went up through the British settlement, but were stopped by guards after a few miles. We turned back and went south-west to Hercules Caves. No one stopped us en route, and after parking the car we got permission from an Arab soldier to visit the caves. When we were about halfway down, someone yelled at us to stop, but I took no notice and went on into the cave. It was about 30 yards long and about 30-40 feet high, with an opening out to the sea. I had only been about a minute and had taken a photograph, when I was surrounded by Arabs who saw my camera. They got very excited and after we had left the cave they insisted on confiscating my camera.

In the end we were taken along to Spartell lighthouse with the Arab guard who had my camera. Here we met a very decent Spanish officer who said he would have to send me to the Spanish Military HQ in Tangier. I was damned annoyed at all this fuss over nothing, but as I could speak neither Spanish nor Arabic, I was helpless.

After hours of telephoning and talking we were sent into Tangier with an Arab officer. Up to now I had been inclined to treat the whole thing as rather a joke, but when we arrived at the Spanish Military HQ and were locked up in a small, very cold room with concrete walls and four wooden chairs, I began to get other ideas. We demanded an explanation and were told that we were not prisoners, but were just waiting to see the Commandant! After another conference they came and asked me to park my car in the car park, as it would be in the way on the road. Never suspecting anything, I did so, putting Gordon-Smith's camera under the seat in case anyone pinched it. I got back to find that the Commandant had arrived, but could not deal with us. We would have to wait till the Colonel arrived. We were all freezing cold and getting pretty mad by this time, but as we were assured that the Colonel would be there in ten minutes, we decided to wait quietly. Outside our window was a large parade ground, with little groups of Arab soldiers sitting around their charcoal fires, cooking their evening meal. We could quite easily have escaped through the window, but I was determined to get my camera back, so stayed in the room. Eventually the Colonel arrived, but said he would have to go out to the cave and see what we had done before he could let us go. On hearing this, we demanded to be allowed to see the British Consul, but were told that there was only an internal telephone, so it was impossible. Without telling us why, they took Absolum, and we were left without any means of communicating with the Spanish.

As they said we were not prisoners, we had objected to having our door locked, so we were allowed to have it open, but a sentry with fixed bayonet was placed outside. Every so often he would open the door and heave an audible sigh of relief each time he saw us still there! This gave us an idea. There was a sort of lavatory affair in the room, so we all got into this after first opening the window of the room. A few minutes later our guard opened our door to make sure we were still there, and after one look out of the window, let out a noise like a steamroller going up a hill backwards. I couldn't help a slight titter, but he was making so much noise he did not hear. He rushed out and told the Arab officer that we had escaped. As soon as he left the room we got out of the lavatory, shut the window, and pretended to be asleep in the chairs. In came the Arab officer and after seeing us all there, was furious with our guard. I wish I knew Spanish just to have understood what he said. The wretched guard couldn't make it out. He was obviously terrified of the officer and I felt rather sorry for him afterwards. On looking out of the window a few minutes later we found another guard with a rifle and bayonet. He seemed quite a decent fellow, but had an unpleasant way of brandishing his bayonet, presumably demonstrating what would happen if we tried to escape!

It was dark by now and terribly cold. As nothing had happened for the last three hours we began to have visions of spending the night there. I wrote a note to the British Consul, but really had little hope that it would ever reach him. When it was written, I walked straight out of the door, the poor sentry being too much taken aback to try and stop me. I found the Arab officer and after much gesticulating, persuaded him to send my note to the British Consul. I saw it given to an Arab who started off with it, and then I went back to our cell. Our guard was obviously relieved to see me return and even smiled. At about 7.30 Absolum returned looking very worried and cold. He told us that he had been out to the cave, and that the Colonel had asked him lots of questions, to which he had replied with utmost caution. Apparently the Colonel would see us in the usual Spanish 'ten minutes'. This time it turned out to be half an hour. Absolum also told us that the Spanish had searched our car and found Gordon-Smith's camera, which they had also taken.

At 8 o'clock the Arab officer called for us and took us to the Colonel's office. The Colonel was a tall, lean-faced man of about 40, with thin, rather cruel lips, and short, thick hair. He seemed quite friendly to us, and told us we were free to go now. After apologising for detaining us so long, he said that the camera would be returned as soon as the films had been developed and found harmless. While all this was going on I had a chance to look round the office, which was very small and rather untidy. The Colonel sat at a desk in the far corner, and had to turn round to speak to us. Above the desk, on the wall, hung a large autographed photo of General Franco, while on the wall nearest the door was a small photo of Hitler. Mussolini was nowhere to be seen. After taking our names we said goodbye, and made a hasty departure while we had the chance. We got the car and went to the British Consulate – which we found was shut, so we took the car on to the garage, where we found Mr Legg waiting for us. He was very interested to hear of our adventures and thought we were damn lucky to get off so easily.

9 December – Gibraltar: After breakfast in bed at 7.30, we dressed and went to the British Consul, Mr Watkinson, to arrange about the forwarding of our cameras. He was a man of about 50, with very scanty grey hair and a charming manner. He told us he had so far heard nothing about the cameras but as soon as he got them, he would send them on. We then packed our bag, paid our hotel bill (320 francs) and went down to the quay. Here we met Absolum and when the motor boat came in we paid him and jumped into the boat. Much as I liked Tangier it was with a definite sense of relief that I left that crowd of shouting, begging Arabs! It was a beautifully sunny day, so I fixed myself up with a deckchair in one of the lifeboats and went to sleep. As we passed Gib harbour we looked eagerly to see if there was a Sunderland, but were disappointed. I can't stick Gib much longer.

On 10 and 11 December, Mac managed to get into the air for a short time and so relieved the boredom a little. He wangled his way into a London II flying boat of 202 Squadron that was responsible for patrolling the approaches to the Mediterranean and keeping watch on German ships bottled up in the ports of southern Spain and Spanish Morocco. Mac flew on one of these patrols with Flt Lt Farrar in K5911 over the Straits of Gibraltar to Cueta, Cape Spartel, Cape Trafalgar and Tarifa. On the second flight, with Flg Off Foot in L7043, they shadowed a French tanker off Cape Tres Forcas in Morocco. He also managed his first flight in a Swordfish:

Diary:

13 December: We tried to get permission to go back to Tangier yesterday, but there seems to be some chance of a Sunderland going to Malta, so we packed. I bought a Hugo's course on Spanish for 3/6d so that I can know enough to get myself out of jail next time. This morning by a bit of wangling, I got permission to fly Lt O'Sullivan's Swordfish [P4271]. Accordingly Gordon-Smith and I went out to North Front and took off. It was wizard to fly again – even in a Swordfish! I did a loop and a few stall turns, shooting up all the boats I could see. That evening I met O'Sullivan and thanked him for the loan of his kite. He then proceeded to tear me off the most almighty strip for looping it! No sign of a Sunderland and the *Ark* has gone out into the Atlantic.

The next evening Mac persuaded Plt Off Richardson to take him as an observer in a 202 Squadron Swordfish (L2808) on a dusk patrol over the Straits. Following a three-hour flight, they landed after dark.

Diary:

19 December: The past few days have been extremely boring as there is absolutely nothing to do. We go through the same routine day after day. Breakfast is at 9am, then a visit to the Tower at about 10am, only to be told that there is still no transport to Malta. After this we wander aimlessly about till 1230 when we go up to the Rock and have a ginger beer. At 1300 we go and eat the same sort of food at the same table, served by the same waiter. After lunch we listen to the news, then sit and read till tea, which consists of two small pieces of toast, three little slices of bread and butter and greengage jam. We then have a choice of five sorts of cake. I always have the same two kinds, as the others are not fit to eat. In the evening we see any new films (i.e. twice a week), or if the *Ark* is in, we get up a party and have supper at the Victoria. As there is still no news of transport to Malta, we have again obtained permission to go to Tangier. We have consequently spent most of the day getting our photographs, temporary passports, and exit permits etc.

20 December – Tangier: On arriving at Tangier, we were met by the usual crowd of Arab guides, small boys asking for francs, and a whole collection of nondescript beggars and sharks. We had decided definitely not to have a guide, but Absolum appeared, seized our bag and rushed off with it to Customs, so we had no choice in the matter. Finally, after much standing about and shouting, we got a taxi and so gained the comparative peace and quiet of the El Minza. After a wash and brush-up, we walked around the cafés till about 8.30pm, when we went down to the Vox for supper. The head waiter was very pleased to see us, and we had an excellent meal, accompanied by an equally fine bottle of red Bordeaux. A violinist played several songs, which brought back vivid and very pleasant memories of Paris in the good old days before the Blitz. After supper we visited the Central, the Shanghai Bar, the Sussex, and finally ended up at the Floriana. We had the odd drink and were immediately tackled by a couple of bints. Mine, a Hungarian blonde, disposed of a couple of half-bottles of champagne in less time than it takes to tell, and was all for having more. Gordon-Smith was in a similar plight, so we called for the bill, and to our horror found it was 940 francs! We paid 800 francs, and said we'd pay the rest tomorrow; no more of the Floriana for me!

22 December: This morning Mr Watkinson rang us to say the Spanish had returned our cameras and that we could collect them from him at lunchtime. Feeling very cheered, we set off for a walk around the Moorish quarter. We were followed by innumerable small boys and prospective guides, but by strictly following a policy of neglect, they eventually left us. At 1230 we returned to the hotel where we met Mr Watkinson and collected our cameras. It was wizard to get them back as I had seriously started to give up hope of ever seeing them again. After lunch at the usual little café, we went

back to El Minza, where I wrote to mother and Chubby Eliot. At
4.30pm we went to the French café, where we shamelessly disposed
of eleven of the most delicious cakes I have ever tasted. It makes my
mouth water to write about them! The gap between tea and supper
was filled by a visit to the pictures, where, for the modest sum of 5
francs we were shown into the most palatial armchairs in the front
row of the balcony (or its equivalent). The film, unfortunately, was
in French, but as Joan Bennett was in it, I did not particularly mind
whether I understood or not. Having come to the unanimous decision
that the Vox is the best eating place in Tangier, we again had dinner
there. The violinist played beautifully, and after a bottle of red
Bordeaux, I began to realise that life is sweet at times! We return to
Gib tomorrow.

25 December – Gibraltar: I'm afraid this Christmas has hardly been
a merry one for Gordon-Smith and me. Yesterday evening was spent
at the Rock feeling sorry for ourselves and wishing we were back in
Malta with our squadrons. We had a bottle of Rye [whisky] which
cheered us up a little, but it still didn't seem like Christmas Eve. This
morning we went down to the *Ark Royal* to get some of the chaps to
come up for a party, but found she was at an hour's notice to sail and
had already got steam up. Anyway we went back to the Rock where
we had our Christmas lunch of roast beef and Yorkshire pud (both of
which I hate). It poured with rain all afternoon so we read 'blood and
thunder' novels in the lounge. After tea, in spite of the slight drizzle,
we went out to North Front aerodrome because I had seen a foreign
plane circling in the afternoon and thought it might have landed. On
arriving, however, we were told it had been shot down and that it
crashed into the sea near La Linea, all the crew being drowned.
Dinner was much more cheerful. We actually got a little piece of
turkey each. Grp Capt Rogers asked us over to his table, and we
moved into the *vino blanco*. After dinner there was a dance and we
organised a series of drunken rugger scrums v the Navy. How no one
got hurt beats me – we broke a huge vase and several chairs etc. The
Group Captain and a Naval commander danced the Charleston and
were almost as amusing as they were drunk. Eventually we all sank
exhausted into chairs and one by one made our way up to bed.

28 December: At lunchtime today HMS *Furious* came in, so we are
hoping she is on her way to Malta with more Hurricanes. This
afternoon we went all round the Upper and Middle Galleries above
the old Moorish castle, and also climbed to the top of the Rock. We
were taken around by a 2nd/Lt of the Black Watch. He took us about
three-quarters of the way up in an army truck and we walked the rest.
The view from the top was most impressive. Looking north, the

Spanish frontier town of La Linea seems almost directly below, and beyond it the mountains of southern Spain stretch away to the horizon. Nestling under the Rock, to the west, is the town of Gibraltar, with its narrow streets and houses of white and yellow. Across the bay is the Spanish town of Algeciras, while beyond it are the Straits with Cape Spartel just visible in the distance. To the east there is a vertical drop of 1,350 feet to the village of Catalan Bay, and beyond it the Mediterranean merges with the sky on the horizon. After duly admiring this panorama, we climbed down to the truck and went to the Upper Galleries. They were very wet after the recent rain, but that did not deter us. I was rather surprised to see so many old cannon in the embrasures, some of them dating back to the 18th century. As far as I can make out the only guns there now are two or three Bren guns and a few rifles!

After going right to the end of the Upper Galleries, we went down to the Middle Galleries. These are much the same as the ones above, but, if anything, are even damper. All the spare rooms and passages are filled with tinned food of every description – sufficient to keep the garrison going for six months. At last we surfaced again and made our way back to their mess. Here we were given a first class tea, during which we all shot our little lines. Most of the officers had been with the Black Watch in the Maginot Line, and later had fought in the rearguard action on the Somme. As usual they asked where the hell the Air Force had been, and we naturally replied, they the army had been running away so hard they didn't have time to see us!

29 December: Today has been a very disappointing one. My hopes were raised to the skies this morning when, on looking out of my window, I saw the old *Argus* tied up to the mole. We took it for granted that she was on her old job, so straight after breakfast we rushed down to see if we knew any of the Hurricane pilots. At the Tower we were told *Argus* had only brought some Fulmars and some 'string-bags' [Swordfish] for the *Ark*, and that she was now going straight back to the UK. This was a terrible disappointment, but we still had hopes that the *Furious* would be going to Malta, so walked round to find out. My hopes were raised still further when I saw Polish sergeant pilots on the quay. On making enquiries I found they were taking Hurricanes out to Egypt, but by way of Freetown and Nigeria. From there they were being flown off the carrier and the pilots were taking them across Africa. I'd give anything to be going with them, but it just can't be done.

1 January 1941: The first day of 1941 has been cold and dismal. Yesterday evening I noticed a layer of alto-cumulus creeping up over the horizon, so was not surprised on looking out of my window this morning, to see misty low clouds and drizzle obscuring even the hills across the bay. To add to the discomforts of the weather, I have been suffering all day from what the French would call a *maladie de l'estomac*. I think the cause may safely be attributed to a pound of figs, which I devoured before going to sleep last night. In view of the inclement weather and my internal troubles, I decided to spend the day quietly at the Rock, reading my latest 'blood and thunder'- a book by John Rhode called *The House On Tolland Ridge*. This evening Gordon-Smith went to the pantomime, so I partook of dinner in lonely state, carefully leaving figs off the menu. Later in the evening (after several very successful visits to the 'little tin shed over the way'), I felt decidedly better, so let off steam by writing to mother. Just as I was going up to bed, Sqn Ldr Middleton informed me that, weather permitting, Gordon-Smith and I would be leaving for Malta by Sunderland at 0600 tomorrow morning. As the weather would very obviously NOT be permitting, I thanked him and said I would see him again at lunch tomorrow!

3 January: Excitement at last! Just as we came out of breakfast this morning we heard all the guns in the place opening up, pom-poms included. On rushing out of the front door, I saw to my amazement, a French kite (a Glenn Martin I think) flying across the bay at about 1,500 feet. Never in all my life have I seen such a shocking exhibition of AA firing. The pom-poms were all going about 200 yards behind, and the 3.7s were all over the place. The Froggy finally disappeared behind Europa Point, but about five minutes later, it re-appeared over North Front at about 6,000 feet and proceeded to dive across the bay at some phenomenal speed. No one got really near to him and he finally made off in the direction of Morocco. We waited around for a little in the hopes of another exhibition. The remainder of the day dragged on in the usual monotonous way, till, just before going to bed, we were told to get our things ready as we would probably be going off at 6 o'clock tomorrow morning. This news cheered us up immensely and we went to bed with light hearts.

5 January – Takali, Malta: Yesterday morning we were called at 0600, only to be told that the weather report from Malta was bad and that, consequently, the trip had again been cancelled. This morning however, we were taken down to the quay by car. There we got into the RAF powerboat and were taken out to the Sunderland. We took off in the pitch dark just after 0700 and headed east at about 1,000 feet. There were seven other passengers not counting Gordon-Smith and myself: one Group Captain, one Lt Colonel, two Majors, a Lt RN and a civilian. We sat facing each other in the wardroom, which was very cold and draughty. I spent sometime up in the pilot's cabin, and then went out to the tail turret, but nowhere could I get warm. We were given a breakfast of horrible greasy eggs and baked beans and rather wishy-washy tea, most of which I deposited again in the heads (the first time I have ever been sick in the air). It was very interesting passing Galite Island and Pantelleria, and they brought back memories of my last trip past them. At about 1500 we sighted the brown cliffs of Gozo and landed at Kalafrana Bay, the seaplane base, at about 1530. There we were taken up to the mess where we had tea, after which we went to Luqa (where we dropped Gordon-Smith) and then on to Takali. Our mess is in a big, square stone building with a courtyard and palm trees in front. It seems very cosy inside and the officers are a damn good crowd. The Station CO (Ginger O'Sullivan) was in to supper and had quite a lot to say for himself.

I am sharing a room with an accountant officer (a flight lieutenant) who gives a good first impression. All the beds are covered with mosquito netting, a system quite new to me. The food here is excellent – a change from the Rock! We spent the evening drinking and talking round a huge fire in the ante-room. I gather I am to be in A Flight [of No.261 Squadron] – obviously the best flight in this squadron. I shall be the second most senior member of the flight, which suits me down to the ground – no responsibility and plenty of flying!

No.261 Squadron had been formed in August 1940 out of the Hal Far Fighter Flight and No.418 Flight, the latter having arrived from the deck of HMS *Argus* in early August. It had a mixture of Gladiators and Hurricanes. It was as reinforcements for the squadron that the two flights had been flown off *Argus* in November. No.261 Squadron, based at Takali, had successfully fought off attacks by the Regia Aeronautica and was now commanded by Sqn Ldr John Trumble. Mac was posted to A Flight under Flt Lt John Waters, one of the original Gladiator pilots.

Diary:

6 January: The day started off with a clear blue sky, which gradually clouded over during the morning, and was almost completely obscured by lunchtime. In the morning I went over to Squadron HQ and read up the pilots' order book and signed the usual 'gen and bullshit bumph'. In the afternoon Trumble [the CO] and I went up in the Maggie [N5428] and had a look at the island. I was to have flown a Hurry-bird, but it stuck in the mud when Trumble was taxiing it, so my trip was washed out. After tea, Trumble took me into Valetta on his motorcycle and I joined the 'Union Club'.

After a haircut and shampoo we had a few drinks till about 8.30pm. The ride back was very exciting and certainly sobered me up, and I was well ready for the sumptuous meal that awaited me. After dinner we had a few more noggins and then talked till about midnight when we retired to bed.

7 January: The weather this morning was pretty bad; however it cleared a little in the afternoon, so I flew over to Luqa in the Maggie and there borrowed a Hurricane [P3330] in which I did 45 minutes aerobatics – very tasty, very sweet. As I was coming into land, the standby flight took off, so I started to formate on the last pair hoping to have a crack at an Iti. I saw the leading Hurrybird coming round onto my tail and suddenly realised that they would not be expecting me and might think I was a bandit. I turned and broke away – just in time, as I found out later!

8 January: This morning I flew over to Hal Far in the Maggie to collect a Hurricane. Here I met Gordon-Smith, who is now on Swordfish again and very brassed-off. We had a beer together and inspected our Gladiators, which look very spick and span in their new Navy camouflage. I flew the Hurricane [V7548] back to Luqa, where I was on standby from 1300 till 1730. I got my old machine V7474 (which I flew off *Argus*) – it is very popular I'm afraid. I shall have quite a job to hang onto it. We stand by in an old bus, which is parked by the Hurricanes at the lee end of the runway. There is an R/T pack set in it over which we get the orders to scramble. Most of the afternoon was spent playing poker dice and line-shooting. At about 1600 we had a scramble and had climbed to 12,000 feet when we were told to land. No sooner had I stopped my engine than I was sent up again. This time we had only reached a height of 9,000 feet when we were ordered to pancake. I must admit I was very disappointed as it was a marvellous evening and I really did expect to see something.

Mac would not be disappointed for long. Two events had been taking place while he had been in Gibraltar and en route for Malta. A new convoy, Excess, had been sent from Britain. Four of its ships were taking supplies to Greece, while one ship, the *Essex*, was earmarked for Malta. It contained 4,000 tons of ammunition and a dozen crated Hurricanes to replace those lost in November during the ill-fated Operation White. The convoy sailed on from Gibraltar on 6 January. It was supported by Force H from Alexandria, while the reciprocal convoy sailed on 7 January, led by the battleship *Warspite*, accompanied by *Valiant* and the aircraft carrier *Illustrious*. As these forces converged on the centre of the Mediterranean, Germany decided to reinforce its Italian Axis partner by sending aircraft to Sicily in order to neutralise Malta and the British Fleet, and would also help safeguard the Axis supply lines to North Africa. By 8 January, the first of 96 bombers, He111s, Ju88s and Ju87s of Fliegerkorps X, had begun arriving in Sicily from Norway. More aircraft would follow including 24 Bf110s, and later still a Staffel of Bf109Es. On the morning of 9 January, the first raids on Malta of 1941 were plotted on the radar. Sixteen MC200s of 6°Gruppo headed for Luqa aerodrome, from where Wellington bombers of No.148 Squadron had undertaken raids on the harbours of Tripoli, Naples and Palermo since the start of the new year.

Diary:

9 January: [Hurricane V7474] The weather was perfect and at 0820 we set off for Luqa in the old bus. F/O Eric Taylor, Chubby Eliot and P/O McAdam were the other pilots. We fully expected a blitz as the Wimpy boys went over and strafed Naples last night and the Itis usually pay us a return visit after such shows. We were not surprised, therefore, to get a scramble order at about 11 o'clock. Eric was leading and we climbed steeply to 22,000 feet well up-sun of the island. Suddenly Eric started to dive steeply towards Grand Harbour and, on following him, I saw a formation of enemy aircraft about 10,000 feet below us and five miles to port. I went straight for them and saw Eric turn to follow me. Ack-ack shells were bursting all around them and, as I closed in, some of these burst unpleasantly close to me! At first I could not make out what type of aeroplane they were and tried to overtake them so that I could do a head-on attack. As I drew closer, however, I realised they were Macchi 200 fighters, so did a normal astern attack on the right-hand man of the second section of three (there were six kites altogether). I opened fire at about 200 yards and saw most of the burst go into the Macchi. He did a steep diving turn to the right, but I managed to follow and gave him two more full deflection squirts while in the turn. The first of these just missed his tail, but I think most of the second squirt got him. Suddenly, to my amazement, the pilot baled out and I nearly hit his half-opened parachute as it disappeared under my nose. Somehow I had expected the kite to catch fire and as it had not done so, I instinctively followed it and fired again. I was very close to the Macchi and could see the incendiary bullets pouring into the empty cockpit as it plunged earthwards in a spiral dive.

For a few seconds I did not realise I had shot down my first kite – it all happened so quickly and was so simple. I must have wasted quite a lot of precious ammo and even more precious altitude, before I abandoned the chase and looked round to get my bearings. Straight in front of me, and about half a mile away, was a lone Macchi trying to catch the other four, which were about a mile in front. He had obviously got his throttle wide open for he was leaving a thick trail of exhaust smoke. Having made sure there was nothing behind me, I 'pulled the plug' and went after him. He rejoined the formation long before I was in range, but I watched him take up his position on the starboard of the formation and decided I would go for him first. It was a marvellous experience sitting there knowing that I was gradually catching them and feeling confident that, with any luck, I would shoot down at least one of them. I took a bead on my selected victim and watched his wings slowly growing till at last they filled the 40 feet base gap on my sight. I waited a little longer to make sure and then pressed the tit. I remember my mouth watering as I saw a jet of incendiary bullets going through him. I expected him to blow up or burst into flames, but evidently my bullets had done no serious damage for he did a terribly tight climbing turn to the right and I only just managed to follow him.

Out of the corner of my eye, I saw two other Macchis turn back towards me, and while making sure they could not get on my tail for the next few seconds, I lost sight of my prey. I banked steeply and caught sight of him going down in a series of aileron turns about 1,000 feet below. I immediately followed and was so relieved to get him in my sights again that I fired lots of hopeless deflection shots, most of which went yards astern. At about 6,000 feet, he pulled out and went into a right-hand turn. I followed him round and got in one long full-deflection squirt. He seemed to drop out of the turn and went into a terrifyingly steep dive. I followed, firing almost continually. At about 3,000 feet my guns stopped and I realised, with bitter disappointment, that my ammo was exhausted. I started to pull out and as I turned, I saw a tall column of water rise out of the sea. I must have killed the pilot with my last burst in the turn for he never pulled out of the dive. I could not see any other aircraft, so turned for home at about 2,000 feet. Suddenly, about half a mile to port, there was a vivid sheet of flame on the surface of the sea. A great column of smoke and water rose into the air and seemed to hang there for seconds before the water dropped back into the sea and the smoke drifted slowly away, leaving nothing but a small patch of burning oil. I flew over and circled the spot once or twice, but could see no sign of life, so once again I turned for home. About three miles off St Paul's Bay, I found the pilot of the first machine I had shot down, still attached to his parachute. I flew low past him and having made sure that a boat was going out to rescue him, returned to Luqa where I landed. I was first down and was amazed to hear that the Wops had done a low level machine-gun attack on the aerodrome and had slightly damaged two Wimpies. Six Macchis had taken part in the raid, while two other formations of six each had stayed upstairs to act as escort. It was one of these I attacked.

The next man down was Eric Taylor, who had also got two (one of which was the one I saw crash in flames). The rest of our pilots came in one by one, none of them however had been able to catch the Itis [in fact, Mac's flight commander, Flt Lt John Waters, also claimed a Macchi as probably destroyed]. Chubby chased three back till he was only about ten miles from Sicily before returning. Later we heard that the AA brought another down in flames, making a total of five. None of our kites were even hit! Later Chubby was heard to say, 'If only I'd had a Spitfire, I could have shot down at least three!' When I returned to the mess, I found that several bottles of bubbly had been opened in our honour, so wasted no time in availing myself of the gesture!

The pilot of the first aircraft Mac had shot down was Capitano Luigi Armanino, a veteran of the Spanish Civil War. He had been wounded in the arm and thigh and was taken to the hospital at M'tarfa.

10 January: I was on the early watch and on again at 1300. I had just run up my kite [V7370] when we were ordered to scramble. We climbed to 20,000 feet and were just beginning to feel safe when the pancake order was given. About an hour later we scrambled again and this time were sent out to patrol over a large convoy coming from the west. Just as we got into position HMS *Illustrious* opened fire about eight miles away. I saw Eliot break away, so I followed him and circled *Illustrious*. I could see no E/A, so climbed to the north, hoping to intercept any stragglers going home. I then saw five little black specks slightly below and about five miles to the north-east. I immediately followed and on closing saw they were CR42s. Hoping they had not seen me I made for the tail of the starboard man. Before I could close to effective range, two or three of them whizzed back over my head and were coming down on my tail. Knowing that I should stand no chance against five kites that could out-manoeuvre and out-climb me, I half-rolled and screeched back towards the convoy. As might be expected from the Navy, *Illustrious* opened up on me with pom-poms. I was well out of range so did not worry. After circling around for about half an hour, I was ordered to pancake.

At about 1700 we scrambled again and patrolled the convoy, which was now about ten miles south of Gozo. When flying over at about 17,000 feet *Illustrious* opened fire on us with her pom-poms and 4.5's, some of which burst right under our formation. If the Navy weren't so easy on the trigger we might give them some sort of protection, but they fire on us as soon as we fly within their range. No E/A appeared and in due course we landed. The *Illustrious* docked this evening, listing slightly and down in the stern. She had a direct hit from a Ju87 Stuka, which was shot during its dive and piled up on the flight deck. [In fact the wreckage on her deck was probably that of a Fulmar, which had been unable to take off and was then hit by German bombs.] I hear there are 150 casualties, 90 dead. The cruiser *Southampton* was set on fire and had to be scuttled. Altogether a pretty good show on the Jerries' part.

Illustrious's captain and crew had every reason to be paranoid. The carrier had begun the day as part of the Mediterranean Fleet with *Warspite* and *Valiant*. This force had made contact with the Excess convoy and the freighter *Essex* had managed to slip safely into Valetta harbour with her precious cargo of Hurricanes. However, the British ships had been spotted and now came in for severe punishment. *Illustrious* had been attacked by over a hundred enemy aircraft and had been hit by six 1,000-lb bombs, her steering gear had been crippled, her lifts put out of action, her flight deck wrecked and half her guns were silenced. She was ordered to pull out of the line and head for Malta steering by main engines. As she struggled towards the shelter of Grand Harbour, the bombers came back four more times and she was hit again. It would be some time before she would be fit for sea again and the period (12-23 January) she was in the dockyard at Malta became known as 'The *Illustrious* Blitz'. To face this onslaught, Malta's Hurricane strength stood at fourteen fighters plus the twelve crated Hurricanes which *Essex* had delivered – and twenty-three pilots to fly them. On the 11th, a single SM79 appeared over Grand Harbour taking photographs. Mac and five other Hurricanes were scrambled, but as he recorded in his logbook: 'Scramble and patrol base at 15,000 feet. No interception.'

Diary:

16 January: The last two days have passed without incident. I have been on night flying for the last three nights and am doing my last stand-by tonight. Last night two formations came over during the first watch and Lambert [Flt Lt Lambert was OC B Flight] took off, but could see nothing, as it was very hazy. The Wimpy boys bombed Catania (Sicily) last night and claim to have destroyed 30 Jerry aircraft, gutted two hangars and blown up the administrative buildings. This may account for today's aerial activity.

At about 1500, the Hurricanes scrambled and we heard there were two large formations coming in from the north and east. Suddenly the AA guns opened up and a swarm of Ju87s came diving down through a hole in the clouds. They dived on Grand Harbour in a continuous stream, releasing their bombs at about 5,000 feet. The noise was simply terrific and great columns of smoke and dust began to rise from the Harbour. Twenty-nine Ju88s came altogether and during the whole attack I did not see one Hurricane! It was enough to make me cry, but worse was still to come. No sooner had the Ju87s gone than the RDF (radar) picked up four more formations coming in at 10,000 feet. Once again the ack-ack opened up and down through the clouds came a horde of Ju87s. Diving almost vertically to 2,000 feet, they released their bombs and slowly turned for home in ones and twos. There was the chance that every fighter pilot prays for and still there was not a fighter to be seen. It was maddening standing on the mess balcony watching single unescorted 87s wandering around at 2,000 feet and being able to do nothing about it. I would have given a week's pay to be up on that scramble!

Chubby and I could stand it no longer. We borrowed John Waters' motor-cycle and rushed off to dispersals where we got into two reserve machines and asked permission to take off. Imagine our consternation when we were told we were not to leave the ground. I've never come across such a panic-stricken, disorganised collection of incompetent lunatics as fighter-control HQ Med. Last night I sat in my kite with the engine running for a quarter of an hour, while a formation of Jerries flew up and down the island in full moonlight, but would control let me go up? Would they fuck! We sit on our backsides for days longing for the sight of an enemy aircraft and when some come, control works up a glorious panic and refuses to let anyone do anything in case something goes wrong and they have to carry the can! It's about time those bastards pulled their fingers out and realised there's a war on! Eventually the Hurricanes returned. Out of the four on patrol, only two had even fired their guns. Heaven only knows where the other two went. Out of sixty Ju88s and 87s we did not shoot down one kite. Honestly, I quit! I don't think I dare go near Valetta for a week or two. The Fleet Air Arm in three Fulmars shot down seven, and even the AA got two or three. The attack wasn't very successful for the Jerries, as they only scored one hit on *Illustrious* and one or two on dock installations and houses. But I'm afraid it will take several weeks' good work to redeem the prestige lost today.

18 January: Last night I went into the big city with Chubby, and had my first bath since arriving here. Feeling very swept and garnished, we wandered into a bar where, amongst others, I met old Lea from No.58 Squadron. He is now a lieutenant on *Illustrious*. Chubby tacked onto a Sub Lt called Noel who asked us to go over and have a look at *Illustrious*. As we had the day off, we went down to the

Customs House where we were lucky enough to find a motor-launch just leaving for *Illustrious*. Having arrived on board, Noel showed us around.

The first bomb, which hit *Illustrious* when she was in the Sicilian Channel, had gone down the after lift and exploded on a level with the hangar. The internal damage was pretty serious, though the actual hull of the ship appeared undamaged. Looking down the lift from the flight deck, we could see a mass of tangled iron and burnt-out wreckage. The whole ship seemed pervaded with the smell of stale cordite smoke and burnt bodies. Inside the hangar, the scene was even more terrible. Lying in contorted attitudes all over the floor, were the burnt-out remains of what once had been Fulmars and Swordfish. Here and there on the walls, were ugly splashes of blood, where limbs of the unfortunate hangar personnel had been flung. The bomb which had caused most of this damage had gone through the 3-inch armoured flight deck, through the hangar, and had burst as it went through the hangar floor. The wardroom, which is immediately below the hangar, received the full force of the explosion and everyone inside was killed. We had a quick look round the rest of the ship and just as we were leaving the air-raid warning went. We were nearly swept off our feet in the mad stampede for the shelter.

We had been there about ten minutes when the guns opened fire and on hearing them, I went back to the entrance whence I had quite a good view of the proceedings. Down through a gap in the clouds came a horde of Ju87s. The AA barrage was terrific, but they never wavered. These Jerries have guts, and I couldn't help but admire them. As far as I could make out, they were attacking Luqa. They seemed to come down in a never-ending stream; their organisation was marvellous. I saw them come down very low with Bofors shells flying all around them. Their leader turned off and flew out to the east smoking badly. There was a flash, a dirty puff of black smoke behind him and down he went, flames and smoke belching from his petrol tanks. At last the guns ceased firing and the smoke gradually drifted away. The 'All-clear' went, but scarcely had we left the shelter when the alarm sounded again. This time however, it was only a recco machine and we were soon on our way round the docks to the ferry. As we arrived, the alarm went again and within minutes the streets were clear. Chubby and I were so brassed-off by this time that we just sat and waited at the ferry pier. After what seemed like ages the 'All-clear' went and eventually we managed to get a boat across to Valetta. It was 6 o'clock by this time, so we went to the Club and then on to Caruana's for the odd noggin. Here we heard that the hangars at Luqa had been flattened and that two Maltese had been killed by a direct hit on their shelter. Two Wimpies were burnt out and all the rest were temporarily u/s. We shot down six Jerries, the AA got five and we lost two Fulmars. One pilot, however, was picked up OK.

The raids of the 18th were a prelude to larger ones on the 19th. They came in throughout the day from 0830 onwards, aiming at the Grand Harbour and *Illustrious*.

19 January [Hurricane V7546]: It was a perfect morning and we took over our kites for the 9 o'clock watch with a definite feeling that our morning would not be uneventful. At about 0945 we were ordered to scramble and had reached about 12,000 feet when AA shells started bursting over Grand Harbour. I saw hordes of Ju87s starting to dive down through the barrage, so led my section round to the west of Valetta and came in behind one of the first machines to leave the Harbour. I gave it a short burst, but I overshot it and had to break away in a climbing turn. I fully expected to hear bullets pouring into my unprotected belly, but either the rear gunner was dead or a rotten shot, for nothing hit me. Having lost the necessary speed gained in my dive, I selected another Ju87 and closed in from the rear and slightly below. The gunner started firing long before I was within range, but after I had fired one well-aimed burst, he packed up and I could see his gun pointing harmlessly into the air. The rest was fairly plain sailing. I closed in to about 100 yards and gave him five or six short squirts. Clouds of smoke came from his engine and, as he rolled into his last dive, I could see livid tongues of flame streaming back from his port wing root. I watched him go in, and then turned for home.

One large, though rather straggly formation, passed me about half a mile to port, and then I saw what I had been looking for. Over to starboard was one lone Ju87 trying to sneak back unobserved. I chased him and after two or three squirts, he started to smoke and dived into the sea. While I was watching him crash, I suddenly became aware that I was being shot at. Little red ping-pong balls were flying past me in a steady stream. I did a steep left-hand diving turn, 'pulled the plug', and went like the clappers. As I turned, I saw to my horror, a CR42 flying dangerously near my tail. I glanced at the clock and saw I was doing over 300 mph, so turned to see if I was being followed. There, almost straight above, was the CR42, obviously unaware of my presence. I pulled up underneath him and got in about a two-second squirt before I ran out of ammo. I did not dare to stay to see the results as he was slightly above me and was quite possibly still OK. I then flew home, passing dozens of wizard shots – lone Ju87s and CR42s who could easily have been attacked unawares. How I longed for another ten seconds' fire. On landing I found there were bullets through both my main spars, through my tail plane and also my rudder. Makes you think a bit! I was first down, but the others soon followed. Burges had got two, MacAdam one, Sgt Bamberger one and Sgt Ayre one, making a total of seven. Sgt Kelsey unfortunately did not return.

We had only been down a few minutes when we [Mac and Sgt Bamberger] were ordered to scramble again [now in V7545]. This time we chased a single plot fifteen miles north-east, but made no interception, so returned. After about half an hour on the ground we scrambled again and were told there was one seaplane, and one fighter, ten miles north of the island. When about twenty miles out, I saw a tiny speck in the distance and called 'Tally Ho!' I lost sight of it but saw another aircraft circling over the sea about five miles away. I closed on it, carefully keeping between it and the sun. At about 100 yards I opened fire. It was a huge three-engined job [a Cant Z506B seaplane], and I could hardly have missed it if I had tried. A sheet of flame burst from its starboard wing-root, so I ceased firing and flew very close to it. It did not seem to be losing height, but flew calmly on for about three miles, with flames and smoke pouring from it. I gave it another short squirt, but it was already doomed. The flames crept back along the fuselage and finally the tail control surfaces. As they burnt off I could see the elevator being pulled back, but eventually the pilot lost control and the machine went down in a spiral dive, blazing from stem to stern. As it hit the water there was a column of steam and smoke, which slowly cleared, leaving a patch of burning oil and debris.

The Z506B was a Red-Cross marked air/sea rescue machine from 612^Squadriglia flown by Sottotenente Ignazio Rossi. Such aircraft were considered fair game despite their markings, since it was believed that in addition to carrying out their designated duties they also undertook reconnaissance sorties.

I flew back and had just stopped my engine after landing, when the alarm went again. The ground crews quickly refuelled and rearmed, and in five minutes I was in the air again. Burges, who had also landed, took off with me and we climbed to 17,000 feet. Again we saw the now familiar sight of AA shells bursting over the Harbour. Down came the bombers, Ju88s this time. Burges went screaming down into the middle of them, but, hoping that Ju87s would follow, I hung around at about 10,000 feet. I saw a Ju88 pull out of its dive and instead of turning straight out to sea, it kept flying south in the direction of Kalafrana. It seemed to be quite alone, so I decided to have a crack at it. I got round onto its tail, but before I was in range it saw me and turned, trying to get me with its front fixed cannon. I followed it round and then, tightening my turn almost to blackout point, I got in a well-aimed full deflection shot. The port engine started to smoke badly and I thought for a moment that I had got it. It straightened out however, and started to climb gently. All this time the rear gunner had been blazing away at me, but I was too excited to worry. I closed to about 50 yards and gave it a five or six-second squirt. Clouds of smoke came back and my cockpit was filled with the horrible smell of burning aeroplane. I pulled out to one side, just missing a salvo of bits and pieces that fell out of the bottom of the bomber. I think the port engine had stopped altogether; it kept emitting showers of sparks and clouds of black smoke and oil. I had a quick look round, but could see no enemy aircraft within a mile, so circled round watching the Junkers crash. At about 3,000 feet, one of the crew baled out and the bomber steepened its dive. Finally it crashed into a little bay near Zonkor Point. As I only had about ten rounds left in each gun, I returned to Takali and landed.

By this time it was 1 o'clock, so B Flight took over watch. I spent most of the afternoon writing out my combat reports and went to Valetta in the evening. The squadron's total score for the day was eleven confirmed and two possibles. A Gladiator from Kalafrana got one and the AA boys got five, making a total of seventeen. Altogether a most exciting and enjoyable day.

Malta's RAF Intelligence signal described it as, 'a good bad day with a fair score'. The Luftwaffe admitted to losing only three Ju87s and two Ju88s, while the Italians lost a CR42 and the Cant seaplane. Following these three days of heavy fighting, the Axis attacks stopped for the time being.

Diary:

22 January: Since the blitz, some of the Navy boys from *Illustrious* have been standing by with us and flying our Hurricanes. Using this as an excuse, I managed to get a trip in one of their Gladiators [N5524] this afternoon. It really was great fun; though slightly heavier on the ailerons than a Hurricane, I think it is the best aerobatic kite I have ever flown.

24 January: Since the 19th nothing very exciting has happened. The *Illustrious* has gone to Alex for repairs, so the aerodromes are the only objectives of any importance. Last night we had one Jerry over but he dropped his bombs harmlessly in the sea. This morning, while I was on watch, the CO drove up and got out. He came over to me and, to my utter astonishment, said, 'Congratulations on getting the Bar to your DFC.' I was completely taken aback and for a moment could think of nothing to say. They certainly didn't waste any time getting it through. Eric Taylor got his well-earned DFC. He has seven confirmed and a good many pretty certain probables. This evening we got five bottles of champagne (8s 6d a time) and had a pretty average party! I also received several letters of congratulations, among them one from His Excellency the Governor [Sir William Dobbie, who just happened to also be a Governor of Monkton Combe School].

It was on the 27th that Mac wrote home with this and other news:

"I am now back in Malta. I am enjoying life immensely, though we don't get quite enough flying for my liking. The first day I flew here, I met a formation of Italian fighters and managed to shoot down two of them. One of the pilots baled out and was taken to hospital with three bullets in his arm and one in his thigh. I have been to see him two or three times and have taken him cigarettes etc. He seems an extraordinarily pleasant type and is not the least bit antagonistic. It makes you realise how futile the whole business is. One day you shoot a chap down and the next you more or less go and apologise! Apparently the Air Officer Commanding took a rather good view of our scrap with the Germans. I have since had a letter from your friend Dobbie, giving me his congratulations.

Our mess here is in an old 16th century château with a walled courtyard and a garden full of orange and tangerine tresses. At the moment I am sharing with another flight lieutenant. We are getting more officers, so another house is being started in the nearest town. I am going to be in charge of it . . . I am very interested that Gordon has started flying and I hope he enjoys it. My last letter from you was dated Dec 4th!"

Mac's brother Gordon, having joined the RAF in August 1940, had been sent to Moose Jaw in Canada for training, after attending the Elementary Flying Training School course at Newmarket in December 1940. It seems that Mac was liked by most who crossed his path, and he certainly had the respect of many of the ground crews, one of whom, Cpl John Alton, later wrote:

"Dear old Mac was the sort of personality that inspired a sense of hero worship in every ground crew member; perhaps this was why I was concerned in helping him to strap into his Hurricane for a scramble from Takali. Normally, as the line NCO, I would have taken up a position where I could observe all aircraft starting up.

Now, the safety harness in a Hurricane comprised four stout woven straps, which passed over each shoulder and over the thighs, and were held in place by a cone-shaped stout pin, which passed through the eyelets on each strap. This pin was then secured in position by a lyre-shaped, strong wire locking piece, which was normally secured to the strap by a piece of cord. On this occasion, Mac drew my attention to the fact that it was missing. There was neither a spare pin nor another aircraft, which could be 'robbed'. I found a piece of fencing wire and, with Mac's help, pushed it through the locking piece and with a grateful smile he waved chocks away and off he went."

Reinforcements for No.261 Squadron had arrived from Egypt on the 20th in the form of four pilots. Nine more arrived on the 29th and a further nine on the 30th, together with six more Hurricanes, which gave the squadron twenty-three serviceable aircraft. During the first six days of February, Mac scrambled on six separate occasions but failed to make any contact although he sighted Ju88s bombing Luqa and Hal Far on the 4th.

Diary:

8 February: Owing mainly to bad weather, we have had very little action during the last fortnight. About a week ago, one Savoia-Marchetti 79 came over escorted by five CR42s. Sgt Robertson got one CR42 which we all saw crash into a hill near Naxxar. One of our new F/Os [Derek Whittingham] also got a CR42. Jock Barber put all he had into the bomber, but apparently without result. Just as B Flight were packing up watch on the evening of the 4th, they were ordered to scramble. I was on my way over to do some night flying when they took off, so I jumped into an aeroplane and had just started the engine when the AA guns opened fire. I screeched off into the twilight and climbed as quickly as I could. I saw bombs bursting at Luqa and Hal Far, but could see no enemy aircraft. The sky was full of Bofors shells and bursting AA. Every time I edged round towards Luqa, I was met by a hail of shells, so had to content myself by waiting around over Filfla in the hopes of catching someone unawares. By this time there were one or two fires going at Hal Far and the flames lit up great clouds of smoke and dust that slowly climbed into the night sky. It was now too dark for me to have any hope of finding a Jerry without the aid of searchlights, so I decided to land. There was no flarepath at Takali, and I could only just make out the runway. Using my landing light, I managed somehow to get down without breaking anything. I taxied up to the dispersal point, and having stopped my engine, I went over to the bus. There I met

Sgt Robertson who had shot down a Ju88. We heard there was
another formation coming in, so, without waiting for permission, we
screamed off again. This time I got up to 12,000 feet, but could see
nothing, so came down to land. Each time I came in I was given a
red, so finally went over to Hal Far and landed there. I found out that
one of our machines had piled up on the Takali runway and all the
other Hurricanes had also landed at Hal Far. Wing Commander Allen
[OC Takali] took us back to his house and we had the odd nip. Jock
Barber had also shot down a Ju88, glowing nicely. One of the Fulmar
boys also claimed one, making a total of three. We had supper at Hal
Far and spent the night there.

Next morning we got up at 5.30 and went over to our kites. We
had a look at A Flight's hangar, which had taken a direct hit. The 6-
gun Gladiator was burnt to a cinder and one of our new Rotol
Hurricanes was distorted beyond recognition. We flew back to Takali
as soon as it was light and there had a very fine breakfast. Eliot and
I went over to Luqa in the Maggie. We went to the mess, or what
used to be the mess. A bomb had burst just outside and the whole
place was a shambles. You only had to take six deep breaths in the
bar and you were all set for a party. The floor ran with the most
amazing cocktail; whisky, brandy, gin, beer, champagne and heaven
knows what else. Broken bottles and glasses lay everywhere. The
side of the officers' quarters had also been blown clean off and the
unfortunate owners were rummaging in the ruins trying to salvage
what was left of their possessions.

The moon is nearly full now and the weather is perfect. Last
night, several Ju88s came over and dropped bombs in the
neighbourhood of Luqa and Hal Far. Young Eliot went up, but the
searchlights didn't manage to catch anything, so he was unlucky.
I am on tonight, so perhaps I shall be lucky. I have got a sty coming
in my left eye.

9 February: No sooner had I taken over my machine [V7671] on the
evening of the 8th, than all flights were ordered to scramble. We
screeched up to 16,000 feet (all six of us), but as it was almost dark
by then, we split up and each stayed at a separate height, mine being
16,000 feet. Two or three raiders came in and dropped their bombs
without being picked up, but at about 7.10pm, I saw a Ju88
beautifully illuminated at about 10,000 feet over Rabat. I 'pulled the
plug' and went screaming after it, catching it as it was just going out
of range of the lights. I could see it quite clearly in the moonlight, so
closed till it completely filled my reflector sight. The rear gunner
must have seen me coming for he opened fire at the same moment as
I did. As soon as I pressed my firing-button, I was blinded by the

flames from my guns, so, fearing that I might ram him in the dark, I ceased fire to get my bearings again. I thought for a moment that he was on fire, flames and sparks seemed to be pouring from his fuselage. Then, to my horror, I realised that the flames were coming from the muzzles of his rear guns and the sparks were tracer and incendiary bullets streaming back unpleasantly close to my head! For some unknown reason I always feel that no one can hit me when I am firing at them, so, with eight guns blazing, I closed to about 50 yards and again ceased fire to take stock of the situation.

This time there was no return fire from the bomber. All I could see was its dark silhouette against the moonlit sky and the pale glow from its exhausts. I realised that the fight was as good as won, so taking careful aim at very close range, I fired a fairly long burst. Incendiary bullets poured into the helpless bomber, but it did not catch fire. My windscreen was covered with oil from one of its engines and I was blinded, so I broke away slightly to see what had happened. A long trail of smoke streamed out behind the bomber, but it did not seem to be losing height. I finished off my ammo in an attack from the rear starboard quarter, but with no apparent result. A feeling of helpless frustration came over me. A few moments before I had been certain of a spectacular victory, but now it seemed as though I was to be cheated. I glanced at my instruments and saw I was only doing 160mph and going down at 1,000 ft/min. Perhaps I had got the bastard after all! I looked at my instruments again to make sure and saw I was down to 5,000 feet. When I took my head out of the cockpit the bomber had vanished. I circled round for a little, but could not find it again, so returned and landed. HQ later confirmed that this aircraft crashed into the sea (how they confirmed it is still a mystery).

In fact, Malta HQ's Y Service had been listening into the crew's final, desperate radio calls. It transpired that the aircraft was not a Ju88, but a He111 of 5/KG26; the crew survived although one had been wounded.

No sooner had I landed than Eliot took off and patrolled for about an hour but without result. Immediately he had landed, I again took off and climbed up to 16,000 feet over Filfla. I had been on patrol for about a quarter of an hour, when the searchlights came on and formed a fairly concentrated intersection over Luqa. I immediately turned towards it and, to my delight, saw a Ju88 beautifully illuminated at about 10,000 feet slowly turning north. My mouth started to water as I opened the throttle, pulled the plug and lowered my seat. By the time I had turned on my reflector sight and put my gun-firing switch in the firing position, I was doing about 340mph and slowly closing on the bomber. In modern aerial warfare it is not very often that one is able to carry out a premeditated, cold-blooded attack, but when it is possible one goes through the most amazing sequence of mental states. When I first sight the enemy, my mind is usually so busy weighing up the situation and deciding on the best target and the best way of attacking it, that I have little time left for committing my mental attitude to memory. It is therefore not until the last few moments before the attack that I have time to analyse my feelings. In this particular case, the tension was terrific. For what seemed like minutes the bomber hung there in front of me, shining tantalisingly in the searchlights.

My mouth watered and my heart beat furiously as I watched its wings slowly growing in my sights. I could feel my aircraft rocking in its slipstream and with great difficulty overcame my natural impulse to open fire. At last, its wings completely filled my sights and aiming at the top of the fuselage I let fly. This time I was ready for the blinding flames from my guns and after a two-second burst, I ceased fire to see what had happened. The Ju88, which was still about 150 yards in front of me, was doing a gentle turn to the left. I could see quite a lot of the upper surface of its wings and fuselage, so aiming about a length in front, I gave it a five or six-second squirt. Clouds of smoke came back and my cockpit was filled with the smell of burning aeroplane. I turned to one side to avoid hitting the Jerry and was immediately picked up by our searchlights. By the time I had extricated myself from these, my target had vanished. I felt almost sure I had got it, so called up 'Banjo' [the Controller] and asked if they could confirm its destruction. Five minutes later, they called me back and said some pongos [soldiers] had seen it crash into the sea.

According to German records, however, the badly damaged bomber, an aircraft from II/LG1, did manage to reach Catania, where it crashed on landing and was written off.

As I still had about one-third of my ammo left, I stayed on patrol for another half hour, but the searchlights failed to pick anything up, so I landed without further excitement. As I taxied back to the dispersal point, Eliot took off past me. I watched the red glow of his exhausts disappear into the night sky and then stopped my engine. Hardly had I got out of my kite when the searchlights went on again and, after a few minutes, picked up a Jerry who they held right across the Island. Unfortunately, Chubby had not had time to climb high enough to catch it, so it got clean away. About half an hour later they picked up another, but, for some unknown reason, lost it again before Chubby had time to close. The poor boy does have the most appalling luck. Eventually, Chubby landed and I took off, climbing to 17,000 feet over Filfla. Two Jerries came in, but were not picked up; then a third approached the Island, and was picked up just before it crossed the coast on its way home. I screeched after it, but the searchlights lost it long before I was within range. I followed it out towards Sicily, but could see no trace of it, so returned home. After patrolling for another half hour, I landed without further incident. Chubby then went up for an hour, followed again by myself, but on neither trip did the searchlights manage to illuminate anything. At about 3am, the all-clear went, so, feeling completely exhausted, we tumbled into the ambulance and slept like logs till we were wakened at dawn by the early morning watch who took over from us. Altogether I did $4^1/_2$ hours' flying.

Mac, who had just taken command of A Flight from Flt Lt Waters, wrote home from Takali on the 10th:

"Until three days ago, we have had a fairly quiet time. For the last few days, however, the weather has been perfect and Jerry has wasted no time in taking advantage of it. I was on night stand-by the day before yesterday and managed to shoot down two Ju88 bombers. Both of them have been confirmed, so my score is now eight. This fighter racket is great fun compared with Battles, though admittedly, I've been very lucky so far . . ."

But there was an ominous note in the next diary entry:

11 February: I have been off flying for the last two days as I have had a very painful sty in my left eye. It has been much better today, however, and this morning I took a Hurricane up and did about half an hour's aerobatics, which I greatly enjoyed. This afternoon B Flight was up at 20,000 feet when they were attacked by Me109s. F/O Bradbury, Flt Lt Watson, P/O Thacker and P/O Pain went in to attack three Ju88s, and were immediately set on. Watson and Thacker were shot down into the sea, and old Brad, though shot to hell, managed to get back and land at Luqa. His kite was riddled with cannon and bullet holes, all the fabric was torn off one side, and his rudder control was shot away except for one strand of wire on one side. Thacker managed to bale out and was picked up by an RAF speedboat after being in the sea for about an hour. Poor old Watson was never found. The appearance of 109s has greatly shaken the morale of the Squadron (and mine in particular). I think the sooner we hack some down the better.

The Messerschmitt 109Es were from 7/JG26 and had only arrived at Gela on the 9th. The Staffel was commanded by Oblt Joachim Müncheberg, one of the Luftwaffe's outstanding fighter pilots with twenty-three victories to his credit. Although 7 Staffel had only nine aircraft, the appearance of Bf109s over Malta gave the Axis powers a tremendous morale advantage.

13 February: Last Thursday night I had two scrambles, but on neither of them did the searchlights manage to illuminate anything. This afternoon I saw 109s for myself and am just as scared of them as I always was. I was leading A Flight south of Comino at about 22,000 feet when I saw four 109s coming straight towards me. I was up sun of them and they did not see me until we were only about 1,000 yards apart. We were in sections, line astern, and for once in really decent formation. We evidently looked *très formidable*, for as soon as Jerry saw us, he broke formation and, turning steeply to starboard, they climbed away from us in a shambles. Our poor old Hurrybirds were no match for the 109s and, though we chased them with throttles wide open, they left us standing. For the rest of the patrol, I suffered from acute twitch, but by the grace of God we were not attacked. This evening there was a great discussion in the mess as to the best way to deal with 109s. If someone doesn't shoot one down soon, the squadron morale will be non-existent.

Shot down . . .

16 February – Imtarfa: As A Flight were on the 9am watch, John [Sqn Ldr Trumble] decided to have all the bloodthirsty pilots on, in the hopes of getting a 109. We arranged that if we were attacked, we would break away and form a defensive circle. At about 0915 we were ordered to scramble and climbed to 20,000 feet. We were still climbing over Luqa, when six Me109s screamed down on us out of the sun. We immediately broke away and formed a rather wide circle. Just as I took my place in the circle, I saw four Messerschmitts coming down out of the sun. I turned back under them and they all overshot me. I looked round carefully, but could see nothing, so turned back onto the tail of the nearest Hun who was chasing some Hurricanes in front of him. We were all turning gently to port, so I cut the corner and was slowly closing on the Hun. I was determined to get him and must have been concentrating so intently on his movements that, like a fool, I forgot to look in the mirror until it was too late. Suddenly there was a crash in my cockpit – bits and pieces seemed to fly everywhere. Instinctively, I went into a steep spiral dive, furiously angry that I had been beaten at my own game!

My left arm was dripping with blood and when I tried to raise it, only the top part moved, the rest hung limply by my side. Everything happened so quickly that I have no clear recollection of what actually took place. I remember opening my hood, disconnecting my oxygen and R/T connections and standing up in the cockpit. The next thing I saw was my kite [V7331] diving away from me, the roar of its engine gradually fading as it plunged earthwards. It was a marvellous feeling to be safely out of it; everything seemed so quiet and peaceful. I could clearly hear the roar of engines above me, and distinctly heard one long burst of cannon fire. I could not see what was happening as I was falling upside down and my legs obscured all view of the aircraft above me. My arm was beginning to hurt pretty badly, so I decided to pull my chute straight away in case I fainted from loss of blood. I reached round for my rip-cord but could not find it. For some unknown reason, I thought my chute must have been torn off me while I was getting out of my kite and almost gave up making any further efforts to save myself. I remember thinking that the whole process of being shot down and being killed seemed much simpler and less horrible than I had always imagined. There was just going to be a big thud when I hit the deck and then all would be over – my arm would stop hurting and no more 109s could make dirty passes at me behind my back. I think I must have been gradually going off into a faint when suddenly I thought of my mother reading the telegram saying that I had been killed in action. I made one last effort to see if my parachute was still there and to my amazement and relief found that it had not been torn off after all. With another supreme effort I reached round and pulled the rip-cord.

There was a sickening lurch as my chute opened and my harness tightened round me so that I could hardly breathe. I felt horribly ill and faint. Blood from my arm came streaming back into my face, in spite of the fact that I was holding it as tightly as I could. I could only breathe with utmost difficulty and my arm hurt like hell. I could see Malta spread out like a map 15,000 feet below me and I longed to be down there – just to lie still and die peacefully. I was woken from this stupor by the roar of an engine and naturally thought some bloodthirsty Jerry had come to finish me off. I don't think I really minded what happened; certainly the thought of a few more cannon shells flying past me didn't exactly cheer me up. To my joy, however, I saw that my escort was a Hurricane, piloted, as I learned later, by Eric Taylor. He had quite rightly decided that he could do no good by playing with the Huns at 20,000 feet, so came down to see that none of them got me.

For what seemed like hours I hung there, apparently motionless, with Malta still as far away as ever. Once or twice I started swinging very badly, but as I was using my only hand to stop myself bleeding to death, I was unable to do anything about it. At about 1,500 feet I opened my eyes again and to my joy, saw that I was very much lower down. For a little while I was afraid I was going to land in the middle of a town, but I mercifully drifted to the edge of this. For the last 100 feet I seemed to drop out of the sky – the flat roof of a house came rushing up at me and just as I was about to land on it, it dodged to one side and I ended up in a little patch of green wheat. I hit the ground with a terrific thud, rolled over once or twice, and then lay back intending to die quietly. This, however, was not to be. Scarcely had I got myself fairly comfortable and closed my eyes, when I heard the sound of people running. I hurriedly tried to think up some famous last words to give my public, but never had a chance to utter them. I was surrounded by a crowd of shouting gesticulating Maltese, who pulled at my parachute, lifted my head and drove me so furious that I had to give up the dying idea in order to concentrate completely on kicking every Maltese who came within range. From what the pongos told me after, I believe I registered some rather effective shots!

Eventually two army stretch-bearers arrived with a first-aid outfit. I told them to put a tourniquet on my arm and to give me some morphia, whereupon one of them started to bandage my wrist and the other went off to ask what morphia was. In the end I got them to give me the first-aid outfit and fixed myself up. At last a doctor arrived who knew what to do. He put me on a stretcher, had me carried about half a mile across fields to an ambulance, which in turn took me to the local advanced field-dressing station. Here they filled me with morphia, gave me ether and put my arm in a rough splint. When I came round, they gave me a large tot of whisky, another injection of morphia and sent me off to Imtarfa as drunk as a lord. When I eventually arrived at the hospital I was feeling in the best of spirits and apparently shook the sisters by asking them to have a drink with me! They wasted no time in getting me up to the theatre and after making them promise not to take my arm off, I gave a running commentary as the ether took effect.

Among the many who witnessed Mac's plight was off-duty pilot Sgt Jim Pickering, also of No.261 Squadron, who wrote:

"I saw Mac shot down when I was at our flat in Valetta. The air raid alarm had sounded and the streets were empty. From the balcony I saw a Hurricane being chased over Valetta by a Me109. The 109 was only about 50 yards behind when it opened fire. Its overtaking speed made it brake almost immediately. The Hurricane turned towards Luqa airfield and out of sight. Mac baled out."

Meanwhile, the other Hurricanes had all returned to base, although Plt Off McAdam's aircraft had been virtually shot to pieces and that flown by Flg Off Peacock-Edwards landed with numerous shell holes and with the starboard aileron shot away. It seems fairly certain that Mac had been shot down by Oblt Müncheberg, who claimed one Hurricane from which he saw the pilot bale out, his 26th victory. In his first pass Müncheberg had also claimed a Hurricane, while Uffz Georg Mondry claimed a second – presumably the aircraft of McAdam and Peacock-Edwards. The appearance of the Messerschmitts had seriously affected the squadron's morale, as noted by Wg Cdr Carter Jonas, OC Luqa:

"Day after day the sirens would scream dismally and already our Hurricanes would be wearily climbing their way up into the sun. And more often than not, out of the sun would come the yellow-nosed Messerschmitts, long before our fighters had had sufficient time in which to gain their best operational height. To anyone interested in psychology, the effect of the Messerschmitts on the Hurricane pilots was obvious. For here was an ordinary average crowd of Air Force youngsters, neither better nor worse than their compatriots in squadrons all over the world. Many of them by now had been in Malta for several months . . . and ever since Italy entered the war, these boys, often in obsolete aircraft, had carried out bravely and unquestioning the task that they had been called upon to perform. Then more Hurricanes had arrived, and encouraged by successes, morale had risen, fiery and inspired, to almost unbelievable heights. By now, not only were many of the Hurricanes tired and scarred, but the pilots themselves were tired. No new fighters ever seemed to come now, no fresh and eager faces appeared in the Takali Mess. Instead, there were empty places at the table, empty beds, cars for sale and dogs that needed masters . . ."

And one of those empty places at the table, and an empty bed, were those until recently occupied by Mac, who was now beginning to feel the pain of his injuries, as confided to his diary:

When I came round I was back in Ward M3, surrounded by screens, with Sister Dempsey sitting in a chair beside me. After a quick glance I was delighted to see that my arm was still there, so I went off to sleep again, feeling very cheerful about the whole thing. The next two days were pretty average mental and physical hell; thank God I cannot remember very much about them. I was having a saline transfusion day and night, and unfortunately my blood kept clotting; this necessitated making fresh holes in my arms and legs.

I remember watching the saline solution dripping down the glass tube from the container – terrified that the drips were becoming less frequent and would eventually stop again. Everyone was simply wizard to me, especially Sister Dempsey. She used to sit by my bed for hours when she was off duty. I got a lot of secret amusement from telling her to leave me, as I wanted to die. She would get really worried and stroke my forehead and plead with me not to talk about dying. Had she known it, I had already made up my mind to get better, and nothing in the world was further from my thoughts than death.

As the first two days dragged on, I began to realise that there was no hope of saving my arm. The blood circulation was all right, but my finger movement was scarcely visible and I could hardly feel anything in my hand. My whole arm began to smell positively revolting. The doctors kept hinting that I would be much better off without it, but I was terrified that, without it, I should never be able to fly again, so refused to let them touch it. By the third morning, however, I was so weak and the pain and smell so unbearable, that they had little difficulty in taking me up to the theatre and performing the necessary operation. When I came to I was in the cabin at the end of M3 and still having a saline transfusion. As I can remember very little about the rest of the day, I presume that I must have been unconscious most of the time.

When Mac finally got round to writing a combat report, the result was brief and to the point:

While on patrol over Luqa at 20,000 feet, we were attacked from above and astern by six Me109s. As previously arranged, the flight broke away to the right and formed a defensive circle. As I took my place in the circle I saw four more Me109s coming down out of the sun. Just as they came within range I turned back towards them and they all overshot me without firing. I looked very carefully but could see no more enemy aircraft above me, so turned back to the tail of the nearest 109. I was turning well inside him and was just about to open fire when I was hit in the left arm by a cannon shell. My dashboard was completely smashed, so I baled out and landed safely by parachute.

Our casualties: One Hurricane.
                   Left arm written off by cannon shell.
                   Shrapnel in both legs.

Meditating in his bed in hospital, Mac reached a determination that he would fly again. There were rumours of bets being taken with Sister

Dempsey and others that he would do so within a fortnight! Some of
the pilots came to see him, but not all were initially allowed entry, as
Sgt Bamberger recalled:

"This stupid officer thing raised its ugly head again. I went to see
Mac in hospital. They wouldn't let me in because I was only a
sergeant."

Diary:

20 February – Imtarfa Hospital: This morning I was moved back
into the ward as I am now off the danger list. Just before lunch today,
the Macchi pilot who I shot down on January 9th was wheeled in and
is now in the next bed to me. His arm is still very bad, though the
bullet wound in his thigh has healed. I think he was even more
surprised to see me than I was to see him. It is certainly a crazy war.
There is a wizard set of chaps here. Opposite me is Lt Gowing RN,
commonly known as the General, who is the life and soul of the
party. He was in *Illustrious* when she was bombed and had his right
leg blown off and the rest of him pretty well filled with shrapnel.
About a week ago he developed phlebitis, which apparently is a
disease of pregnant women. He is certain he is going to give birth to
twins and is very worried as he does not know who the father is!
Next to him is a Lt Janvrin, who was also in *Illustrious* and had his
backside removed by a piece of red-hot bomb. The poor boy goes
through hell every day when his dressings are done, but is very
cheerful about the whole thing. On my left is an extraordinarily
decent warrant officer who was in HMS *Hyperion* when she hit a
mine south of Pantelleria Island. He has a leg and an arm broken and
is fixed up with a marvellous set of weights and pulleys. Further up
the ward is a chap called Logan who was chief engineer on the SS
Essex. He is horribly burnt, and looks more like a skeleton than a
human being. The ward sounds more like a torture chamber than a
hospital when the poor fellow has his dressings done. After looking
round at these chaps I'm beginning to feel almost well again. With
any luck I should be out of here long before most of them.

22 February: I am really beginning to feel a little better, though
I still have morphia at night. Yesterday Ginger O'Sullivan [OC
Takali] came to see me and says he has written to mother. I hope he
hasn't told her I've lost my arm. This afternoon Chubby and Terry
Foxton came up and gave me all the squadron news. Everyone else
got back OK when I was shot down, but McAdam's kite was just
about shot to pieces. P/O Langdon, who saw me being shot down,
says that as soon as I turned back after the 109s, two more came
down out of the sun onto my tail. They were going at well over

400mph, but the first managed to get in a quick squirt before he overshot me. Yesterday a formation of Dornier 215s [*sic*] came over and Hamilton got one and the rest of the boys shared another. One or two of them collected the odd rear gun bullet but no one was seriously damaged. These enemy aircraft were more likely to have been Me110s. This evening I had an extremely interesting conversation with 'Macchi' about the performance of various Italian aircraft. He says he was flying CR32s in the Spanish War and then went on to CR42s, which he much prefers to Macchis. Incidentally, his proper name is Luigi Armanino. He really is a charming fellow and very interesting to talk to.

That same day, Mac wired mother and told her of his accident – just in case Wg Cdr O'Sullivan had contacted her. In fact he had written but his letter was not sent until the 29th, so Mac was able to reassure her for a short time, at least:

"As far as I can see, there is no reason why I should not fly again. I am feeling very much better already and I hope to get up in a few days."

Mother replied two days later:

"You can imagine with what joy and thankfulness and intense relief we received your own wire this morning and heard that you are going splendidly! It was an anxious moment when the Air Ministry wire arrived last Tuesday morning. They said you were on the seriously ill list, so I feared there must be something more than the fractured arm . . . I am so thankful it is not your right arm and trust the surgeon has set it satisfactorily and that it will recover completely so that you will have full use of it again . . .We are all hoping you may be sent home to convalesce . . . Take extra care of the wee Bible and do read it faithfully . . . The Prayer book version of Psalm 119, verse 75, reads, 'I know, O Lord, that thy judgments are right: and that Thou of very faithfulness hast caused me to be troubled.' I think it is a sweet thought . . . God knows just what is best for us and He makes no mistakes and I have trusted you to His faithfulness and His loving care all through the years, so I am not going to doubt Him now . . . hope you are a good patient and not grumpy or troublesome."

He had obviously succeeded in pulling the wool over her eyes for the moment.

Diary:

25 February: I am really feeling very much better now, though I get a lot of pain at night. The piece of shrapnel that was touching the nerve in my ankle is apparently working its way to the surface, as I can now walk without any pain. Yesterday there was a wizard scrap at about 3,000 feet over Imtarfa. The Hurricanes were on patrol in the usual sections in vic formation when down came about four 109s at a simply phenomenal speed. The Hurricanes did a very spectacular breakaway, Sgt Bamberger coming down in a spin and the 109s disappeared into the sun again. One of our kites got separated from the rest and was immediately set on by a 109. As usual the Hun came screaming in at about 400mph and got in about a two-second burst before he had to break away to avoid overshooting. He must have been a rotten shot for, in spite of the fact that he closed to about 50 yards he never hit the Hurricane once. The pilot, Sgt Davies, apparently knew nothing about it until he saw the Jerry breaking away and then it was too late to do anything in the way of a counter-attack. There were several other rather 'shaky-do's', but no one got badly shot up.

My public is rising far above expectations and I have now been visited by almost everyone of importance on the island. Yesterday afternoon, General Dobbie [the Governor] came to see me and made the usual sympathetic remarks. This afternoon almost the entire squadron came round. Just as they were leaving, Sqn Ldr Moore (who had just been promoted) and Johnny Warfield (now a Wg Cdr) also appeared. In the middle of their visit Air Vice-Marshal Maynard (AOC Malta), Air Commodore Sanderson [SASO] and the usual following arrived. Apparently half of Malta watched me coming down and as far as I can make out I am the first man to land actually on Malta.

26 February: Today we had one of the biggest, if not the biggest, blitz ever experienced. At about 1300 the alarm went and eight Hurricanes, led by Eric Taylor, roared off into the blue. They had reached about 28,000 feet (hoping to catch the 109s) when a terrific formation of Ju87s came in at about 10,000 feet As usual the AA guns opened up and the first machine to dive went straight into the road at Luqa without ever releasing its bomb. The Hurricanes, who started to come down as soon as they saw the AA fire, were now at about 10,000 feet just south of Luqa. As the Junkers pulled out of their dives and emerged from the barrage, they were immediately set on by the Hurricanes, who were in turn attacked by 109s. This evolved into a series of little processions which, led by the Ju87s, all headed south towards Filfla. On two occasions I saw an 87, a Hurricane, and a 109 in almost perfect line astern formation. After the Junkers came a large composite formation of Ju88s, Do215s [*sic*] and Heinkel 111s, all escorted by Me110s and Macchis. None, or very few of these, ventured below 6,000 or 8,000 feet and, as the Hurricanes were all well below 3,000 feet, they were pretty safe. The AA however, got a Ju88, which dived vertically into the sea from about ten grand, making a row like the souls awakening. The whole attack was directed against Luqa and by the time the last Jerries arrived, the column of smoke and dust had risen to about 4,000 feet and completely obscured the north-east end of the island. As the last Jerries flew off, the Hurricanes, most of whom had expended all their ammunition, returned one by one and circled Takali. Suddenly one of them started smoking and looked as if it would burst into flames at any moment. It went into a shallow dive and finally disappeared behind Imtarfa Hill. I heard later that the pilot was Terry Foxton and that somehow he managed to crash-land it on Takali, writing the kite off but escaping unhurt himself. He had apparently been hit in the radiator and his engine seized up.

This raid has, I'm afraid, been highly successful from Jerry's point of view. Six Wimpies were burnt out and all the others put u/s by bomb splinters. Hardly a building is left standing and all the hangars are smashed. It cost Jerry fourteen planes definitely destroyed and several probables. Our losses were four Hurricanes and three pilots, one of whom was poor Eric Taylor. He was last seen chasing a Ju87 with a 109 on his tail. Later his Mae West was washed up with a cannon hole right through the chest – he certainly couldn't have known much about it. Langdon and Plt Off Kearsey were the other two casualties. Young Eliot got his first Hun since he's been here – a flaming Ju87 and another 'probable'. Terry Foxton also got a cert, and a probable, before he was shot down. Sgt Robertson got a 109 – the first to be shot down in Malta. Altogether a most exciting day.

Luqa airfield was rendered unserviceable for nearly forty-eight hours and before long both Wellington and Sunderland aircraft had to be withdrawn from the island.

Diary:

27 February: This afternoon I got up and dressed for the first time. I managed all right except for my tie, which I eventually managed to do by holding one end in the drawer of the dressing table, so keeping it tight, while I tied the knot. I feel pretty shaky on my feet and I get pins and needles in my arm if I move about too quickly. This morning 'Macchi' [Capitano Armanino] had his arm operated on again and has been feeling pretty bad all day. He is really damn brave about it and hardly ever makes much noise. He stuffs his mouth full of blanket and bites that when his arm hurts very badly. It makes me feel terrible to see him going through so much pain and know I am responsible. Lying here and seeing all these mutilated chaps makes me realise more than ever how utterly mad this war is. This morning I went through to M4 and had a game of poker with Wyatt-Smith [also a No.261 Squadron pilot] and a Maltese Naval officer. I made 6s. Sister O'Connell and Peggy Lane are on night duty and we have great fun ragging them when they come round in the evening. I sleep without morphia now and can even lie on my left side if I arrange the pillow properly.

28 February: This afternoon I got up after lunch and had just finished dressing when P/O Hammond arrived with Jock Barber's car. I got permission from the Sister to go for a short walk and then drove the car down to the dispersal points at Takali. I found I can manage quite well, though of course, there is very little traffic on the road! When I arrived I saw the AOC's staff car and our brake. On closer inspection I saw to my surprise and secret joy that I had run into one of Ginger O'Sullivan's Sunday luncheon parties. I was greeted, with surprise, by Ginger, who introduced me to Lady Barbara Strickland (wife of General Sir Edward Strickland). The AOC then emerged from a Hurricane and was amazed to see me up so soon. I shot them a pretty good line and have no doubt that my fame will spread through the length and breadth of Malta. At last, after much talking, they drove off and I was able to transfer my attention to the boys. They were equally astounded to see me as none of them knew I had been allowed up. This morning Jock Barber was up with A Flight when they ran into four Me110s. Apparently, Jock and the boys came round a cloud one way, and the Messerschmitts came round the other. Although Jerry passed within 50 yards of them, both parties were so surprised that neither had time to have a decent squirt at the other. I had tea in the mess and went back to Imtarfa at about 6pm. No one had missed me, so I hopped into bed feeling very pleased with myself.

3 March: I felt very tired after last Sunday's exertions and have consequently been taking it easy for the last two days. Yesterday the *Illustrious* boys left by hospital ship for an unknown destination – they seem to think they are going home via the Cape. The ward seems terribly quiet without them – especially the 'General'! This morning Chubby came up for me in Jock's car and I drove down to the mess where I had lunch. In the afternoon we went into Valetta and I did a spot of shopping, after which, we went to see Dorothy Lamour in *Jungle Princess*. I don't think they ought to show films like it in Malta! Just before the show finished the air raid warning went and a few minutes later the guns opened up. We stayed in the cinema for a little, but as the guns went on firing, we decided there must be a bit of a blitz on so went out to see what was happening. The sky was covered with little white puffs of AA smoke. Just in front of the nearest puffs was a Ju88 flying slowly across the island in the direction of Hal Far. As it arrived over the aerodrome, it went into a shallow dive, dropped its bombs and flew on. There was silence for a minute or two and then the guns roared into life once again.

The shells started bursting well to the north of the island. After searching the sky very carefully, I saw three more Ju88s coming in at about 10,000 feet. We decided that we could just reach the Bastion before they were overhead, so ran in that direction. As we emerged at the top of Merchant Street we heard the roar of engines and saw a 109 dive down and attack a Hurricane at about 15,000 feet over Grand Harbour. Just as the attacking Messerschmitt opened fire, the Hurricane pulled up into a vertical climb and I saw, for the first time, another 109 flying just above the Hurricane. The attacking Messerschmitt was going far too fast to follow the Hurricane and apparently missed it altogether. Our kite, however, opened fire on the second 109 while still in a vertical climb. Then, keeping its sights on, it half-rolled out onto the tail of the Messerschmitt, firing all the time. The whole manoeuvre was marvellous to watch – certainly some of the best flying I have seen in this squadron. Unfortunately, Jerry was too well-armoured to fall victim to what must have been a rather inaccurate attack. No sooner had this little sideshow finished than the three Ju88s commenced their dive, this time on Luqa. The usual shower of shit was thrown up at them, but as far as I could see, they all got away with it. After waiting a few minutes without further excitement, we went over to the War Room, where we found that all the plots were going out. About sixty Ju88s and 87s had come over, escorted by 109s and 110s and had attacked Luqa and Hal Far.

After the Hurricanes had pancaked, War Room phoned Takali to ask for the aircraft serviceability state and got the following answer: 'Eight Hurricanes serviceable. One Me110 unserviceable.' On hearing this we jumped into John's car and rushed back to Takali. As we drove up the road past the mess, we passed hundreds of Maltese going to see the Messerschmitt. We found the remains still burning in a field just across the road from the north-west corner of the aerodrome. The Jerries had come down to machine-gun Takali and had been attacked by a Hurricane and Bofors guns at the same time. It caught fire at about 500 feet and went in at about 45°. The majority of the machine, including three horribly burnt and mutilated bodies, were smouldering in the middle of a small clover field. Both engines and some of the heavier debris, however, had been flung over the road into a field on the other side. As usual on such occasions, the air was sickly with the stink of burning flesh and that peculiar smell that all German aircraft seem to have. I took off the number plate of one of the engines as a souvenir and then John ran me back to hospital.

6 March: Yesterday I hitch-hiked down to Takali, hoping to fly the Maggie [N5428]. Unfortunately it was u/s, so I had to content myself with lunch in the mess and a game of poker in the afternoon. Today I have been more fortunate. Chubby came up for me just before lunch and in the afternoon, I did my first flight since I was shot down – exactly fifteen days since my arm was amputated. The Maggie was back in service, so Chubby did a circuit and a bump first, then I did one, during which I shot up Imtarfa Hospital, flying past M3 with my wing-tip not more than 10 feet from the windows. It shook the sisters, but not nearly as much as it shook me! After I had done two or three satisfactory landings, Chubby got out and I did about twenty minutes' solo flying, during which I went and had a look at the field where I landed by parachute. I can't describe the marvellous feeling of satisfaction that I got from flying again. During my first few days in hospital I went through untold mental agony – fearing I should never be able to go back to the old game. Now I know I can cope I'll fight heaven and earth to get back onto fighters again. My one ambition now is to get a 109, and, God willing, I'll do it. When I arrived back in M3, I found a letter from mother, and the shilling bet I had won from Sister Dempsey by flying within three weeks of my accident. I certainly am a happy man tonight!

Fellow-pilot Sgt Jim Pickering recalled:

"Sqn Ldr Lambert [who had just been promoted to command] was one of five pilots at readiness that morning, and it was suggested to him that some matter away from the airfield needed urgent attention. He knew, of course, what was going to happen, but it was best he did not have to either agree to or forbid an unauthorised flight. When the coast was clear, Mac came from the hospital and got into the Magister that already had a pilot in the other seat to provide a brief dual trip. This completed, Mac then made a solo flight. He had to prove to himself he could do it. It was kept quiet."

Mac now felt it safe to write to mother to enlighten her about the true state of affairs:

"I have just received your letter . . . Apparently, the Air Ministry did not tell you that my arm had to be amputated just above the elbow.

I know it sounds pretty grim, but actually it's not as big a handicap as you would imagine. I can dress myself completely and yesterday I flew solo to the amazement of the hospital staff. I can drive a car with comparative ease and when I get my artificial arm, I should be almost as good as new. Actually, it is only by the Grace of God that I am alive at all . . . a cannon shell entered my arm just above the elbow and went right down my arm, finally emerging about six inches above my wrist. The bones were smashed to pieces and though they left my arm on for two days, I slowly realised that I should have to lose it. I don't know exactly what is going to happen to me, but it seems probable that I shall be coming home soon for my new arm. I am amazed to hear that Gordon has gone to Canada [to learn to fly under the Empire Air Training Scheme]. He is certainly lucky!"

Diary:

17 March – Takali: Nothing of any importance has happened during the last ten days. I have now done five hours flying on Magisters and have been doing my best to get permission to fly a Hurricane. Unfortunately, old Ginger O'Sullivan has got to hear of my intentions and has forbidden me to fly one! [which was hardly surprising, since he had looped the Magister, had a dog-fight with a Hurricane, 'shot-up' a Bofors gun and practiced forced landings and low flying!]. Today I left Imtarfa. It's grand to be back with the boys, though 50% of the squadron are new to me.

Mac's path was about to change – and a great African adventure about to start.

CHAPTER VII

AFRICAN SAFARI

Diary:

22 March – HMS *Defender*: Without any preliminary warning, I received a signal after breakfast this morning, telling me to report at Customs House at 1630 this afternoon for embarkation on the destroyer HMS *Defender*. Fortunately I had so much to do in the short time available that I did not feel as miserable as I should otherwise have done. Although I have not been here quite three months, I have grown to love this little island more than I ever thought was possible. The squadron itself is the best I have ever been in. From the CO down to the most junior sergeant pilot, there is not one chap who is difficult to get on with and very few who are no use as fighter pilots. It hurts more than I can tell to leave such a fine lot of chaps. I feel that if only I could stay with them, I could get my old flight organised to such a pitch that we could even cope with the 109s. The raw material is there, but they need intelligent leadership and, above all, absolute confidence in their leader.

Having watched Jerry's tactics for the last month, I am convinced that, in almost every case, I could put our squadron in a position to attack Jerry without always waiting for him to take the initiative. At the moment the average scramble is pathetic to watch. The boys scream off in a straggly formation and then fly around at about 3,000 feet waiting for one of the braver 109s to pick off any stragglers. I know it is very difficult with machines which are vastly superior to our old Hurricanes, but I'm sure if we used a little more imagination and climbed to the south of Malta instead of over it and did not return till we were at about 30,000 feet, we could fox the Jerries – for the first time or two anyway! The squadron morale is very low at the moment, but that is only to be expected. So far, each time we've met 109s, someone has been shot up and in very few cases have we been able to retaliate. As Derek Whittingham wrote in his last combat report, 'Malta must have bigger, better, faster fighters if we intend to maintain air superiority.' Perhaps I think like this because I'm jealous of the boys. When I hear the phone ring in the old crew bus, and the telephone operator say, 'All sections, scramble!', I long to jump into the nearest kite and roar off in a cloud of dust with Chubby and Sgt Bamberger close on my tail. I long to feel that peculiar sinking feeling as we climb into a bright blue sky and hear the first message from 'Banjo' [the Controller]. It's a dangerous game, but I wouldn't change it for any other in the world.

Having got that all off my chest, I will return once more to facts! I spent a busy morning packing and paying final visits to the orderly room and the accounts section. Before lunch I went over and said goodbye to the Bofors gun boys near the mess. They are a grand lot of chaps and were genuinely sorry to hear I was going. Everyone insisted on my signing various photographs etc. and before I left, I really felt like a hero! After lunch I said goodbye to A Flight who were just going on watch. Then I borrowed Jock's car to go up to Imtarfa and said goodbye to 'Macchi' and the other boys there. I went into Valetta by service transport and had just arrived at the War Room, when the alarm went. I went into the plotting room where I was told that two large formations were approaching from the north-east. Not wishing to miss any fun, I climbed up onto the roof. Here I met Grp Capt Sanderson [the SASO] complete with binoculars. We waited for about five minutes and then saw four 109s at about 20,000 feet going south across the island in wide line abreast. A few minutes later they returned apparently keeping up a standing patrol. A short time later the AA guns opened up and I saw first, three, then six and finally fourteen Ju88s coming in on Grand Harbour from the north-east. The shells were all bursting about 1,000 feet below the Jerries, but were otherwise very accurate. Suddenly the leading bombers started to dive at about 45°. They pulled out at about 15,000 feet and flew off to the west. The bombs came screaming down and as usual, sounded as if they were coming straight for us. Then, as the scream reached a crescendo, we saw flash after flash of dirty red flame, followed by tall columns of smoke and dust rising above the houses on the other side of the harbour. The bombs had apparently been aimed at the two destroyers in the harbour, one of which was HMS *Defender*.

After this farewell demonstration I went down to the Customs House, where I met the embarkation officer and a Capt Hayes, who was also going to Alexandria. We embarked at about 1730, just as a second warning sounded. Nothing came of it however, and some fifteen minutes later, the 'All-clear' sounded. We heard that eight

Hurricanes of A Flight, led by Terry Foxton, had gone north after a plot of ten-plus and had been attacked by 109s. Terry was last seen going into the sea in flames and four others [Sgt Richard Spyer, Flg Off Johnny Southwell. Plt Off Dennis Knight and Plt Off Micky Garland – the last three pilots had only been on Malta a few days] were never heard of again. Chubby, as usual, saw them just in time and managed to get home. He'll go a long way if he has average luck. Poor old Terry was caught the same way as I was. He attacked a 109 and actually shot it down before he was killed by another.

We sailed just as the sun was setting and as we passed out of the harbour I took my last look at the little island, which might have been my grave. As the light faded and Malta finally disappeared into the night, my misgivings gave way to a feeling of anticipation as once more I set out on my travels.

Mac was being despatched to Middle East HQ at Cairo prior to being sent back to Britain via the Cape.

23 March: HMS *Defender*, as the name implies, is one of the D Class destroyers – the first to be built after the last war. The accommodation is extraordinarily comfortable, especially for me as I am in the Captain's day cabin! It would be difficult to find a more hospitable lot of officers. Everyone is extremely friendly and there is none of the smoking that is sometimes found in HM ships. The food is good, especially for a destroyer, and the bar is delightfully cool. We sighted the fleet at about 1020 this morning and took up our position in the destroyer screen shortly after lunch. The flagship [HMS *Warspite*, Admiral Cunningham] was leading followed by *Formidable*, *Barham*, *Valiant*, *Orion* and *Ajax* bringing up the rear. The sea was pretty calm though the sky was overcast and there was a fair wind blowing. We spent most of the day either on the bridge or the quarterdeck and in the evening watched the phosphorescence in the ship's wake.

25 March – Alexandria: Yesterday the weather was perfect and in the afternoon, Hayes and I sunbathed on the rear gun platform. At teatime a signal was received that *Defender* was to proceed north at dusk. In the end however, we went into Alex with the fleet and tied up alongside an oiler at 1030. After refuelling, we went out and dropped anchor in the harbour where we spent the night. This morning we said goodbye to the crew and went ashore in a naval pinnace. Eventually we found the embarkation officer and were posted to Middle East Pool at Geneifa. I, however, had very different ideas. I persuaded Hayes to spend at least one night in Alex, and off we went to the Cecil [Hotel].

Mac's intention was to wait for a ship going down the Suez Canal, round the Cape and so safely back to Britain. But he wanted to stay away from Britain for as long as it would take to fill his logbook with as many flying hours as possible, so proving to the Air Ministry that he was fully capable of flying operationally once more.

Diary:

As I was going up to the reception desk, I was surprised to see Jas Storrar of 73 Squadron shooting a line to some Naval chappies. We immediately removed ourselves to the bar, where I discovered that Jas had come down to ferry a Hurricane back to the squadron near Tobruk. He told me that there was another Hurricane, which should be ready in two days, so my mind was made up!

28 March – Bu Amud aerodrome, Egypt: After breakfast yesterday, we went out to Aboukir aerodrome by taxi. There we found, to my bitter disappointment, that neither of the Hurricanes was serviceable. I am, however, a strong believer in the saying, 'Where there's a will, there's a way', and refused to give up my intention of going to Tobruk. In the evening I met Flt Lt Belgrove, who is a test pilot here. We went to the flicks together and, after supper, had the odd noggin. I learned from him that there were two serviceable Maggies on the station and he thought I stood every chance of borrowing one. Accordingly, after breakfast, I went down to Wg Cdr Donkin's office and spun my tale of woe. He was extraordinarily decent and gave me permission without hesitation. Jas Storrar decided to come with me and at about 10am we took off [in R1884], heading west for Mersa Matruh. As we left Aboukir, the palm trees along the beach became fewer and further between until finally there was nothing but miles and miles of white and brown sand. For most of the way the road follows the coast, but in places it cuts inland to avoid marshes, or it cuts off corners. We amused ourselves by flying low above the road and chasing any camels or goatherds that we flew over. When we arrived at Matruh, there was a wild sandstorm blowing and the air was very bumpy.

Having refuelled we set off again, intending to make Tobruk in one hop. We circled the ruins of a few buildings, which, to my surprise, I found were the remains of Sidi Barrani. About twenty miles further on we passed a convoy of Aussies who had stopped for lunch. They all waved as we flew past at about ten feet. Just this side of Sollum, Jas took over and showed me the remains of a CR42 that had been shot down by No.274 Squadron. We then flew inland over the Libyan plateau trying to find the remains of a Gladiator, but the sandstorm was so thick that we had to turn back and land at Sollum. Here we had a look at another CR42, which had been left by the

Top: Mrs MacLachlan with the children. From left to right: Helen, Gordon, Archie, Liz, Jay (Mac) and Hugh. Taken at The Spurs, Styal, in July 1928, shortly after the premature death of her husband.

Middle left: Jay (Mac), Hugh and Gordon at Southampton, circa 1935.

Middle right: The young Acting Pilot Officer in Mess dress, 1937.

Bottom: Fledgling pilot, No.10 Elementary and Reserve FTS, RAF Yatesbury 1937. First flight – Mac in the rear cockpit of Tiger Moth G-ADOA; he soloed seven days later.

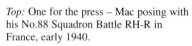

Top: One for the press – Mac posing with his No.88 Squadron Battle RH-R in France, early 1940.

Bottom left: A squadron artist captures a likeness of Mac in this caricature.

Bottom right: Mac with his motorcycle surrounded by admirers.

Top: Mac in RH-D (K9250) leads a vic of Battles from No.88 Squadron for the cameras, while two French Curtiss H-75As provide escort.

Middle left: Mac in the cockpit of a Battle.

Middle right: A nice shot of RH-P with Mac at the controls.

Bottom: LAC Les Davies was Mac's regular air gunner and was awarded the DFM. He later remustered as a pilot, was commissioned and flew Mosquito night fighters with No.96 Squadron. Seen here as a flight lieutenant at RAF Yelverton later in the war. Mac had hoped to recruit Les to join his Mustang Flight.

Top: A No.88 Squadron Battle having force-landed following battle damage. The crew was unhurt.

Middle: The same aircraft showing flak damage.

Bottom: A low level attack by Battles on horse-drawn German transport in France 1940. Note two figures running away. Photo taken by Battle's air gunner.

Onwards to Malta – Hurricanes being loaded onto the old aircraft carrier *HMS Argus*. Three views show V7548 being hoisted aboard. Mac flew V7474 to Malta; V7370 (bottom) also reached Malta but eight others ran out of fuel and crashed into the Mediterranean with the loss of seven pilots.

Top: Group of No.261 Squadron pilots at Malta – Mac, in white flying overalls faces Sgt Bam Bamberger (in sunglasses), who was his No.2 when he was shot down.

Middle left: The last picture taken of Mac shortly before his near fatal combat with Messerschmitts of 7/JG26 on 16 February 1941.

Middle right: Mac's victor, the illustrious Oblt Joachim Müncheberg of 7/JG26. Mac was his 26th victim.

Above: The locally-made badge removed from Mac's flying overalls following the action in which he was shot down on 16 February.

During his half year 'out' – March to August 1941 – following the loss of his arm, Mac travelled intensively around North, Central and South Africa, war permitting. Some snapshots of this period.

Top left: Home again. Mac with Mother at Haywards Heath.

Top right: Mac with his fiancée Muriel.

Bottom left: Younger brother Gordon, a

Spitfire pilot with No. 616 Squadron. He was shot down and killed in combat with FW190s of 1/JG2 over Brest on 16 April 1943.

Bottom right: Gordon and Mother.

CO of No.1 Squadron – Mac in the cockpit of his Hurricane IIC.

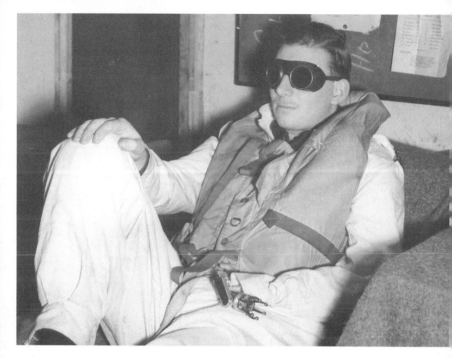

Top: No.1 Squadron was a night intruder Hurricane unit when Mac assumed command. Here Mac accustoms his eyes to the darkness before a night sortie.

Bottom: While waiting to go on duty Mac enjoys a game of cards with some of his pilots.

Top: Commandant André Jubelin, a Free French Naval pilot, had flown Spitfires with No.118 Squadron before joining No.1 Squadron, where he and Mac became great friends.

Bottom left: Another pose for the camera as Mac climbs aboard his Hurricane.

Bottom right: Ready for action.

Top: The President of Czechoslovakia Dr Edvard Beneš congratulating Wg Cdr Max Aitken DSO DFC following the presentation of the Czech Military Cross, flanked by Mac on the left who received a similar decoration, while Flt Lt Karel Kuttelwascher DFC (on the right) received a fourth bar to the Cross. London, 30 July 1942.

Bottom: Posing for the cameras after the presentation.

Top: Mac with film stars Orson Welles and an admiring Joan Fontaine.

Bottom: Another young American admirer.

Top: Mac giving a talk to an audience of young American women munitions workers at Atlanta, Georgia.

Right: Posing with P-36 Mohawk 'Minnie Pearl'.

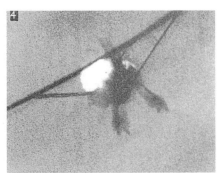

Top: (1&2) The first of the two FW56A trainers of JG105 to fall to Mac's guns on the 29 June 1943 sortie – thought at the time to have been Henschel 126s.

Above: (3&4) The end of the second FW56A.

Left: Mac's first Ju88 on 29 June 1943 – a training aircraft from IV/KG6; a second Ju88 from this unit was shared with Flt Lt Geoffrey Page, who also accounted for two more FW56As.

Bottom: Mac and Flt Lt Geoffrey Page at the BBC studio recount the sortie of 29 June 1943 when they shot down two Ju88s and four FW56As in 10 minutes over France.

Top left: Mac with Mustang FD442 of the Air Fighting Development Unit, the aircraft in which he claimed his final victories. On 18 July 1943 he was critically injured when this machine was shot down by ground fire.

Top right: One of the last photographs taken of Mac before his death in July 1943.

Middle: CWGC headstone commemorates Mac's last resting place at Pont-l'Évêque Communal Cemetery, France. On the tombstone are the words 'In proud and loving memory of our dear Jay "Death is swallowed up in victory".'

Bottom: Picture taken in early 2003 showing author Brian Cull with Liz Scratton (Mac's sister).

Italians. I took some photographs and we flew on round the coast, turning in again to have a look at Fort Capuzzo and the aerodrome nearby. There were the remains of some Bredas, SM79s and Fiats. As we passed Bardia, we saw wadis littered with derelict Italian transport and tanks. All along the road were guns, lorries and other equipment left by the Italians in their flight. Further on we passed a long column of Indian troops going up to the front. We flew low past them at first, but one of them fired at us with a rifle and another followed us round with a Bren-gun, so we decided to keep at a safe distance.

After miles and miles of endless desert, we eventually arrived at Sidi Mahmud – No.73 Squadron's aerodrome. It certainly was a welcome sight to see the old Hurricanes again and know that we had actually arrived. I shot the mess up in the approved style and touched her down a perfect 'three-pointer'. We left the Maggie at the Ops room and went in to see the boys. I was met by Garton and Maurice Leng, who were delighted to see me. Later we went to the mess where I found old 'Hooligan' and 'Market' Harborough, the Adj, not to mention a number of new officers. After tea, Scotty, Smith and McFadden arrived in a tractor, which they had found. They then produced some parachute flares, which they had acquired in an Italian dump. We had great fun letting them off, till some Aussies phoned up to say they had seen some parachute troops landing near our 'drome. Alan Murray [the CO] then told us to pack it up, which we actually did. McFadden then drove up in his Italian tank and gave me some dual, after which I went off solo and nearly turned the contraption upside-down by taking a trench at about 15mph. When darkness came and we went to the mess (which consisted of a rather ramshackle and sandy hut, another gift from the Italians), two bottles of whisky were produced for the occasion and I was not allowed to buy a single drink. Mike Beytagh was there, as palatial as ever and, if possible, even more likeable. Inevitably it was a case of, 'I shot lines and they shot lines, and we all shot lines together!' but it was one of the best parties I've ever had. I was given one of the best beds in the place and could not possibly have been better treated. I honestly think there are few joys in life greater than meeting old friends, and, above all, an old squadron. When at last I got to bed I was so tired that I fell asleep as soon as my head touched the Irwin suit that served as my pillow.

29 March: After a typical 73 Squadron breakfast of baked beans, bacon and fried bread, Milly [Plt Off Ken Millist] and I set off on a twenty-mile drive to Tobruk in a Ford lorry. As we drove along we passed innumerable derelict lorries and tanks and, occasionally, rows of Italian guns and other equipment. After some fifteen miles we reached the outer defences of Tobruk. They consisted of an anti-tank trench about ten feet across and about five feet deep. Beyond this was a barbed-wire entanglement some twenty feet in depth. Behind this again, were innumerable machine-gun and anti-tank positions, some of them defended by thin areas of barbed-wire. As we drove nearer to Tobruk, we passed several AA and heavy artillery positions, all surrounded by barbed-wire and sand-bags. How we took the place beats me. The town itself was rather disappointing. After all the papers had said, I really expected to find quite a reasonably-sized town complete with docks etc. In actual fact, the place in no bigger than a fair-sized English village and the docks are nothing more than a quay with one wrecked crane and a few sheds. Anyway, the papers say its capture is a great British victory – and the papers are always right! We had a quick look round and I bought a shirt from some army stores. I then sent off wires to mother and Chubby Eliot and we drove to El Adem for lunch. This was one of the most important Italian air bases in Libya and lies on the edge of the plateau about fifteen miles south of Tobruk. It was still showing the effects of the recent moonlight raids by Ju88s, though very little serious damage was done. Before lunch we went round the aerodrome and had a look at the remains of CR42s and SM79s left by the Italians. We then returned to the bar where we finished off the last two bottles of Australian beer. The bar and ante-room were beautifully decorated by one of the Italian prisoners who had drawn the most tantalising females in various stages of undress on every bare piece of wall. Definitely the wrong sort of thing for the Western Desert! Lunch itself consisted of spaghetti and bully, cooked and served by Italian prisoners who really seemed to be enjoying the job. After satisfying our appetites, we went to 70 Squadron mess on the other side of the 'drome and had a look at some more Italian aircraft. Milly had knocked back about half a bottle of whisky by teatime, so I decided it was time we departed.

We arrived back at 73 Squadron at about 1730, and with Milly in the condition he was, I had little difficulty persuading him to lend me a Hurricane [V7380]. Accordingly, I borrowed a parachute and helmet and got cracking. After being forbidden to fly one in Malta, I began to wonder whether it really was going to be as easy as I had first imagined. I was therefore very pleasantly surprised when I found myself at 500 feet with wheels up and the engine and airscrew at correct boost and revs. Apart from manoeuvres where the throttle must be used at the same time as the stick, such as aerobatics, or coming into land, it is just as easy to fly with one hand as it is with two. I climbed up to 4,000 feet and then dived at the mess till the clock showed 260mph. Holding the stick between my knees, I quickly opened the throttle and pulled her into an upward roll. The old Hurricane went round perfectly and as I straightened out at the top, I realised that my fighting days are by no means over. If I can get an artificial arm to open and close the throttle, I can be as good as new with a little practice. I proceeded to give the boys a comprehensive aerobatics display and then flew off low, back in the direction of El Adem, beating up all the camels I met en route. After about half an hour I came in and did a safe, if rather bumpy, landing.

One of 73 Squadron's ground crew, LAC Ken Rumbold, who witnessed Mac's performance, recalled:

"He might have had trouble convincing the authorities, but none of us had any doubts after he had borrowed one of our kites and put on a memorable display of aerobatics, beating up the camp at low level."

Diary:

In the evening I had a long and interesting talk with Murray. We discussed the possibility of my going onto experimental work at Boscombe Down for a couple of months while I got used to my new arm. He is going to give me a letter of recommendation in the morning to make even more certain that I get back onto fighters.

30 March: I really should have gone back to Aboukir today, but we all thought there might have been a sandstorm en route, so Milly and I decided to go to Barce instead. We set off at 10am and flew low over the Italian POW camp just this side of Tobruk. I then flew up the coast road between the telegraph posts, hopping over any lorries we passed. Poor old Milly stuck it as long as he could and then waggled the stick and pointed pleadingly upwards. We climbed to about 200 feet and he was quite happy. Just after Gazala the coast turns north, so we flew inland in order to cut the corner off. Gradually the land scrub became thicker and, occasionally, we saw dried-up shrubs and bushes. The ground became much more hilly as we passed south of Derna and we kept crossing great wadis, sometimes 2,000 feet deep. Eventually we came to the road that runs inland between Derna and Barce and saw, for the first time, green fields and trees with little white houses dotted here and there along the road. The Italians may not treat the people of their empire very well, but they certainly open up the country to a greater extent than I have ever seen in a British possession. This road, built by Mussolini as part of his scheme to invade Egypt, is a typical example. With a beautifully tarmacked surface, it winds for the best part of 200 miles from Derna to Benghazi. Every few miles are the pretty white farms of the Italian settlers, each with their cultivated fields and flocks of goats and cows. After flying for almost an hour over these tree-covered hills, we came to the coastal plain and saw the little white town of Barce. The aerodrome itself lies on the north-east edge of the town and is very small and bumpy. Milly insisted on landing as I don't think he really held with my one-armed flying!

He parked the Maggie near some Lysanders from 6 Squadron and then we walked into town for lunch. This we had in the one and only hotel, which was actually still run by its Italian owners who had remained after the British occupation. As usual, the food consisted mainly of spaghetti, with some greasy pork chops to follow. We had a couple of bottles of Chianti and then went out for a walk around the town. The railway to Benghazi was working again, so we stopped to watch the tiny engine pushing some trucks around. After a short doze in the sun, we went back to 6 Squadron where we had a lovely cold bottle of Aussie beer before starting back for home. The journey back across the desert was very boring and by the time we reached Gazala our bottoms were so stiff that we decided to land and stretch our legs. We taxied over to the eastern edge of the 'drome and had just got out to inspect the remains of an SM79, when some Aussies drove up in a car. Milly asked them for a cigarette and was given a tin of baccy and some paper. After vainly trying to produce something looking like a fag, poor Milly gave up in despair, whereupon the Aussie took over and after much spitting and licking, produced a horrible 'salivating' affair, which Milly tried to smoke. After wasting about six matches vainly trying to light it, he looked at his watch and decided that he hadn't time for a cigarette anyway, so once more we got cracking. We landed just as the sun was setting and went straight to the mess for a well-earned drink.

31 March – Alexandria: I woke up with the definite beginnings of a sore throat, so paid a visit to Doc Evans to get some quinine and a gargle. Sqn Ldr Murray then ran me down to his office where he wrote me out the most complimentary letter of recommendation, saying he would gladly have me back in 73 Squadron as soon as I am passed as OK for ops. I then gathered my kit together, said goodbye to the boys and set off for Aboukir. When we reached Bardia I circled low over the town to have a good look at the defences, which were even more formidable than those of Tobruk. I really must take off my hat to the troops who took the place. If Jerry had been there, we should never have done it. Just after we passed Sollum, I saw three huge sharks in the shallow water about ten feet from the shore, and a little further along, we saw a Lysander which had landed on the sand flats between the road and the sea. We flew past it at about ten feet and saw there were two men apparently camping under the wing. They waved at us and as they looked quite all right and there was nowhere to land the Maggie safely, we flew on. I discovered later that it had forced-landed with engine trouble and that the two men were guards waiting for a servicing party to come out and repair the engine. When we landed at Mersa Matruh, a very obliging flying officer came out and asked us over to his tent for some lunch. There we met another flying officer who had had very little chance of flying, so I said I would take him up for a short trip in the Maggie. We climbed up to 2,000 feet and I did a flick-roll. This chap then took over for ten minutes and flew around, after which I shot up the Matruh track at 0 feet to the consternation of some troops who were sunbathing! Shortly after two o'clock I took off again and after a long and exceedingly boring journey across the desert, finally arrived at Aboukir at 4.30pm. No one seemed to have noticed that I had been away for an extra day, so I refrained from drawing their attention to the fact.

1 April – Geneifa: My sore throat was definitely worse, but I dared not go sick at Aboukir, so I went down to Wg Cdr Donkin again and asked if I might borrow the Maggie to go to Geneifa. To my delight he again said yes. He had heard that I was on Battles in France and as he had been in charge of the training squadron at Hucknall, he was eager to hear if I had any news of his officers that went out to France. At about 3pm we set off for Heliopolis. It was quite interesting flying up the Nile delta and seeing the native villages etc. One thing that impressed me was the abrupt edge of the cultivated area where the irrigation system finished and the desert started. As we got near Cairo I could see the Pyramids in the distance. After refuelling at Heliopolis we flew east across the desert to Geneifa, which is situated on the south-western border of the Great Bitter Lake. The aerodrome buildings are not yet finished, but the tarmac landing strips have been there for some time. I went round to the officers' mess on the fire engine. I discovered that MEP [Middle East Pool], to which I am posted, was a camp about half a mile away across the railway line. A squadron leader kindly rang up for transport and gave me a drink while we waited. After about ten minutes a Ford utility truck arrived and I was taken over to the camp. I went in and saw the adjutant, who was a very cheery Australian. He said no one had noticed my absence for three or four days, then Hayes had told them I had gone to Libya on duty! So all was well. I was billeted in a fairly comfortable tent, which I shared with Hayes and two other officers. Our beds were the most amazing wickerwork affairs, which, provided they did not collapse, were moderately comfortable. Having tidied myself up I went to the three interconnected tents which served as a mess and there found a number of Australian officers who had just arrived and were awaiting postings to squadrons. They were a wizard crowd and in true Australian fashion, they insisted on buying me drinks, and generally treated me as an old friend. Supper was typical desert fare – bully-beef fritters and tinned pineapple – simple, but appetising to a hungry man. Then I suddenly realised it was my birthday – a fact which very definitely called for celebration. We got a really wizard party going, but unfortunately, my sore throat was too sore to take part in any of the singing!

2 April – Cairo: In the morning I went down to the shores of the Great Bitter Lake with Hayes. We sat in the sun till lunchtime and then walked to the camp. At lunch I discovered that some of the Aussies were going up to Cairo in the afternoon and, as luck would have it, they had a spare seat in their car. Martin, one of the other officers in my tent, was also going, so I put my razor and toothbrush in his bag and off we went. Arriving in Cairo at about 1630, we booked in at the Metropolitan Hotel and, after a drink and a wash, Martin and I set off to see the great city. At dinner, we met some of the guys from 73, including Leng, who was most amusing and insisted on providing us with wine and an unceasing flow of humour. We went on to Tommie's Bar and from there to the Bardia. We had the most stupendous piss-up and, just as we were leaving, I met two chums who had just flown across from Takoradi. They accordingly took me back to the Continental where Dudley was reported to be in bed. We went up to his room and I did a 'calamity drunk' outside the door. In a second, Dudley opened it and greeted me with a loud, 'Hey, Hey!' I sat on his bed and we each related our experiences since the good old days of '38. He was on night fighters before he came out here and has got three and a half confirmed. I eventually got a taxi back to the Metropolitan at about 1.30am.

3 April: After a late breakfast, Martin and I went round to HQ Middle East, where I managed to collect £7 advance pay and got permission to go on leave to Palestine, provided I could fix myself up with transport . . . We went up to the mess for lunch, after which I introduced myself to Flt Lt Stacey-Smyth, one of the No.267 Squadron flight commanders and asked what the chances were of a trip to Palestine. He was extraordinarily decent and said he would arrange a seat for me in a Valentia which is going up next Tuesday (No.267 Squadron were involved transporting passengers, mail and freight between Egypt and outlying bases). He then introduced me to Flt Lt Booth who said he would lend me a Maggie to go to Geneifa tomorrow to collect my kit. The whole thing was fixed in about five minutes, so Martin and I went back to Cairo as I had some shopping to do.

5 April – Heliopolis: For the last two days the Maggie has been u/s. I discovered, however that there was a Percival Proctor [P6116] serviceable . . . I had never flown one before and had certain misgivings about the landing. These however, did not deter me from flying between the Pyramids – a thing I have always wanted to do. I had never realised that the Sphinx was so small in comparison. I returned to the aerodrome and after a little difficulty with the flaps, managed to bring off a fairly good landing . . . I had flown another type and also got another two hours solo for my logbook.

9 April: As I was sitting in the ante-room after breakfast this morning, one of the waiters came in and said that the OC of No.216 Squadron (another squadron which devoted themselves to transport tasks) would like to speak to anyone who could fly a Hurricane. Like a flash, I answered the phone and was told that there was a Hurricane that needed testing if I could go over to 216 hangars. In due course I arrived and though the Squadron Leader viewed my empty sleeve with some suspicion, he was too polite to send me away. The Hurricane [W9243] had just arrived from Takoradi and had been re-assembled after a forced landing in the desert through lack of petrol. It now needed an engine and airframe test. It was fitted with long-range tanks, so I decided not to try any aerobatics. After having tea in the Sqn Ldr's office I got into the old kite and taxied out. It was grand to see the familiar cockpit layout again. I really have a great affection for the old Hurry-bird. I opened the throttle and roared off in a cloud of dust and sand, raising the undercarriage as soon as I dare. Owing to the long-range tanks, the lateral control was very sloppy and the machine was inclined to 'porpoise'. I flew up to the Pyramids of Memphis and then came back past the others, landing again after about thirty minutes. To my surprise and personal satisfaction, I found that almost the entire squadron had turned out to watch the landing (which for once was as per the book). The Sqn Ldr seemed favourably impressed for he said the aircraft had to be ferried to Abu Sueir (near Ismailia on the Suez Canal) tomorrow and asked if I would like to do it. Of course, I left no doubt in his mind as to the answer!

10 April – Heliopolis: As arranged I flew the old Hurry over to Abu Sueir this morning. After lunch I was collected by the squadron's Vickers Valentia transport, which took fifty minutes to fly back to Heliopolis – a trip that took just over ten minutes in the Hurricane.

12 April – Heliopolis: Yesterday morning I plucked up sufficient courage to expose my stump to the public and go swimming at the Hellis Club. I must admit, I felt rather self-conscious at first, but once I was in the water, I didn't mind people staring. I am delighted to find I can really cope quite well, especially the side-stroke. I tried crawl but it ended up in what must have looked more like an exhibition of someone drowning! I can dive fairly well though it is quite difficult to keep my balance in the air. I was so thrilled with the knowledge that I can still swim that I went bathing again in the afternoon. All this exposure to the sun was too much for me; my back and shoulders are quite sore as a result.

73 Squadron's Sgt Maurice Leng, who watched Mac trying to swim, recalled:

". . . it was an amazing sight, never to be forgotten, to see Mac's determination to relearn to do the crawl, but this time with one arm. He was like a slow-rolling porpoise . . ."

Diary:

This morning I went in to HQ M.E. in Cairo and, after collecting another £7 advance of pay, I dropped in to see a Sqn Ldr Jolly and asked him if there was any more news of my date of embarkation. He told me that there was no possible chance of leaving before the 21st. I then asked if there were any spare seats in machines going to Palestine, but was told that the weekly service has now been stopped, so my chances of going by air are negligible.

16 April – Heliopolis: Today at lunchtime I had another pleasant surprise. I was standing in the mess hall, when old Lough walked in [with whom Mac had trained and flown at Yatesbury and 3 FTS]. He had brought over some Italian motor-boat from Crete and is going back there by air tomorrow. In the afternoon I took him up to Cairo and we went and saw The Great Dictator (Charles Chaplin). I must say, I was very disappointed after all I had heard about the film. We were both pretty broke, so we went back to the mess for dinner. While having a drink after supper, I suddenly decided to try and go over to Crete with Lough and, if possible, go on to Greece in the Bristol Bombay, which was taking him. I was unable to find the pilot of the aircraft, so decided to turn up at 7am the following morning in the hope that there would be a spare seat.

Unbeknown to Mac, he was actually entering a very dangerous war zone. On 6 April, the Germans had invaded Yugoslavia and Greece to aid their Italian ally. Four British and Commonwealth divisions from North Africa were sent to aid Greece. Already, the RAF had eight squadrons of Blenheims, Gladiators and Hurricanes there, following the Italian invasion in October 1940. These were now reinforced by four more squadrons. By the 16th, the front-line in northern Greece had been broken and the British army was in full retreat. By that date, too, the RAF only had forty-six combat-worthy aircraft left in the face of the onslaught by Luftflotte IV.

Diary:

17 April – Athens: I got up at 6 o'clock and after a hot bath and a shave, walked over to No.216 Squadron hangars with Lough. When we arrived I found the flight commander in charge of the operation. Smiling sweetly, I asked if he could fit me in somewhere without anyone noticing. I took one look at his face and knew I was out of luck. Both Bombays were already overloaded and he said I hadn't a chance in hell. After getting up at 6am I was not going to be put off as easily as that, so waited for the pilot of one of these kites to arrive and tackled him. He didn't seem too keen on the idea and went off to ask [the flight commander] who, of course, said he had already told me I was going to be unlucky. I began to wonder myself how I was going to manage when [the flight commander] himself arrived. I decided to try the sympathy act, so stood under the wing of the Bombay and endeavoured to look the picture of dejection. It worked! He looked through his list of passengers again and just before the aircraft [L5856] taxied out, he told me that one of the officers on his list had not turned up and that I could go in his place. Whether there ever was a 'missing officer' or not, I don't know, but I certainly wasted no time in climbing into the Bombay and in less than five minutes we were off. Before leaving Africa, we landed at Mersa Matruh to refuel. There was quite a dust storm blowing and when we took off, visibility was not much more than twenty yards.

After a little I got browned off with the canvas benches that were provided for the passengers, so went back to the rear gunner's turret. I had just settled down and was enjoying the warmth of the sun, when the second pilot, a New Zealander, came charging down the fuselage and told me to come back at once. Thinking enemy aircraft had been sighted. I wasted no time in complying with his request. When I eventually reached the passenger compartment, he proceeded to tear me off the most 'ginormous' strip, saying that it was a court-martial offence to leave my seat while the aircraft was climbing, as it was liable to tail-slide. I, of course, apologised profusely and refrained from asking what happened if we were attacked and the rear gunner was unable to go to his turret? After a very long, cold and extremely boring flight above cloud, we eventually reached Crete. It is more mountainous than I had expected, the highest peaks being snow-covered. It was a marvellous

sight to see trees and green fields again after the endless desert.
Maleme aerodrome, where we landed, is situated on the north-west
coast and is extremely small and muddy (it had been raining all the
previous night). The Fleet Air Arm was in possession and as might
be expected, the edge of the aerodrome was littered with the remains
of Fulmars, Swordfish, Gladiators and even Martlets.

They said it would take at least half an hour to refuel, as it all had
to be done from four-gallon tins. We took off again at about 1400 and
flew north towards Greece. We passed innumerable small islands
before we eventually sighted the mainland. Then, making a wide
seep round Athens, we approached Menidi drome from the north-
west. After landing we taxied up to the hangars where I was dropped
to make arrangements about transport to Athens, while the others
dispersed and picketed the Bombays. We all met again at the hangars
and were taken up to the mess for tea. This plain, but welcome,
repast finished, we duly admired a brassière and pair of panties that
had been given to the squadron by some female they had rescued
from the desert after a forced-landing. They were displayed in a glass
case above the mantelpiece and really looked rather out of place in
an officers' mess! A squadron leader then drove us to RAF HQ in
Athens, where F/O Priest (the Bombay pilot) had to report and where
I changed some Gyppo money into drachmas. I think I got about 540
to the pound. Having fixed up everything at HQ, we went out on the
town. At a hotel bar – I think it called itself the Windsor – I was
greeted by a party of *Illustrious* boys and from then on the drinks
were on the Navy, and the party was truly nautical. We went on to
Maxine's for dinner and saw one of the best cabarets I have ever
witnessed.

18 April – Heliopolis: We got up at 6 o'clock and without any
breakfast, set off for the aerodrome in an open Ford truck. The air
was very cold and I was frozen to the bone long before we arrived.
Priest and co went and got the Bombay, while I did my duty to God
and the King in a little tin shed near the aerodrome. While I was
waiting for them to taxi the aircraft out, I had a look through the
hangars and was amazed to see an almost undamaged Italian SM79
in one of them. It had apparently been captured from the Italians in
Albania. There were also several Junkers 52s and a Heinkel training
aircraft with a swastika on its tail. I was just about to wander back
when to my amazement, I saw an old French Potez 25A, complete
with spoked wheels and scalloped trailing edges. The Greeks are
certainly very brave people if they go to war in it! We took off from
Menidi at 8am and after an extremely cold and uninteresting trip,
landed at Maleme an hour and a half later. Lough came down to meet

me and as we were walking back across the drome, the air raid
warning sounded. Shortly after, we saw the smoke of bombs bursting
in the distance, but no attack seemed to be developing in the
immediate vicinity, so we took off again as soon as the machine had
been refuelled. The five-hour journey from Crete to Cairo was
incredibly cold and boring, as for some unknown reason, the pilot
would fly at about 8,000 feet. All these bomber boys seem to have a
sort of stratosphere complex. Personally, anything above 500 feet is
too much for my liking. It certainly was marvellous to emerge into
the blazing sun at Heliopolis, though I wouldn't have missed the trip
for anything.

19 April – Heliopolis: Today has been one of surprises. As I was
walking back to my room after lunch, I heard a rather unfamiliar
engine noise and on looking up, saw to my horror three Savoia-
Marchetti 79s flying around the drome at about 1,000 feet, closely
followed by two Dornier 17s! Having safely reached the entrance of
a shelter, I stood and watched. No one fired at them or took any
particular notice. Then, to my amazement, they started lowering their
undercarriages and making the usual preparations for landing. The
first machine came in, stalled at about 20 feet and made a very heavy
touchdown, bending one of its propellers, as I found out later. The
others followed in quick succession, all of them making shocking
landings. They taxied up to No. 267 Squadron's hangars. So, seizing
my camera, I rushed up to have a look at them. Apparently, they were
all that was left of the Yugoslavian Air Force and had just come over
from Greece. The crews, most of whom had not shaved for the last
four or five days, looked a pathetic sight in their marvellous gold-
braided uniforms, which were now all oil-stained and dirty. Each had
a kitbag or suitcase in which he kept all that was left of his worldly
possessions. I think it reminded me more of the refugees in France
than the retirement of a modern air force to 'pre-arranged positions'.
I suppose they will join the Czechs, Poles, Belgians and French in
this cosmopolitan shambles that we call the RAF.

21 April – Heliopolis: I was sitting in the mess after dinner when
I was introduced to two South African Air Force pilots who had just
come up from Nairobi in a Junkers 52 and are going back in a day
or two. Here was a chance of flying down Africa, which, though
rather slender, I was certainly not going to miss. Accordingly
I accepted their invitation to go in to Cairo and found that they were
both extremely good chums, and were flat out for taking me back if
I could get permission.

22 April – Heliopolis: Straight after breakfast this morning, Dicky
Dunn (the 1st pilot of the SAAF Ju52), Eddie Pedder (2nd Pilot) and

I went in to HQME. Dicky went to fix up the arrangements for the return journey, while I went up to Sqn Ldr Jolly's office to try and get permission to fly south. Jolly, as I had rather expected, sent me up to Wg Cdr Moore, who said that as far as he was concerned, there was no reason why I shouldn't go, but that actually, Jolly was responsible for my passage home and I must get his permission. That was just what I wanted, so I went down to see Jolly again and told him that Moore said that I could go as long as he didn't mind. Jolly, thinking Moore was taking responsibility, was only too delighted to get me off his charge so easily and even went so far as to wish me a pleasant trip! It all seemed too good to be true and I determined not to let myself look forward to the journey until we actually took off.

24 April – Heliopolis: In the afternoon I borrowed a Maggie [P6379] and flew up to Alex, intending to collect an Italian rifle I had left there. As soon as I was clear of Cairo, I went down to 0 feet and greatly enjoyed myself beating up everyone in the fields and on the banks of the Nile. They can't have seen many low-flying aircraft there, for they all fell flat on their faces. Some of the braver ones threw stones and mud at me! I landed at Aboukir at about 1600, only to find that my rifle had completely disappeared. I didn't really mind as it is now a court-martial offence to have loot in one's possession. As it was getting fairly late, I had the Maggie refuelled and set off back to Cairo. I really enjoyed the trip back as the sun was just setting as I landed and the air was beautifully calm. After supper I did my final packing and had an early night.

25 April – Wadi Halfa, Sudan: At 0800 this morning we took off from Heliopolis bound for Nairobi. After climbing through the thin cloud layer at 5,000 feet, we set course for Assuit. Once on course, Dicky Dunn let me take over controls of the Junkers 52 [No.664 of the SAAF], to the great surprise of some of the passengers! After flying south for some twenty miles, the clouds disappeared and we could see the Nile away below on the starboard side. After an hour and a half's flying we crossed the river and came down to 1,000 feet so that we could not miss the aerodrome, which, as Dunn had told me, was very hard to pick out. After landing we taxied up to the refuelling point, and while some natives filled up the tanks from four-gallon tins, we had some tea and biscuits in a little café on the aerodrome. Just after 11 o'clock, we took off again and flew on to Wadi Halfa in the Sudan, landing at about 3pm. Here we were met by a Ford truck, which took us across the three miles of desert to the town. The hotel itself was full up, so we slept in tents on the lawn. After a late lunch, Dicky, Eddie and I walked into the native part of Wadi Halfa and had a look round the market. We then went to the hospital to see two Glenn Martin boys who had crashed in a sand storm while flying up from Khartoum. They both seemed very cheerful and apart from a few broken bones, were not very badly damaged. On the way back to the hotel we had a look at the remains of their aircraft, which had piled up just outside the town. After supper, Miles Johnson (who was shot down by CR42s in Eritrea when we invaded Ethiopia in March and who is flying down with me) and I went out and walked through the hotel gardens to the banks of the Nile where we sat in the moonlight listening to the frogs and crickets and dreaming of the good old days of peace.

26 April – Khartoum: After an excellent breakfast of grapefruit, bacon, eggs and sausages, we went out to the aerodrome, taking off at about 0915. The journey from Wadi Halfa to Khartoum was extremely dull as we left the Nile and cut across 300 miles of arid, mountainous desert, where a forced landing would have meant almost certain death. After flying Battles and Hurricanes, it was very comforting to see three engines in front and to know that if one packed up, there were still two more to keep us in the air! At last, after what seemed more like three days than three hours, we saw in the distance the junction of the Blue and White Niles, with Khartoum on the left and dark brown native houses of Omdurman on the right. After landing we found several members of Miles' old squadron (No.237) were up there collecting some new (or rather less-antiquated) Lysanders. So we rushed off to the mess to celebrate this unexpected reunion! After lunch, Miles and I got a taxi and went over the White Nile to Omdurman, where we went all round the market. Miles, after some rather expert bargaining, bought a set of leather mats and a handbag to take home to Bulawayo with him. I unfortunately dare not spend money unnecessarily as I have no idea how long my present supply will have to last. After supper in the mess and several drinks, all of which were on various members of 237 Squadron, a party of us went to the cabaret. The show was by far the best I have seen since France, most of the girls being Hungarian or Greek. It really was an extraordinarily enjoyable evening.

27 April – Kisumu, Kenya: We were called at 5am by a Sudanese batman, and after a quick shave and breakfast, I went to pay my mess bill. I went to the Paymaster General's office, where I found an extremely dim pilot officer. After talking to me for a minute or two, he suddenly realised my arm was missing and said, 'Good God, what's happened to your arm?' I looked down, and pretending that I had expected to find it there, said, 'Heavens, it's gone!' Then he, thinking I was quite serious, said, 'How terrible, didn't you know it wasn't there?' Unfortunately, I couldn't help smiling and so spoiled the whole thing!

We walked out to the Junkers, which we found with its engines running waiting for us. We were in the air by 6am and as we flew south towards Malakal, I watched with interest the gradual increase of vegetation as we approached the equatorial rain belt. Khartoum itself is surrounded by an infinite expanse of bare, arid desert, stretching away to the distant, sandy horizon; but as we got further south, there were occasional patches of camel scrub which later gave place to low, stunted bushes and even small trees. The animal and bird life, too, became more abundant and as we neared Malakal, huge hawks and buzzards zoomed past us three or four thousand feet above the ground. I saw for the first time, the now familiar round mud huts of the natives with their thatched roofs and wooden enclosures. The aerodrome itself was rather small, but Dicky managed to put the Junkers down with plenty of room to spare. The refuelling had again to be done from four-gallon tins, so while it was being done, we went over to the aerodrome café and had a very welcome breakfast. On our way back we passed a secretary bird, which greatly amused me as I had never seen one before.

We took off again at about 1000 and, after flying over the Sud region of the Nile, arrived at Juba for lunch. The heat and humidity were terrific and I literally dripped with perspiration the whole time. We went into the hotel for lunch and a very welcome ice-cold beer. We had originally intended to reach Nairobi today, but there were some very heavy storms over the mountains, so Dicky decided to go round via Kisumu and spend the night there. Shortly after leaving Juba we ran into 10/10 cloud and flew blind for about half an hour, eventually emerging about fifty miles north-north-west of Mt Elgon (Uganda) whose top was unfortunately obscured by cloud. Just before crossing the equator I took over and, after passing one very heavy local storm, we had our first glimpse of Lake Victoria through the mountains. As we approached the aerodrome we could see the little town of Kisumu nestling on the edge of the lake and an Empire flying boat at anchor in the bay. On landing we were met by one of the aerodrome officials who kindly took us to the Grand Hotel in his car. The hotel was very comfortable and the food excellent. We had some simply delicious fried lake fish for supper and the usual variety of paw-paws, avocado pears etc.

28 April – Nairobi, Kenya: For once we were able to rise at a gentlemanly hour. After a hot bath and leisurely breakfast, we were taken out to the aerodrome in the official's car. The lake was still pretty choppy after yesterday's storms though the wind had died down during the night and the sky was almost cloudless. We took off at about 10am and headed south-east over the mountains to Nairobi. We cleared some of the high ground at little more than 20 feet and I saw several herds of game rush off into the bush as we roared overhead. Just before Nairobi the sky became overcast and we landed in one of the heaviest downpours I have ever seen. On the way down I had entertained vague ideas of organising a trip out to Abyssynia while waiting for another aircraft to take me south. On making enquiries however, I found that by a stroke of luck there was a Rapide going south tomorrow, with two spare seats – an opportunity which, of course, I could not overlook! Accordingly Miles and I said goodbye to Dicky and Eddie and went into Nairobi where we booked rooms at the New Stanley. After lunch we both did the odd spot of shopping and I put on blue uniform while my khakis went off for a much-needed visit to the cleaners. As we were coming back for tea, Miles met one of his many female friends who very kindly leant us her car. Once equipped with transport, we rushed around visiting more of Miles' friends, finally fixing quite a party for the evening. At about 6pm we went out to a very artistic old English restaurant where we met another friend of Miles and his wife, who was one of the most attractive creatures I have ever seen since leaving England. John, the husband of the comely wife, asked if we could have lunch with them tomorrow. After a lengthy discussion on times and distances we (or rather Miles) decided that we could just make it!

29 April – Dodoma, Kenya: We surfaced at about 10.30am. At 12 o'clock we met John who took us out to his house, which proved to be almost as pretty as his wife. The outstanding thing about the whole party was the sweet, which consisted of the most marvellous chocolate mousse I have ever tasted. After lunch John ran us to the aeroplane [Rapide No.302 of the SAAF], which took off promptly at 2pm. I managed to get the best seat (the one immediately behind the pilot on the right) and consequently had a very good view of the country. As we flew over the plains of Nairobi we passed countless herds of every kind of game imaginable – springbok, eland, waterbuck, kudu, zebras and even an elephant and giraffe, not to mention the odd rhino. We passed within thirty miles of Mount Kilimanjaro, but again, the top was obscured by cloud. Further south we passed one or two groups of volcanic mountains rising almost vertically from the surrounding flat country. After nearly three hours flying we reached the little town of Dodoma, where we landed for the night. Tea and sandwiches were waiting for us at the little café on the drome. There was also a huge bunch of lovely little thin-skinned bananas, which I moved into in no mean way! After gorging ourselves to the full, we were taken to the local hotel, which was a dirty, ramshackle, one-storey building run by an enormous, rather motherly, old German woman. Our bedrooms (if they could be called rooms) were situated in a long whitewashed outhouse behind the main building. We were sleeping two to a room and no electric light, no washing facilities and no carpet on the bug-infested stone floor. We would gladly have put up with this, but to make matters infinitely worse, the whole place was literally infested with mosquitoes. They dive-bombed us from above and settled in swarms on our legs and arms. If I don't get malaria, it will be a miracle! We spent the evening in the dimly-lit bar drinking tepid beer and telling stories of our adventures. Having nothing better to do, most of us retired to bed at a fairly early hour, thankful to pull down our mosquito nets and at last be free of that host of flying insects.

30 April – Salisbury, Southern Rhodesia: We were woken at 5am and having paid our bills, went out to the aerodrome where we had tea and more bananas before taking off for Mbeya in Tanganyika. This leg of the journey was, I think, the most interesting from the point of view of game. Nash, the pilot of the Rapide, flew most of the way just above the tree tops, giving us an excellent view of almost every imaginable kind of animal and bird. We beat up one herd of elephant and sent them charging off through the bush at a terrific speed, crashing through the thick undergrowth and trampling small trees as if they were grass. At one salt-pan we found twenty giraffe and flew so low past them that we had to look up to see their heads! After about two hours flying we came to the end of this plain and climbed up to the little town of Mbeya in the hills. The aerodrome itself is situated right in a valley with hills rising eight or nine thousand feet all round. It must be very tricky to get into in bad weather. We only stayed here long enough to refuel and then took off, this time for Mpika. At first the ground was very mountainous, but gradually levelled off, finally becoming the same monotonous, bush-covered plain that we had crossed south of Nairobi. At Mpika we stopped for lunch and I saw for the first time the little brown and blue lizards that are so common in that part of Africa. So far I have not seen any snakes and am rather disappointed after all I have heard about African jungles! After lunch, we set off for Lusaka, crossing the Zambezi where I saw several hippos and I think some crocs. From Lusaka, we set out on the final lap of our journey at 2.30pm and arrived at Salisbury shortly after 4.30. Here we said goodbye to Nash, thanked him profusely for the trip and then scrounged a lift round to Miles's brother's house in a friend's car. Dick is Miles's oldest brother and is, I should think, about 35, very well-built and an extremely good type. Sheila, his wife, I like enormously. She is one of the few women who really think logically and do not speak unless they have something worth saying. Dick is a Sgt Major in the Local Defence Volunteers (or its Rhodesian equivalent) and had just been doing some rifle practice with his boys. Supper was miraculously produced, after which we had the odd noggin and shot lines.

Mac signed his own logbook summary for April 1941 as 'OC Sweet Fanny Adams'!

1 May – Salisbury: This morning Miles and I paid a visit to the Air Force HQ in order to change some money and try and fix free railway warrants to Durban, both of which we succeeded in doing. At about 6pm, several friends came round for drinks. Amongst them was a Sqn Ldr de Sallus who works at Group HQ. I told him I was very keen to do the odd spot of flying and he suggested my doing a ferrying trip from Durban as there were several Harvard and Oxford trainers to be collected and a definite shortage of pilots for them. He promised to see Wg Cdr Hamilton about it tomorrow.

2 May – Salisbury: After breakfast Dick took us . . . on a conducted tour of a tobacco factory. We saw the drying, stripping, sorting and packing sheds. It's really amazing the time, trouble and money spent on this smoking racket. Each leaf is treated with the same care as a silk handkerchief in the laundry (in fact, a darn sight more care than most of my handkerchiefs ever get!). After finishing our tour we left this sickly-smelling establishment and I went to Air Force HQ, while Miles did some more visiting. I found Sqn Ldr de Sallus who took me in to Wg Cdr Hamilton. He said if I could produce my logbook to prove that I could fly with one arm, he was so short of pilots that he would be only too glad to let me do the trip up from Durban. So, returning in the afternoon and having shown them my old logbook and my letter from Murray, I was officially attached to No.22 Flying Training School, Thornhill for ferrying duties (it's nice work if you can get it!). As Miles was going down to Bulawayo that night, we both caught the 6pm train, and after thanking Dick and Sheila for their kindness, I once again set off on my travels.

3 May – Thornhill: The train arrived at Gwelo at 2.30 this morning. Feeling cold and tired, I said goodbye to Miles and emerged onto the small deserted platform. I had rung up and arranged for transport to meet me and to my utter astonishment found it had actually turned up! I dumped my baggage in the back and soon we were tearing along the two miles of dusty strip road to the camp. Just before 3am, feeling cold and dirty, I was dumped at the officers' mess. After a brief and unsuccessful search for a bed, I finally spent the remaining hours of darkness huddled up in my great coat on some cushions on the anteroom floor. I don't think I slept very much as, apart from the cold, mosquitoes kept up a continuous dive-bombing raid in my vicinity, some of them pulling out of their dives no more than an inch above my ear. Just before sunrise I walked over to the hangars where the machines were being D.I'd. [Daily Inspection] and run up ready for flying to commence at 6am. I returned to the mess again at about 0700 and after a wash and shave, went in and devoured a very welcome breakfast. After this I was introduced to Sqn Ldr Mills, the Chief Flying Instructor. He explained the nature of my duties and he agreed with me that a little Harvard-flying would be an excellent thing. I was then introduced to Flt Lt Porteous, whom I had met at Montrose last September. He is now D Flight Commander and the proud possessor of some eight or nine Harvards (two of which are occasionally serviceable at the same time!). After waiting for about an hour in his office, during which time he effectively kept me awake by singing (he tells me he has a beautiful voice), we managed to capture one of his few serviceable machines [P7162] and prepared to aviate. I may ridicule his singing, but his flying is definitely exceptional. We climbed to 4,000 feet and he performed some of the smoothest aerobatics it has ever been my fortune to experience. Having duly impressed me, I was allowed to take over, but, though I managed to cope reasonably well, I'm afraid I was nowhere near his standard of perfection. We smooched about for an hour and then I brought off quite a passable landing, thus adding one more type to my list of aircraft flown!

5 May – Thornhill: This morning I borrowed a Harvard [P5794] and went up by myself. After a quarter of an hour's fairly successful aerobatics, I saw an Oxford floating along about a mile away, so went over and did several head-on and beam attacks to cheer the pilot up. I then flew north up the railway line to Que Que and returned at low-level. At lunch the Chief Flying Instructor told me he wanted to see me in his office at 2 o'clock. Accordingly I wandered round and had the most 'ginormous' strip torn off me for beating up the Oxford. Honestly, anyone would think this place was a prep school for the mentally deficient the way they treat you! In this particular case the wretched instructor was vainly trying to teach his pupil instrument flying, so I suppose it was a bit of a 'black' on my part. Anyway, the net result of the whole thing is that I've been grounded for two days till I can learn to be a good boy. I suppose I'm lucky I didn't have to stand in the corner or write out a hundred lines!

9 May – Johannesburg: At 1030, I set off with two other pilots in a Rapide [No.305] bound eventually for Durban where we had to

collect some Harvards and ferry them back to Thornhill. We stopped
at Bulawayo for tea and then took off for Pietersburg. F/O Bowker,
the pilot, was a damn good type and let us all take a turn in flying the
machine. Just after we crossed the Matopo Hills, we climbed to
5,000 feet as it was rather bumpy low down. The country is very flat
in this region and the monotony of the bush belt is only broken by
the occasional dried-up river, whose yellow, sandy beds wind their
way southwards to the Limpopo River. As we neared Pietersburg the
ground started to rise and the bush became less dull, finally ending
in the grass-covered plains that fringe the northern edge of the
mountains. Pietersburg itself is a typical South African town, laid out
in squares with all the streets running parallel or at right angles to
each other. The aerodrome, which lies to the south-east of the town,
is small and exceptionally bumpy and has the usual little filling
station, offices and café. We took off again at about 3pm and Bowker
let me take over. There was a fairly strong headwind, so using this as
an excuse, I got right down onto the deck as soon as we had crossed
the mountains. We flew over a large citrus estate which looked very
pretty as the oranges were just beginning to turn red. It made me
think of the poor chaps at home who are paying God knows what for
each orange. The country over most of the route is dead flat, but
round Pretoria there are hills rising to about 1,000 feet above the
surrounding country. Johannesburg itself looks a very modern city
from the air. Great white skyscrapers rise precipitously from the vast
suburbs of the 'Golden City', which itself is surrounded by dozens
of flat-topped yellow sand hills dug out from the mines during the
last fifty years. After landing at Germiston Airport we taxied up to
the control tower to find that a terrific parade was in progress. After
an inspection of all the troops, each unit started doing regimental
drill and the most amazing chaos followed. Sections of WAAFs did
head-on attacks on pupil pilots. Air gunners fixed bayonets, while
cooks and butchers staged a tactical retreat through their lines. If
South African organisation is no better than this on a battlefield, God
help them when they meet the Germans! After much signing of
names, we were given transport, which took us to the Carlton Hotel
where we had a few drinks before catching our train to Durban.

10 May – Durban: The journey from Johannesburg to Durban is
simply wizard from the point of view of scenery and railway
engineering. The track is electrified and winds in and out of the
Drakensberg like a snake on heat. Often we could see the engine
going in the opposite direction across a gorge, so steep were the
corners. We arrived in Durban just after dark and went round to the
Mayfair Hotel where we were booked in.

12 May – Pietersburg, South Africa: We left the hotel at 8am and after signing wads of bumph, eventually took off at about 9 o'clock [in Harvard N7073]. I ran my engine up very carefully before I finally taxied into position and, closely followed by my No.2, roared across the aerodrome and climbed steeply into the bright blue sky. We circled Durban to gain height and then set course for Zwartkop, some three miles south of Pretoria. As we crossed the Valley of a Thousand Hills, the air became very bumpy and I was thankful that I had told the sergeant who was following me to keep at a safe distance. Each time I looked back I could see the stubby little yellow wings of his Harvard dropping first on one side and then the other as the swirling air currents tossed and buffeted him like a piece of paper in the wind. After we had crossed the Drakensberg, the country levelled out and with the exception of small chains of hills to the east, the great grass-crowned plain stretched away to the misty horizon. At last we struck the railway, which runs north-west from Sanderton to Jo'burg, and broke the monotony by flying on each side of the telegraph poles which followed the track into the distance. At last the great, flat-topped sand hills of the Golden City appeared and we passed it to the east. We landed at Zwartkop in good time for lunch and arranged for our machines to be refuelled.

We were to have taken off again at about 2pm, but the sergeant had great difficulty in starting his machine and it was not till well after 3pm that we finally got cracking. Having missed the hills at Pretoria and settled onto our course for Pietersburg, we came down to ground level and amused ourselves by skimming over the little farms and mealie patches, watching the goats dashing off into the bush. After hedge-hopping for about an hour, we climbed to 500 feet and started looking for the mountains which should have been in front of us. Away on the port horizon I thought I saw hills, but in front of us, nothing but bush veldt for as far as the eye could see. I began to get a little worried as once one is really lost in this part of the world, there is very little hope of finding one's position and there are no aerodromes to land at. We climbed still higher and there away on the horizon I saw mountain peaks glowing crimson in the setting sun. As we flew further north I became more and more worried – ruins appeared where they shouldn't and the railway line just wasn't there at all. However there was nothing for it but to go on and hope for the best.

As we crossed the mountains I looked eagerly for the grass-covered slopes of Pietersburg, but instead I saw more mountains and between them, nothing but bush. Even a belly landing would mean almost certain death in this country and all the time the sun was sinking lower and lower over the western hilltops. Suddenly, with a terrible feeling of helplessness, I realised that I was lost. Nothing I could see bore any resemblance to my map and in less than an hour it would be dark. A few weeks, possibly months, trekking over the mountains to civilisation would be rather fun. I thought even the idea of baling out didn't really worry me, after all, I had got away with it once! But what really terrified me was the knowledge that if I crashed my aircraft, my chances of getting back onto operational flying would be greatly reduced and I should certainly be very unpopular in Rhodesia! There was nothing for it but to pray, so I prayed harder than I've ever prayed before. When I opened my eyes and looked down, I saw a little river with a single railway line winding along beside it! Now all I had to do was to fly up the track till I hit a town and then I thought I should be able to find out my position from the map. After flying north-west for some twenty miles however, the mountains became even steeper and higher, so I decided to go back and try and find a town the other way. By this time the sun was just disappearing behind one of the large peaks and it was obvious that we must land or bale out very soon. I started searching desperately for any sort of clearing that we could crash-land in, and at last saw a mealie patch which looked a little larger than usual and which appeared to be fairly flat. I circled once and saw that it was about 250 yards long and on a gentle hill, so I decided to land. Putting my wheels and flaps down, I approached with motor on and skimmed the ground with my wheels. It seemed fairly smooth, so after one more circuit and several prayers, I tightened my straps and came in to land. I touched down about ten yards inside the clearing and after a very bumpy run, came to a standstill with my airscrew chewing the leaves off a bush at the other end of the clearing.

As if by magic a crowd of natives appeared from the bush and stood around talking and gesticulating. Then to my intense relief a white man pushed his way through the natives and shouted something in Afrikaans. I asked him where I was, but he only shrugged his shoulders. However, he came and pointed on my map to a little station called Gravelotte, about fifty miles east of Pietersburg. Fearing the Sgt Pilot might crash if he tried to land, and hoping that we could make Pietersburg before it was completely dark, I decided to try and take off again. By this time the natives had surrounded the plane and were starting to climb onto the wings. I put the Harvard's airscrew into fine pitch and holding the stick, ran the engine up to full throttle. When I throttled back they had all disappeared as miraculously as they had come. I then faced the aircraft downhill, lowered the flaps about 15° and with the brakes on, opened her up, releasing the brakes as I put the throttle through the gate. The roar of the airscrew was deafening as the Harvard plunged through the long grass, slashing small shrubs to pieces as it went. About half way down the clearing I suddenly saw an anthill, but was too close to it to avoid it. There was a dull thud as my starboard wing cut it in half, but the Harvard never wavered in its headlong rush through the undergrowth. Just as I was about to crash into the trees at the downhill end of the clearing, the aircraft hit an unusually large bump. It leapt drunkenly into the air, started to sink back and then somehow, skimmed over the trees and started to climb. It was certainly with an intense sense of relief that I raised the flaps and undercart and climbed westwards for Pietersburg. At 7,000 feet it was still quite light and after twenty minutes' flying we saw the lights of Pietersburg in the distance and knew all would be OK. It was practically dark when we landed and taxied up to the aerodrome café. The aerodrome staff were almost as glad to see us as we were to be back and we were soon on our way to the local hotel to celebrate our safe arrival. We booked rooms, and after supper went to the local flicks.

13 May – Thornhill: After a huge breakfast of bacon, eggs and oranges, we went up to the aerodrome where, to my horror, I found several WAAFs who assured us that we had promised to take them up. Realising that a promise is a promise under whatever circumstances it was made, we fixed them up with parachutes and took off. It was one of those lovely sunny mornings with puffy little cumulus clouds at about 2,000 feet just asking to be shot up. Automatically there followed the most incredible beat-up of the drome, the town and the whole district in general, till the place became positively unsafe. Harvards were mingling with traffic on the main street, slow-rolling across the aerodrome at 200 feet and chasing each other round the church spire. At last, dropping our rather sickly-looking passengers and topping up our petrol tanks, we took off on the long and rather monotonous trip to Bulawayo. I asked another pilot to lead, as yesterday's boob had rather shaken any faith I ever had in my navigating ability. As usual, we flew at ground level and beat up the numerous herds of vildebeest, zebras and buck that we passed. Just before reaching Bulawayo we climbed to about 2,000 feet and started a running dogfight which ended up at about 100 feet over the middle of Kumalo aerodrome, much to the annoyance of the wretched Oxfords who were doing circuits and bumps, and much to our own amusement. Scarcely had we landed when I was sent for by the Chief Flying Instructor and had a very

juicy strip torn off for bad flying discipline – always in the shit, that's
me! As it was painfully apparent that our popularity at Kumalo was
not all that might be hoped for, we refuelled as quickly as possible
and took off on the last leg of our journey to Thornhill. This time
I decided to lead myself as, if the worst came to the worst, there was
always a railway line to follow. As it happened, we did follow the
railway and as usual, flew at 0 feet. It was rather fun cutting off the
corners and keeping overtaking each other. Before reaching
Thornhill, we climbed to 3,000 feet and formed a close 'vic'
formation. When we approached the aerodrome, we dived to 1,000
feet and I half-rolled off the top while my Numbers 2 and 3 did
outward stall turns. It must have looked OK as no one took a poor
view.

14 May: I borrowed a Harvard [P5913] today and flew up to
Salisbury where I had lunch and then went to Training HQ to do a
spot of organising. I have arranged to go back to Durban on the 16th.
In the meantime, I have been asked to give the boys at Thornhill a
lecture on air-fighting tomorrow, so I spent the evening trying to
think of something to say.

16 May: Although I felt a little self-conscious at first, the lecture
went off very well both yesterday and today. I started off by shooting
a few lines about the battle of France and then got cracking on Malta
and ended up by reading a few extracts from my diary. It's really
rather nice to feel that I'm doing something to earn my keep for a
change! This afternoon, one of the instructors was rather busy and
asked if I would like to take up one of his pupils for some instrument
flying in an Oxford [T1003]. The pupil, Sgt Chater, turned out to be
the brother of a chum who was at Flying Training School with me at
Yatesbury in 1937, so we got on very well. I never did believe in
instruments, so we skipped all that nonsense and went and beat up a
poultry farm near Shabani. By the time we'd finished, there were
hens all over Southern Rhodesia, clucking and laying eggs as never
before!

Mac returned to Durban by train on 19 May. Once there, it would seem
that his conscience began to trouble him.

20 May – Durban: As I have now been completely out of touch with
any RAF Embarkation authorities since 22 April, I felt it was high
time I wandered round and saw the local embarkation officer. After
extensive enquiries I found his office and was ushered in to a dear
old boy by the name of Sqn Ldr Rowe. I told him I had come down
from Egypt by air for onward transit by sea to the UK. As I had
hoped, he knew nothing about me, so we went round to the Durban

Club to have a drink and to talk the situation over. Apparently there is no ship going home for at least a week, so I have plenty of time to do a little organising. In the normal way I should have been attached to a trans-shipment camp outside Durban, but the idea did not appeal to me in the slightest, so this afternoon Sqn Ldr Rowe and I went to the camp and after shooting one of my better lines, I got permission to live out at the Mayfair Hotel. Now I'm all set for a week's leave in Durban!!

28 May: By God it's good to be here! I've spent the last week having the most marvellous time of my life – lying in the sun and bathing all day. I'm getting very sunburnt and have never felt fitter since I left Malta. I think I'll come to Durban for my honeymoon if anyone's ever sucker enough to marry me. It's certainly got the right atmosphere. It spite of the great time I'm having, I'm longing to fly again, so was delighted when some pilots from Thornhill walked into the Mayfair at lunch time today. If I can get permission to fly another kite up to Rhodesia, I shall miss my boat home, which suits me right down to the ground. Knowing how keen Thornhill's Sqn Ldr Webster is to deliver the planes once they are assembled, it should be a piece of cake.

30 May: Yesterday evening I went round to see old Webster and after buying him a double-whisky, asked how he'd like me to take an Oxford up to Rhodesia for him. He said it sounded reasonable, as I was obviously doing damn-all in Durban and might just as well do some ferrying! He promised to fix it at RAF HQ at Salisbury, so, feeling very pleased with myself, I said goodnight and went to bed. This morning he rang up to say I was to report to the aerodrome on Monday and crack off for Salisbury in either an Oxford or a Harvard, whichever I liked!

1 June – Pietersburg: I got out to the aerodrome at 8am and after filling in the usual bumph, installed myself in the Oxford [V3317]. I had only one passenger, a flight sergeant fitter, so we took off very easily and set course for Zwartkop. I had only flown in an Oxford twice before and was consequently glad to have the fitter with me to correct instrument readings and throttle settings. The air was beautifully calm and the Oxford, being a very gentlemanly sort of crate, more or less flew itself. The journey, apart from a rather frightening attempt at cloud flying, was uneventful. After refuelling at Zwartkop, we flew on to Pietersburg, this time at a good 500 feet, and keeping a careful check on our position! Fortunately, the gremlins had left all the mountains and rivers in their proper places and I found the aerodrome without any difficulty!

2 June – Thornhill: This morning we flew on to Thornhill where we had lunch and, after refuelling, went on to Salisbury where I dumped my passengers and then got transport to RAF HQ. Everyone was very amused to see me back, as they naturally thought I was well on my way to England by now. After a little wangling I managed to book a seat in a Rapide going south next Wednesday and after a little more bullshit, they arranged for it to call in at Thornhill for me. This organising is a piece of cake if you know how. I then flew back to Thornhill where the chaps were equally surprised to see me. Life's too amusing for words these days! If I play my cards properly and don't put up any major 'blacks', I see no reason why I shouldn't keep this up for months. After all, they probably won't let me fly when I get back home and every hour I can put in here will all help to fox the doctors when the real fight comes. I'd like to see the man who says I can't fly even now!

4 June – Johannesburg: Before leaving Thornhill this morning, I went and saw Grp Capt Chick, the Station CO, and he wrote me a terrific letter, saying what a good type I was and that there is no reason why I shouldn't go straight into a fighter squadron. It's damn good of everyone to take such an interest in me. After all, I'm not much more than an aerial tramp at the moment! I haven't done a stroke of work since I was shot down. At 10am, as arranged, the Rapide landed and taxied up to the watch office. I shall now go via Bulawayo, Pietersburg and Zwartkop to Germiston and Johannesburg.

6 June – Johannesburg: This morning I went out to the aerodrome and had a look at some South African Airways Lockheed Lodestars which were fitted with Sperry automatic pilots. It's rather discouraging to think that after four years' flying experience, a little box of tricks can cope better than I can. Still, an automatic pilot can't shoot a line, so what the hell! Apparently when the machines have been fitted with 'George', they go on to Lagos to be tested. As they generally go almost empty, I see no reason why I shouldn't get a lift up to Lagos and catch a boat home from there; I might even get over to the States! Anyway, it's worth a try.

7 June – Durban: I caught the 4.20pm train from Jo'burg yesterday and arrived in Durban at 9am this morning. At the Club I was introduced to Captain Gordon Davies DFC who is on the Intelligence Staff at Defence HQ at Pretoria. He has just written a book [in fact, a paper entitled 'Identification of Aircraft and Air Tactics'] on fighter tactics and we had an extremely interesting discussion on the subject. Before leaving, he gave me a copy of the book, which I am going to read and tell him what I think of it. He also suggested my going back to Pretoria with him to give a series of lectures at the South African Flying Training Schools. I see great possibilities ahead!

9 June: This morning at 10am, I met Gordon Davies and his staff sergeant and told them I thought the book was terrific (actually, it was damn good and made very interesting reading). This pleased him no end and he determined to get me up to Pretoria to put over his book and give some lectures. I pretended to be very keen on getting home and said I would only come if he would fix up an air passage to Lagos for me. It all looked too easy! The next job was to get permission from the Air Force Embarkation Officer. This was not so easy, as I had already missed one boat and he was determined to get me on the next one. Eventually we managed to fix him by getting a signal from the Air Commodore in charge of South African Training Command, authorising me to proceed to Pretoria on an official lecture tour. This life is incredibly good fun. It's really most amusing not knowing how or where I'm going to be next. Nobody wants me or gives a damn what happens to me! If I'd been a good little boy and stayed at Geneifa, I'd probably still be sitting in that fly-infested camp on the Suez Canal feeling as miserable as sin.

10 June – Durban: This morning, just to make sure I could cope when I got up to Pretoria, I gave a typical lecture to the Anson pilots at Durban aerodrome. I must admit I felt horribly self-conscious as I'm not used to this organised line-shooting. Luckily, there were no bad eggs or rotten tomatoes handy, so I got away unscathed. Everyone said it sounded quite reasonable, but I think that was just to cheer me up. Thank God there was no one from any of my old Squadrons there – I really shot a shocking line! In the evening I had dinner with two very charming nurses from Maritzburg. I have promised to go and beat them up on my way north tomorrow.

11 June – Pretoria: After getting up at 7am this morning I went out to the drome by car and eventually took off at 1030. As this was the last I was to see of Durban, I beat up the aerodrome, finally flying the Harvard [P5698] between the hangars in fine pitch. I then followed the railway up to Pietermaritzburg where I did justice to June's hospital, as arranged last night! I then set course for Zwartkop and landed with only ten gallons left. I parked the Harvard and then got transport over to Waterkloof mess where I was to live. This afternoon I went in to Pretoria and met Captain Davies who introduced me all round and really made quite a fuss of me. I am to have full use of his office and clerical staff, so with the aid of these I rewrote my lectures and made out a provisional programme for my tour. This evening I went to dinner with Gordon Davies and his wife at the Zwartkop Country Club. The hospitality in South Africa is simply amazing. Several people in the mess, who I don't even know, have asked me to spend the weekend with them, or go to Jo'burg for a party. I can see I'm going to enjoy myself here.

12 June – Pretoria: This morning I went in to Defence HQ, where I saw Air Commodore Frew. He has a terrific collection of gongs including a DSO, DFC and Bar and I think an MC. He was damn nice and says I can borrow aircraft from Zwartkop Air Station to fly round on my lecture tour. I also mentioned the possible use of an air passage to Lagos, but nothing very definite was decided on. This afternoon I went and had a tooth pulled out as I'd had trouble with it for some time. After making fairly extensive enquiries, I find there is a Lodestar going from Germiston to Stanley in the Congo every week. From Stanleyville I could get to Lagos by Suliva Airways, provided I can talk these types into sending me. If I wait here another week I can accuse Training Command of making me miss my boat and tell them the only way to make up time is to fly across West Africa. Once I get to Lagos I'll find some way home in a flying boat. I don't trust ships these days – they're far too dangerous.

14 June – Pretoria: The last two mornings I have spent at Zwartkop Central Flying School lecturing the pilots. The whole thing has gone off very well, though I don't suppose the chaps learned much. They all sit there and lap it up. These South Africans are terrifically keen and ask the most tricky questions. Luckily, being a believer in the saying that 'bullshit baffles brains', I've managed to cope so far! This afternoon I had an unusually strong desire to fly, so I walked up to Zwartkop aerodrome where I had been promised a trip in an Avro Tutor [No.732]. A WAAF job with wings on [a Miss Slabbet] said she'd come up with me, so, thinking this was my chance to shoot a real line, I took off and held the kite about two feet above the ground till we'd got to 100 mph on the clock. I then did a steep climbing turn and staggered up to 2,000 feet where I carried out a series of fairly ropey (though what I hoped were impressive) aerobatics. Having frightened myself sufficiently for one day, I let the WAAF job take over, expecting a few gentle turns and a bad landing. Instead, she put up the most superb aerobatic performance I have ever seen in a light aircraft; looping, rolling, spinning and flicking, without losing an inch of height. To cap it all, she did a perfect tarmac-landing and then got out and smiled sweetly at me. I told her, condescendingly, that she was quite good and asked her if she'd done much flying. Only 4,000 hours she said. Still, I always was a sucker!

For almost a month the diary was not written up and it is unclear what Mac was doing, apart from a lot of flying in a variety of aircraft around South Africa, presumably as part of his lecture tour. Eventually, however, the authorities caught up with him and he was ordered to return to the Sudan. His logbook records the following flights during this period:

17 June: Lodestar ZS-ASN from Germiston to Beaufort West and Wing Field, Cape Town (passenger).

18 June: Glenn Martin No.1667 back to Zwartkop (passenger).

19 June: Leopard Moth No.1407 from Waterkloof to Kimberley and Bloemfontein (flown with Lt Blinkhorn).

20 June: Büker-Jüngman No.1467 – Solo local flying and aerobatics.

21 June: Leopard Moth No.1407 from Bloemfontein to Vereeniging and to Zwartkop (with Lt Blinkhorn).

24 June: Taylorcraft No.2006 – Solo Zwartkop to Germiston, to Baragwanath and Vereeniging.

25 June: Taylorcraft No.006 – Solo back to Zwartkop.

28 June: Piper Cub No.1583 – Zwartkop to Waterkloof to Warmbaths (with 2/Lt Campbell, landing on main road); back to Waterkloof and Zwartkop.

At the end of June, when he updated his logbook, Mac stated that he was then stationed at No.23 Air Station at Waterkloof in the Transvaal. That same day, he wrote home for the first time since leaving Malta, summing up what he had been doing:

"I don't know if this letter will arrive before me or not. Needless to say, I have had no letter since I left Malta as they have not been able to catch up with me . . . From Malta I went to Alexandria where I borrowed an aeroplane and flew out to my old squadron, 73, in Libya. I spent a few days with them and then returned to Cairo where I spent three weeks officially waiting for a ship home. As no boat appeared, I went over to Crete with Lough who was stationed there. I then went on to Greece for a short time, returning again via Crete. As there was still no sign of a boat, I got permission to fly down Africa, intending to get a boat at Durban or Cape Town. When I got to Rhodesia I found they were short of ferry pilots, so I did two trips to Durban and back ferrying aircraft. After this I waited three weeks at Durban for a boat home, but none came, so I got permission to go up to Pretoria to give some lectures on fighter tactics, hoping to get an air passage home in return. I have had my own aeroplane here and have been all over South Africa giving lectures and having a marvellous time. My arm is quite OK now and I have done over 100 hours solo flying since my accident."

His logbook records the following flights for July:

2 July: Miles Hawk No.2008 Zwartkop to Waterkloof and back (with P/O Beattie).

8 July: Miles Hawk No.2008 Zwartkop to Waterkloof (aerobatics), on to Baragwanath (with F/O Barber).

Hornet Moth No.1535 local flying to see crashed Tiger Moth (with F/O Barber).

Miles Hawk No.2008 back to Zwartkop (with F/O Barber).

11 July: Douglas DC2 NA12674 Germiston to Zwartkop, Kumalo and Lusaka (passenger).

12 July: Douglas DC2 NA12674 Lusaka to Kasama and Nairobi.

13 July: Douglas DC2 NA12674 Nairobi to Juba and Khartoum up the Nile.

14 July: Bombay L5829 Khartoum to Port Sudan (passenger).

15 July: Bombay L5829 Port Sudan to Asmara, returned with engine trouble.

16 July: Bombay L5829 Port Sudan to Khartoum.

17 July: Rapide SU-ABR Khartoum to Kassala, and to Asmara (passenger).

18 July: Wellesley L2645 Air Test with F/O Aldis.

Rapide SU-ABR Asmara to Agordat via Keren and on to Kassala and Khartoum (passenger).

Apparently Mac then received orders to proceed to Takoradi for posting back to England. At Khartoum he boarded a BOAC Lodestar (G-AGBS) captained by Captain Bowes-Lyon, a cousin of the Queen, and commenced the long flight to Takoradi via El Fasher, Geneina, Fort Lamy, Kano and Lagos, arriving on the 23rd.

Diary:

22 July – El Fasher, Sudan: After breakfast I packed my bag, paid my mess bill and at 1115 we took off for El Fashar in one of BOAC's Lodestars. As we flew further from Khartoum, the sand scrub and thorn bushes became more numerous and at El Fashar itself, the flooded riverbanks were lined with palms and bright green bushes and trees. After landing we were taken up to the BOAC hostel where we had lunch. In the afternoon I tried to get my diary up to date as it is now over a month behind.

23 July – Lagos, Nigeria: We were called at 4am and after a bath and an early breakfast, we took off at 6 o'clock. Our next stop was El Geneina, where we had a cup of cocoa each and refuelled the kite. After about an hour, during which time we inspected the remains of a Blenheim, a Tomahawk and a Hurricane and watched big red spiders chasing each other, we took off for Fort Lamy in French Equatorial Africa. The runway here was actually made of bricks and must have taken ages to lay down. Outside the hangars, two French Potez 29s were being run-up in true French style with the usual crowd of natives and Froggies standing around watching. After refuelling we flew on to Kano, where we went to the hotel for lunch. All over the hotel walls and climbing up all the trees, was the most amazing collection of lizards I have ever seen. There were some big jobs nearly two feet long with orange heads and tails. There were blue and brown ones and grey ones with green and yellow heads. It was better than any zoo. After lunch I went for another look at them and to my astonishment found the back yard was full of brown vultures, as tame as chickens. They were fighting over the dustbins and more or less queuing up outside the kitchen door waiting for the refuse to be thrown out. Apparently they are protected by the government, as, of course, they are marvellous scavengers. We took off again at about 2pm on the 500-odd-mile journey down to Lagos. As we flew south, the vegetation got thicker and thicker till, apart from the many swamps, the whole country was covered in tropical jungle. Lagos itself is almost surrounded by water, as the whole coast is a mass of rivers and interconnected lakes. After landing at what I think must be the smallest aerodrome on the route, we taxied over to the BOAC HQ and unloaded. After waiting around for half an hour, we got transport up to the RAF mess where I met all the boys from 228 Sunderland Squadron which used to be in Malta. The climate is horribly sticky in spite of the fact that this is their cool season. The humidity is so bad that nothing will ever get really dry and one's clothes feel wet and clammy the whole day.

24 July – Takoradi: Weather permitting, we hope to go on to Takoradi. After an early lunch and a favourable weather report, we drove out to the aerodrome and having collected my luggage and ensconced myself in the nose turret of the Bombay, we took off. To my great satisfaction, we flew for the first twenty miles down the palm-fringed beaches at about ten or fifteen feet. As we approached the Vichy-occupied territories of Dahomey and Togo, we flew out to sea, keeping well outside the three-mile limit. The clouds were pretty low and we were forced to fly below 1,000 feet the whole way (not that that worried me much). When we reached the Gold Coast we again went down to twenty feet and flew along the beach. Every two or three miles we passed villages and invariably the natives rushed out onto the beach to wave frantically as the old Bombay staggered past at the terrific speed of 125mph. At last we sighted the harbour of Takoradi and, soon after, saw the aerodrome with its tarmac runways lined with Tomahawks, Hurricanes, Glenn Martins and Blenheims – a perfect target for a German strafing raid. After landing we went up to No.2 mess where I met old Mike Beytagh sitting in his shirt-sleeves trying to catch malaria so that he can go home. After fixing myself up with a room and having a spot of tea, Mike and I went down to the club and got cracking. I've no idea what time we left, but I know it was somewhere around 11pm. On the way back I walked into a car or something and was stiff for the next three days. When we arrived at the mess, we met a crowd from 73 and 261 Squadrons, including [David] Thacker and Tiger Pain from 261 and Humphries from 73. We were all frightfully palatial and started getting rough. I smashed a little table and Tiger Pain started throwing glasses at some crests on the wall. Mike then suggested turning the table upside down, which we did, then tried to balance any other available furniture on the table legs. Finally, amidst smashing of glasses and hoots of merriment, we staggered back to our rooms and went to bed.

25 July – Takoradi: I woke up this morning feeling ghastly and with a very guilty conscience about last night's party. I had no mosquito net last night either, and to my horror, saw four bloated mosquitoes sitting on the wall just above my head. I squashed them and found they were full of blood, so I expect I shall have malaria in a day or two. I was sitting in the ante-room after breakfast when the Padre came up and asked if I was in last night's party. I said I thought I must have been, so he said, 'We don't mind you breaking our glasses, we don't mind you breaking our tables, in fact we don't mind you pulling the crests off the walls and throwing them out of the window, but if you want the mess furniture inverted, we must have a mess meeting first and put it to the vote. Apparently there's going to be a hell of a row about the whole thing!' In the morning I played poker and lost £4 so with that on top of my hangover I felt pretty green. In the afternoon it was still pouring with rain, so I decided to go and have a bathe. To the great amusement of the mess I walked down to the beach in pouring rain, dressed only in my bathing costume. The sea was quite warm and I stayed in almost an hour, finally getting rid of the last traces of hangover. In the evening I drank lime juice and water and went to bed early!

26 July – Takoradi: After racking my brains since I arrived here, I have at last thought of a story which I think will get me an air passage home. I went and saw the Senior Medical Officer this morning and said that I had been invalided home four months ago and had been detained in South Africa at the request of Training Command. As a result I have had no treatment for my arm and I am afraid that if I have to hang around much longer, I shall gradually lose the use of it. The Doc said he could do nothing for me until

I was actually attached to Takoradi and reported sick. I then went to
the Adjutant and got him to signal Pretoria for authority for me to be
attached and after lunch I went and reported sick. The flight
lieutenant on duty took a brief look at my stump, wrote out a wizard
report, recommending that an air passage be arranged for me
immediately. Now if the SMO says OK, I shall be home in a
fortnight. Before lunch today I borrowed a Hurricane [Z4086] from
Station Defence Flight and did half an hour local flying and
aerobatics. I tried to do a half-roll off the top, but pulled her round
too tightly and she rolled out going up vertically. I ended by hanging
on my prop and shoving the stick forward cutting the engine, but just
saving myself from tail-sliding. I enjoyed the trip immensely and in
the afternoon did some more aerobatics, this time quite successfully.
28 July – Takoradi: This morning I went to the SMO's office and
found that he had strongly recommended my air passage home and
had sent my letter on to the CO for his approval. Eventually he OK'd
it and a wire has been sent off to Cairo to reserve a seat for me. Now
with any luck I shall be home within a fortnight and I suppose my
travels for the time being will be over. After getting my air passage
finally fixed I went over to the servicing flight, where I managed to
get a trip in a Blenheim [V6189] with a Pole, Flt Lt Slodkiewicz,
who, I found later, had never flown one before! Boy, was I scared!
How we got down in one piece is still a mystery to me and I think to
him, too. Anyway, all's well that ends well. We played poker in the
evening and I won 7s 6d.

This was the last entry in Mac's diary. He flew home, courtesy of
BOAC Clipper G-AGCB via Lagos, Bathurst in Gambia, Lisbon,
Foynes and Dublin to Bristol arriving on 7 August. His African 'leave'
had helped him achieve the aim of filling his logbook with the evidence
that he could still fly. All he had to do now was to get the Air Ministry
to accept that evidence and for the experts to design an arm which
would allow him to fly operationally.

CHAPTER VIII

NEWLY ARMED

Having arrived back in England, Mac reported to No.1 Depot, RAF Uxbridge two days later, and was then requested to attend No.2 Central Medical Board on 13 August, where he was pronounced Category A (Temporarily); and was ordered to return to Uxbridge for 'fitting limb at nearest centre'. Within days of returning to Uxbridge, Mac managed to get a flight in a Spitfire II (P2406), his first experience of the type. The next day (21 August) he flew a Tiger Moth (T7027) down to RAF Ibsley near Bournemouth to see his brother, Gordon, who was now a pilot officer flying with No.501 Squadron. Mac reported this in a letter to mother as well as telling her where he was, and the progress being made on his new arm:

> "I am now stationed at RAF Uxbridge, while being fitted with my new arm. Last Tuesday I went down to see 'Baked' [Gordon's nickname]. I stayed in his squadron mess till yesterday afternoon. Baked's squadron leader let me fly one of their Spitfires [P2410] and I actually had a dogfight with Baked on Thursday evening. We flew over Southampton in formation . . . I've also been to Boscombe Down to see all the batmen etc. Several of the old-timers were there. I shall have my first fitting for my arm next Monday or Thursday."

Mac visited his brother again on 30 August – on this occasion flying a Defiant (N3392) of No.3 Squadron – shortly after Gordon had been posted to No.616 Squadron at RAF Westhampnett. Gordon wrote to his sister Helen telling her about this visit and describing how Mac managed to fly one-handed.

It was at Queen Mary Hospital, Roehampton, headquarters of the Ministry of Pensions' limb-fitting department, that Mac was being equipped with his new arm. The limb and attachments were made at Steeper's factory in Putney, of which Mr Hugh Steeper was Managing Director and Mr Dansie Hoare the Works Manager. Mr Hoare had already designed and provided artificial arms for other amputees including a young typist who had lost both her arms in an air raid. She was able to resume her job and was not greatly incapacitated. The first example he offered to Mac, however, was a rigid, cosmetic hand, which provided amusing moments, but was clearly not suitable for flying an aircraft. The next was a standard hook, which was similarly unsuitable. But the third was unique, as Mac recalled:

> "I explained the layout of a Hurricane and together with the designers we worked out what was wanted. They designed a marvellous arm which enabled me to operate the engine throttle while taking the control column and the firing button with my right hand."

They spent many hours studying the cockpit layout and controls of the Hurricane in order to produce an effective instrument. This arm had a special device with four spring-loaded pins – rather like fingers – which would allow Mac to use the controls on the starboard side of the Hurricane. They secured his left arm to the levers of the throttle quadrant: throttle, propeller pitch control, supercharger control and mixture control. In the Hurricane the landing gear control was on the starboard side as well and required a fair amount of muscular effort to move it. This special arm had, therefore, to interact with the control column while the undercarriage was being retracted and lowered. Together with all the other controls in the cockpit, manual dexterity was essential and could tax that of an able-bodied man, let alone a one-armed man. When interviewed by a reporter from the *Sunday Express*, he said:

> "It locks itself automatically in six different positions. I can do almost anything with it. And you will note the mobile thumb; so useful when you're playing cards! I use it chiefly for the throttle; but, at a pinch, I cab steer with it as well. And now they're building me a special flying hand. When I get that, I shall feel like a kid with his first pair of long pants!"

He added:

> "I am standing by, waiting for the final word from the Air Ministry, and just itching for another real party like the last one."

His cousin, John Orr-Ewing remembered:

> "James had the habit of twisting his artificial arm which squeaked a bit. One day he was travelling in a tram and was twisting his arm absentmindedly. A small girl sitting opposite him was fascinated at what he was doing. The girl's mother, who had been looking

elsewhere, turned round to see her daughter holding an artificial arm in her lap. James had unscrewed his arm and handed it to the girl!"

Mac's youngest sister Liz recalled another occasion when he was playing with a dog. It bit and tussled with the glove on his artificial hand. He then released his arm. The dog dropped the gloved hand and shot off with its tail between its legs! Mac's letters home now contained news as to the progress on his new arm. On 11 September, he told mother in his latest letter:

"As you will see I am now at Hunsdon attached to No.3 Squadron. I was fitted for my new arm on Wednesday and should have it in about a fortnight. Yesterday the attachment designer from Roehampton came and took measurements for the hand and says he can make a wizard one. In the meantime I shall probably have to go to an RAF Hospital to have my stump treated and toughened-up, as it is still rather tender."

He wrote to his sister Helen on the 20th:

"I am now in No.3 Squadron, flying night-fighting, cannon-Hurricanes. I am not allowed to do operational flying till I get my artificial arm (which will be in about four or five days). Then I hope to be pretty busy settling off a few little scores with our friends across the Channel! I haven't yet decided how many Huns my arm was worth, but I hope to have some idea in three months' time!"

Then finally, he was able to tell mother on the 30th:

"I have now got my arm and can work it quite well already. I have my final medical board tomorrow at about 10 o'clock and, if all goes well, shall then be passed fit for operational flying. You may have seen a little write-up about me in the *Telegraph* or the *Sketch* yesterday, saying that I am already on ops. That unfortunately is not yet true – where the papers got the story from I have no idea . . ."

To impress the Air Ministry, Mac had been doing a lot of flying in a variety of types during his time with No.3 Squadron at Hunsdon – Defiants, Havocs, Bostons, Cygnets, Magisters, Masters and Tiger Moths. Every day throughout August and September he was in the air. He even managed to visit No.88 Squadron at Attlebridge near Norwich; had been night-flying to test the Turbinlite fitted in the nose of a Havoc, which was supposed to illuminate enemy bombers for night-fighters to shoot down; done searchlight co-operation; fired at gulls off Bournemouth; and had fired his Hurricane's cannon at a target wreck off Orfordness.

He had also visited Monkton Combe with his brother Gordon, to see their youngest brother Archie. On this occasion (25 September) Mac landed their Tiger Moth (T6300) on the rugger field. This was in the nature of being a 'compassionate' exercise, as Gordon had been shot down over the Channel four days earlier. Gordon recorded the incident in his logbook: 'Had a squirt but was hit myself in glycol. Engine caught fire and seized up. I baled out into the sea. Picked up after an hour.' The visit to Monkton was Gordon's first flight since being shot down. Mac had also experienced some 'near-misses' during this period. His logbook shows that on 7 September he force-landed Hurricane Z3464 at RAF Wattisham in darkness during a searchlight co-operation exercise. Ten days later he landed Magister T2744 in a field near Newport in Essex, en route for Duxford from Hunsdon, having lost his way. Then, on 28 September, while flying Magister P6360, he nearly hit a Blenheim in low cloud, no doubt terrifying his passenger, Plt Off Mitchell. He was also involved in lecturing, as he told the family on 30 September:

> "I seem to be very busy these days. I was lecturing last Sunday week and have another one at 8pm tomorrow. I am also flying most of the day. I really am happy here and shall be certainly sorry when the time comes for me to leave 3 Squadron. As I expect Baked [brother Gordon] will have told you, our CO is a wizard type. All we want now are a few Huns to shoot at."

Having been passed fit by the medical authorities, he now had to await the decision of the Air Ministry. On 15 October, he flew from Hunsdon to Hendon to hear their verdict. It was just what he had hoped and planned for – he was returned to operational flying. To celebrate, he flew aerobatics in his Hurricane (Z3165) over the Hunsdon airfield. There was even more reason to celebrate on the 18th, as his brother Gordon reported to their mother from RAF Kirton-in-Lindsey;

> "I have had two visits from Jay this week. One today on his way back from Scotland and one on Saturday when he was going up to Scotland. He just got up there by 3 o'clock having flown through pretty terrible weather. He has been posted down to No.1 Squadron at Tangmere as a flight commander."

CHAPTER IX

IN OMNIBUS PRINCEPS – No.1 SQUADRON

No.1 Squadron, which had been part of the Advanced Air Striking Force in France in 1939 and 1940, and had taken part in the Battle of Britain, now started flying Rhubarbs, fighter sweeps and bomber escorts over Occupied Europe. Its personnel was now being leavened by a sprinkling of Czechs and Poles. In July 1941, the squadron, commanded by Squadron Leader R.E.P. Brooker DFC, was posted to RAF Tangmere near Brighton in Sussex, an airfield badly bombed during the Battle of Britain, which was only just beginning to look itself again. The role of the squadron was now that of night fighting, especially the interception of enemy bombers, and in August it had been re-equipped with Hurricane Mk IICs armed with four 20mm Hispano cannon instead of the usual eight Browning machine-guns. Training for night operations continued all through August, September and October on every night when the weather was suitable. It was then that Mac joined them. He wrote home excitedly:

"I have been frightfully busy the last few days as I have taken over a flight in No.1 Squadron and have been trying to do as much flying as possible, in addition to all the ground work that goes with a flight. We are on the same job as No.3 Squadron – four cannon, night fighting Hurricanes, so I feel quite at home. The chaps in my flight are simply wizard – in fact I doubt if I could find a better crowd . . . I seem to know half the people here already."

Twice a day at least, sometimes three times, the squadron worked up its preparedness for night operations. In November it was declared fully operational as a night-fighter unit. Then, on 3 November, Mac was promoted to squadron leader and given command when Squadron Leader Brooker was posted to the Far East. The newspapers had a field day:

'One-Armed Pilot As Leader.'
'One-Armed Pilot Leads Fighters.'
'One-Armed Pilot Leads. Skill Unhampered.'
'A Fighter pilot who had an arm shot off by a Messerschmitt cannon shell over Malta in February, has been appointed to lead a famous Hurricane squadron in Britain.'
'The squadron of which he has been given command destroyed more than 100 enemy aircraft in France.'

One of the first things Mac did was to get his own personal emblem painted on the nose of his Hurricane, BD983/JX-Q. It showed a left arm with a cannon shell passing through the forearm and the fingers giving the 'V' sign!

As a squadron commander, he proved to be an inspiration. Commandant André Jubelin, an officer in the Free French Navy who had escaped from the Japanese in Indo-China by flying a light aircraft to the Philippines and who had then reached England by various means was attached to No.1 Squadron, having previously flown Spitfires with No.118 Squadron. He paints this picture of Mac in his book *The Flying Sailor*:

"Of all single-minded men Mac seemed to me the purest and loftiest I had ever met . . . Slender, with an obstinate expression in his triangular countenance, he exhibited a broad black line round the irises of his luminous eyes and wore a slight reddish moustache under a sharply pointed nose. Mac was a born leader. In a branch of the Service where, one may as well admit it, true discipline did not exist except in battle, Mac introduced it with ease into the smallest details of squadron life. A short scene, on the very day of my arrival, convinced me of the fact. The pilots were assembled round their leader, taking his orders. One of them answered one of Mac's questions with a cigarette in a corner of his mouth. The Squadron Leader's reproof struck him like a blow. 'Your cigarette, please.' The other was taken aback and blushed to the roots of his hair. Then came, in the quiet tone of an indulgent sovereign: 'Don't mention it.' He meant: 'I've told you what I had to. I shan't enlarge on it. No more to be said.'

Mac was fundamentally gentle and good-tempered, a charming companion. He was worshipped by everyone in the squadron. But he was capable of sharp outbursts of anger. I noticed this when, one evening in Brighton, we had asked for two gins a few minutes after the sacred hour of closing time. The repulsive ass of a barman gave us the following brilliant reply: 'As you know, sir, there's a war on.' Mac was behind the bar in three strides. He took the idiot of a fellow by the throat with his hard wooden, cripple's hand and would have positively strangled him if they hadn't been separated. We loved and admired him. Mac added a new significance to our notions of human valour. He was cast in the heroic mould."

The squadron spent November and December in intensive night-fighting training, particularly searchlight co-operation, and co-operation with Havocs using the 'Turbinlite.' These were the methods used then to try and pick up enemy bombers and guide the fighters to their targets. One pilot described the exercise thus:

"The idea was that the Havoc took off at night with a Hurricane formating on each wing tip. The three aircraft were then directed by a Ground Control Station (GCI) onto the target aircraft. The flying called for all three aircraft to keep tightly together, through thick cloud if necessary. Once the target was judged to be in range, one of the Hurricanes was instructed to attack and some seconds after going forward the light would be switched on to illuminate the target. The second Hurricane would then go forward also, to 'finish off' the bandit. Such was the theory! In practice, the first thing that the lead Hurricane found was the slipstream of the target, then he was blinded by the brilliant light from behind obscuring the windscreen. There then followed a series of involuntary aerobatics terminating several thousand feet below, each Hurricane looking for the black Havoc in a very black sky."

Mac flew several of these exercises, culminating in an incident on the night of 12 December, when his Hurricane JX-Q collided with a stationary Havoc while landing at Tangmere. Neither aircraft was seriously damaged although Mac's aircraft was unserviceable until the end of the month. The only Turbinlite 'success' achieved was when Plt Off Fred Murray shot down a returning Stirling in error for a German bomber; fortunately the crew baled out safely. On one occasion there was excitement as the squadron was scrambled to patrol Dover where Ju87s were reported to be operating but none were encountered. Mac recorded an accident in a letter home:

"I wonder if you saw my last write-up in the papers? I force-landed in a field near Staines owing to a rough motor and bad weather [on 10 November]. I managed to fly the Hurricane [JX-Z] out again without doing any damage. We had a rather unfortunate accident yesterday afternoon. One of my new pilots came down in cloud and flew into a hillside. I have had the unenviable job of writing to tell his mother. This afternoon I went up on an experimental flight in our latest four-engined bomber [Lancaster L7528]. It really was extremely interesting and quite easy to fly."

However, night fighting was a role that was becoming frustrating for there was very little to do. The Germans seemed to have called off their massed bomber attacks and were sending over smaller groups which were much harder to intercept on this side of the Channel. A new tactic was now considered – intruding. The idea was to destroy the enemy bombers as they left their home bases under cover of darkness. Mac prepared his mother for his re-commencement of operations:

"We are starting operations very soon and there is an awful lot of organising etc. to do. Please pray extra hard for me from next Sunday on. We've got a fairly safe job and with any luck shouldn't lose any of the boys. If we are successful you will no doubt read of our doings in the papers."

Unfortunately, the weather closed-in:

"Owing to the shocking weather we have not been across to France yet, but are greatly looking forward to the first clear night. So far the squadron has gone very well – I really do love it here. It is good of God to give me such marvellous opportunities. I only hope I shall be worthy of it all. Yesterday evening, the Station Commander [Grp Capt A.B. Woodhall] and I went out to dinner with Anthony Eden [Foreign Secretary] and his wife, and tomorrow I am going to the Worshipful Company of Tin Plate Workers banquet in London. I hear Churchill will be there, so it's quite a big do. I have spent most of today trying to get another one-armed chap into the Air Force. He is frightfully keen, so I am doing all I can for him."

The airman he had been helping was French pilot Sergeant Jacques Guillou de Mezillis from Brittany, who had lost his left forearm while flying a Blenheim with the Free French GRB1 Squadron in Libya. Following a crash in which his left hand had been almost severed, he cut it off with a knife and then walked close on 30 miles in the desert under a relentless sun until he eventually reached safety. Repatriated to England, he was fitted with an artificial arm similar to the one that Mac used, the young Frenchman achieved his aim and eventually joined the Free French No.341 Alsace Squadron based at Westhampnett, flying Spitfires. Mac had given him much encouragement, support and, of course, inspiration, while de Mezillis obviously possessed the necessary determination to succeed; fellow French pilot Pierre Clostermann wrote: ". . . by an incredible effort of will [he] learnt to fly with his artificial arm." He obviously had the same willpower and strength of mind as Mac. Sadly, within a few weeks, de Mezillis was killed in a flying accident, on 13 March 1943, aged twenty-five, when the wings of his Spitfire folded up in a dive. His CO, Cmdt René Mouchotte, was particularly saddened by his death: "I was grieved by the loss of my very dear comrade . . . Jacques is a great loss to all of us. He was such an example of courage; he wanted to fly and fight again, despite the amputation of his left arm." He was made Chevalier de la Légion d'Honneur posthumously.

Apparently, Mac also personally offered encouragement to a Polish fighter pilot who had lost an arm and inspired many others including Flg Off O.B. James MM DFM. As a Sergeant Pilot, Oliver James had been shot down in March 1941 while flying a Hampden bomber on a mine-laying sortie off Brest. He suffered serious injuries and his left arm was amputated by the Germans following his capture. Despite his injuries he later escaped and arrived back in England in March 1942. Inspired by what he had heard about Mac's new arm and acceptance by the RAF to continue operational flying, he too had an artificial limb fitted. Having retrained to fly single-engined aircraft, he joined a Typhoon fighter-bomber squadron but, sadly, was shot down and killed in October 1943. Of Mac's inspiration to others, André Jubelin wrote:

"The Squadron Leader was already a legendary figure. Other cripples gravitated to him as to one who had been the subject of a miracle. They gained new strength when they saw him spring in triumph from the cockpit of his black aircraft."

Meanwhile, mother was shocked to learn that Gordon had experienced a nasty flying accident on 15 November, when he was being flown in a Magister to North Coates from Kirton-in-Lindsey, to fetch a Spitfire. His companion, Sgt 'Ben' Gunn, thought Gordon had taken over the controls, which in fact he had not. The result was a crash. He broke his nose, had a black eye and fractured his back. He was sent to Grimsby Hospital and then to the RAF Hospital at Torquay, where he had to wear a plaster jacket for some time. He was not fit to fly again until 23 March 1942.

Owing to the poor weather, the first night-intruder operation by No.1 Squadron was not carried out until 16 December, when Sgts Gerry Scott and John Smith set out from Manston in Kent. While one flew over France looking for flarepaths, the other patrolled over Dover. Neither saw any enemy aircraft, though flak and searchlights were both active. After an hour they returned with nothing to report. The first success for the squadron occurred on the night of 28 December, when Plt Off Karel Kuttelwascher, a Czech with three victories to his credit, attacked a tanker and a flak ship off Ostend. Shortly after Christmas, Mac wrote to his sister:

"I seem to have simply thousands of letters to write this Christmas –

all sorts of old dames sending me socks etc. It's very kind of everyone, but I do hate writing letters. We've had some simply wizard parties. The night before last, we had a dance in the mess here and last night the Duke and Duchess of Norfolk invited us round to the most palatial do in Arundel Castle. I shot a hell of a line to an old boy, who had also lost his arm and later found he was the Earl of Cowdray or something. There really were some very [nice] little jobs there – the type that Grandma would approve of for a MacLachlan's wife!"

He was to enjoy another 'party' on 10 February – at Buckingham Palace – when he was invested with the Bar to his DFC. But in the letter to mother confirming details of the arrangements for the great day, he ended by saying:

"We had a dance in the Mess last night to say goodbye to Grp Capt Woodhall who is going to Malta. I wish No.1 were going with him, we're terribly fed up here."

On 11 February, Mac departed for a course at the Searchlight School at Shrivenham. In his absence, his squadron was called into action, but not for a night operation. On the morning of the 12th, reports were received that the German battlecruisers *Scharnhorst*, *Gneisenau* and *Prinz Eugen*, together with their escort of six destroyers and torpedo boats had broken out of Brest under cover of bad weather, to make a dash for German ports through the English Channel. Above them was an umbrella of low-flying fighters. The force was not detected until late morning and then frantic efforts by Bomber, Coastal and Fighter Commands were made to stop them, although the main effort came from the Fleet Air Arm, which despatched six Swordfish. Led by Lt Cdr Eugene Esmonde, the Swordfish were all shot down, Esmonde being awarded a posthumous VC. In the poor visibility few aircraft were able to find the German warships. Hurricanes from 1 Squadron were ordered to attack the escort vessels. Taking off at 1330, six Hurricanes of A Flight led by Flt Lt Bill Raymond, flying at less than 300 feet, spotted three destroyers. These put up a heavy flak barrage as each pair of aircraft strafed. White Section – comprising Sgt Errol Blair (Z3774), a South African and Lithuanian-born Plt Off Romas Marcinkus (BD949/JX-J) – was shot down, the former pilot being killed and the latter captured, although he was later shot by the Gestapo following his escape from Stalag Luft III in March 1944. The three German battlecruisers reached their harbours before dawn on the 13th. Only mines had inflicted any serious damage to them. Mac returned to Tangmere next day.

As if the loss of two pilots was not bad enough for the morale of the squadron, there followed an unfortunate accident which cost the life of another. No.1 Squadron had been 'adopted' by the town of Brighton and in order to cement good relations, the Mayor, Alderman M.W. Huggett and other dignitaries were invited to pay a visit to Tangmere on 16 February and to have lunch in the officers' mess. After spending an interesting time at the aerodrome and discussing ways in which the town might help the squadron, such as extra furnishings – comfortable chairs, carpets, rugs, tables and books for the dispersal huts – the Mayor was invited to take a short trip in a Magister (V1013) so that he could view his town from the air. Mac piloted the aircraft. After landing, the Mayor's secretary, Mr George Martin, asked if he could have a trip, too. He was taken up by Plt Off Eustace Sweeting. On coming in to land after ten minutes, the Magister was seen to go into a steep left-hand turn. The nose dropped and the aircraft crashed into an open field just west of Tangmere. Both men were killed. The papers appear to have got their facts wrong, for Mac had to write another re-assuring letter home:

> "I'm sorry people thought it was I who had crashed the other day – the papers certainly did make rather ambiguous statements. As you can probably imagine, I've had a pretty grim time interviewing the wives and relations of the pilot and passenger and have been horribly busy arranging funerals, attending courts of inquiry and coroners' courts etc. Yesterday morning I drove up to town to see my new flight commander getting married. We went on to the reception after and really had a grand time. He is a Czech by the name of Kuttelwascher."

To his sister on the same day (22 February), he confessed:

> "We had some very unfortunate accidents in the squadron last week – five people being killed. Two of them were lost in the *Scharnhorst* affair which I luckily missed as I was on the searchlight course. I am trying to get the squadron posted overseas, but so far have met with little luck. It really is getting very boring doing nothing. Now I am on a special course at Old Sarum for three days. I am the junior officer here, most of the others being air commodores or brigadiers. The course is a Senior Officers' Army Co-operation Course."

The remainder of February and the whole of March were spent in intensive training, carried out under favourable conditions by night and by day. As if to point out the need for new night-fighting tactics, Mac's logbook records a number of searchlight interceptions of German raiders, but the lights never held the target long enough for him to go into action. At least the weather was improving and that was a hopeful

sign that the squadron's new sphere of operations might soon
commence. In the meantime, Mac had been doing his bit for the war
effort:

"I have just returned from Slough where I have spent a most
interesting day visiting the Hurricane factories and talking to the
employees. We watched the whole process of production, right from
raw sheet metal to the final assembly. I had to talk for about ten
minutes in each shop. I was really amazed to see women working
great lathes and presses as well as, if not better than, men. By the
way, you might put up a special prayer for me next Tuesday night as
we may be going across to the other side. Please don't bother about
my birthday (you've already given me my watch). I'm getting
terribly old – I feel quite grown-up now."

It was on Mac's twenty-third birthday – 1 April 1942 – that the
squadron's first successful intruder mission was carried out. The moon
was now full which assisted night flying, as well as helping in the
location of enemy bombers. In preparation for the new tactics, long-
range, forty-two gallon drop-tanks were fitted to the Hurricanes. The
aircraft had also been painted in a matt-black camouflage. The pilots,
too, had to make their preparations. Eyes had to get their night vision.
Nerve ends began to jangle. Mac (flying BE215/JX-I) and newly
promoted Flt Lt Kuttelwascher took off from Tangmere just after 2000
for the bomber airfields of northern France, some of which Mac would
have known from his time there in 1940. They crossed the French coast
near Le Havre. Mac flew to four airfields – Evreux, St André, Dreux
and Chartres, but saw no activity at any of them. Disappointed, he
returned to Tangmere, landing at 0030. When Kuttelwascher returned
at 0135, there was cause for celebration. At Melun airfield, on the far
side of Paris, he had found the flarepath lit and a Ju88 in the process of
taking off. He slotted in behind it as it climbed into the circuit pattern,
raked it with cannon fire and watched it dive into the ground. He then
saw another Junkers on the runway and strafed it before the aerodrome
defences at last woke up and he broke off his attack to return home.
No.1 Squadron was in business at last.

   The next night, Mac was to add something new to the repertoire of
night-intruding. He and Kuttelwascher went out again. Mac, taking off
at 2340, crossed the French coast east of Cherbourg. He flew direct to
Rennes airfield, but saw no activity there. He did spot the dummy
airfield nearby with flares lit, but was not fooled. He flew on to Dinard
and orbited the aerodrome there at 2,000 feet, but there was no activity
there either. He returned to Rennes with no reward. On his way home,
though, he caught sight of an alternative target – a goods train travelling

south of Cherbourg with open trucks. He proceeded to carry out two low-level attacks, giving the train a five and two-second burst from his cannon. He left it enveloped in steam with two trucks burning. But here was an interesting variation for the intruder who could not find any aircraft to hit. Railway lines stood out well in the dark and trains gave themselves away by the sparks and smoke from the engine. Night was the obvious time to move freight traffic around and so trains seen after dark were fair game and their destruction was certainly a way of impeding the German war machine. Subsequently, train-busting became something of a speciality for No.1 Squadron. Mac sent a note to his mother:

> "Your prayers for my safety have been well-answered during the last two nights, as I have been far into France and on neither trip was a single shell fired at me. Last night I attacked a goods train and blew up the engine and set fire to two of the trucks. It really was wizard fun."

Bad weather over France prevented any more intruder missions for a fortnight. It was not until 16 April that Mac and Kuttelwascher tried their luck once more. Taking off at 2225, Mac crossed the French coast at Fécamp at 8,000 feet. He flew to the airfields at Evreux, Dreux and Bretigny, encountering flak and searchlights but no enemy aircraft and so returned to Tangmere. However, this was not the end of his activities or his frustration for the night, since some thirty German raiders were active over Portsmouth, but none was illuminated, even though he was flying over the region for more than an hour. Kuttelwascher had had better luck over St André-de-l'Eure, where he came across two Do217s orbiting the airfield and shot down one of them.

German bombing activity over England was in fact being stepped up. On the night of 18 April, the squadron was scrambled once again over Portsmouth, but while Do217s bombed the city, none was illuminated as targets for the night-flying Hurricanes. The reason for the increased Luftwaffe activity was the Bomber Command raid on the Baltic port of Lübeck on the night of 28/29 March. The town had been chosen as a particularly suitable target for testing the effect of a very heavy attack with incendiary bombs – or 'fire-raising'. 234 bombers dropped 144 tons of incendiaries and the old wooden Hanseatic town burned furiously, resulting in the deaths of 312 of its population. Attacks were planned on the similarly old town of Rostock, beginning on the night of 24/25 April. Coinciding almost exactly with these raids, Hitler launched his own revenge for the attack on Lübeck with his *'Baedeker* Blitz' against the historic towns of Exeter, Bath, Canterbury, Norwich and York, which were attacked in turn, with the loss of over

1,600 civilian lives and a great amount of damage done to historic buildings. That same night of full moon, when Exeter was receiving its second visit from Do217s and Ju88s, saw the next batch of intruder missions initiated by No.1 Squadron. This time, seven pilots were to be given the opportunity of attacking the German bomber airfields. However, the net result was disappointing. No one saw any enemy aircraft and a Czech pilot, Sergeant Vlastimil Machácek in BE573, was lost over the Channel.

It was the turn of Bath to receive two attacks from eighty bombers on the night of 25/26 April, and they came back again for a third time early in the morning of Monday the 27th, a total of eighty-three aircraft from Fliegerkorps IX participating. Late on the 26th, Mac took off in JX-I for the Evereux-Dreux group of airfields. His combat report records what happened:

" . . . took off at 2205 and crossed the French coast at Fécamps at 9,000 feet above cloud . . . I came down through cloud and found I was over the River Seine, fifteen miles west of Paris. I flew to Bretigny aerodrome which was illuminated, but although I circled it for half an hour, no E/A were seen. Was caught by searchlights for half a minute, but there was no flak to follow and the lights lost me again without any special evasive action on my part. Set course, still at 2,000 feet, for Dreux but found St André and Evreux alternatively illuminated and considerable activity at both. I circled St André at 2,000 feet but the lights were soon switched off, so I flew north for five minutes and returned to St André when I saw the lights come on again. I saw one E/A take off with navigation lights on and went in to attack it, but lost sight of it when its lights were switched off. A second E/A was taking off and I attempted a head-on attack but this aircraft, too, switched off its navigation lights before I was in range.

Flying on to Evreux, I circled at 200 feet over the end of the runway and watched a third E/A take off and climb to about 500 feet. It passed above me and switched off its navigation lights but I identified it as a Do217 as it was silhouetted against the moon. I closed in to 600 yards dead astern and attacked it with three short bursts. Hits were observed, but the E/A continued on course. My two port cannons had jammed so I closed in to 200 yards and gave several short bursts, whereupon showers of sparks came from the starboard engine, the nose dropped and it went in a shallow dive to crash in a field about two miles north of the aerodrome. While returning to St André at 1,000 feet, I saw a second Do217 on the port side slightly below and behind me, flying on a converging course. I throttled back, allowing it to pass and dropped below it. When 250 yards dead astern I opened fire. Steady aim was difficult as only the starboard cannons were functioning, but after a series of very short bursts, the E/A started to emit smoke. I broke away and the E/A had disappeared when I returned to the attack. It is claimed as damaged as several shells were observed to hit it."

Mac returned to base at 1,000 feet, crossing the French coast just north of Le Havre and landing at Tangmere at 0105. An entry in the squadron ORB suggested that the enemy aircraft claimed as damaged would possibly be upgraded to 'probably destroyed'. German records show that three bombers failed to return from the raid on Bath, although it was believed these fell to UK-based night fighters. However, a Do217E from I/KG2 was severely damaged near Evreux that night and it seems probable that this was one of Mac's victims. Kuttelwascher also claimed a Do217, as it orbited Boos airfield near Rouen, but was then attacked by a Ju88 night fighter. However, as it overshot him he gave it four short bursts and saw it go into a steep left-hand turn, before it disappeared from view. It was claimed as damaged. Mac told André Jubelin:

"If only you knew what it feels like when he's so near that he fills my reflector sight and I'm going to fire! Oh boy!"

Jubelin commented in his book:

"I was not surprised at his hatred of them. It dated from the time when his arm had been smashed by the enemy's fire. He was the gentlest of men. But he had an account to settle. It was the price of his lost arm. No one will ever know what perseverance and heroism that rehabilitation required. And victories in the air soon came . . . on return from a successful patrol he would unscrew his leather arm and throw it up in the air for the others to play ball with, whooping with joy."

In the morning a telegram arrived from AOC No.11 Group, Sir Trafford Leigh-Mallory, which read:

'Heartiest congratulations on highly successful intruder operation last night. Well done.'

Mac sent his own telegram off to Steepers, the company that had built his artificial arm, informing them of their mutual success, as he had promised to do when he scored his first victory. His success was duly reported in the press as well. *The Times* printed the following:

'Squadron Leader J.A.F. MacLachlan DFC and Bar, who is a fighter pilot, has shot down his first enemy aircraft since being equipped with an artificial arm specially devised to handle the controls of a

Hurricane. His left arm was amputated above the elbow after it was hit by a Messerschmitt cannon-shell during a fight over Malta last year. When he returned to Britain, MacLachlan, who is 23, was appointed to the command of a famous Hurricane squadron.'

Over the next two nights Sgt G.S.M. Pearson was sent out on his second intruder mission and Plt Offs G.H. Corbett and Fred Murray on their first. They went to the same areas where Mac and Kuttelwascher had enjoyed such success, but returned without seeing anything. André Jubelin described the frustration of the lottery of intruding:

"Would one pilot be near the airfield concerned? That was the first throw in the game of chance. It might very well be that all would return empty-handed. The next chance would be the one each of us had to take. One man might see nothing and circle for hours over a base that would be fast asleep until daylight. Another might be delayed too long by searchlights or flak and so be prevented from arriving in time for the bombers' return. Another might grow tired of waiting and leave too soon. Still another might be deceived by the lure of dummy runways marked out in open country, while the bombers touched down on the real airfield in a less conspicuous place five miles away. Then again, there would be the man whom destiny had marked for its own."

In the meantime, the *Baedeker* bombers hit Norwich and York. The final day of April saw Mac (in JX-I) and Kuttelwascher in action once again. Mac went over to Evreux, Dreux and Rouen, departing at 2305. He was followed by the Czech some 25 minutes later. Mac saw no aircraft at the airfields he visited, so he picked up the railway line from Rouen to Le Havre and shot up two goods trains, damaging both. He also gave a tug the benefit of some cannon-fire on the River Seine. He landed, refuelled and went out once more, this time to Chartres, Orleans and Evreux. Again, no aircraft were to be seen, but he spotted another goods train starting from a station east of Yvetot. He attacked the engine with one long burst from 500 yards, closing to 200 yards, whereupon the boiler appeared to explode. He returned to Tangmere landing at 0245. After Kuttelwascher had set out, six more pilots followed at intervals throughout the early hours of 1 May. They all returned safely and most had successes to report. Flt Sgt C.F. Bland had taken to the art of train-busting with a vengeance and reported attacks on the engines of five goods trains. Four more trains were reported damaged by other pilots, but it was Kuttelwascher who had achieved the main objective once again, downing a Do217 as it took off from Rennes. On his way home he saw lights at Dinard airfield and caught a He111 as it took off, silhouetted against the moon. This, also, was shot down.

Later on 1 May, Mac flew to Oatlands Hill, a satellite airfield near Stonehenge for Old Sarum. The large 100-acre field had belonged to the J. Arthur Rank Organisation, but it had been requisitioned in 1941. It was the base for No.41 Operational Training Unit, where pilots were being trained to fly the new North American Mustang fighter. Always keen to add another 'type' to his list of aircraft flown, Mac was given permission to fly one of the new fighters. Wg Cdr David Annand, the Chief Flying Instructor, described what happened next:

"Mac was strapped into the cockpit and I gave him the cockpit drill. I was standing on the starboard wing and I have never heard a pilot absorb all the details so quickly. Mac's dummy left forearm was firmly attached to the throttle. Engine was started up, run up and 'chocks away.' Mac taxied to a position where he could have maximum take-off run. All this time other Mustangs were taking off and landing. Mac took off, but as he became airborne, the aircraft 'porpoised' as he got the undercart up, lifted flaps and changed the propeller from fine to coarse pitch. He held the aircraft down, instead of climbing up. The aircraft disappeared over the brow and the small village of Stoke Wake. I anticipated an accident and black smoke from a burning aircraft. Much to our relief, Mac, from a speed of well over 240mph put the Mustang into a vertical climb, then into half a loop and half-rolled the aircraft over Oatlands field at a height of 2,000 feet. He then proceeded to outshine even the Instructors at Oatlands Hill with a display of aerobatics in an aircraft in which he was doing his first solo."

Having diced with death twice already that day, he gave the 'Grim Reaper' a third chance on his return to Tangmere, when the engine of JX-I cut south-west of Worthy Down. He carried out a forced landing but the Hurricane flipped over onto its back, and he had to be dug out. Fortunately, he was not hurt, only shaken.

More and more pilots of the squadron were now becoming involved in intruding missions. Flt Lt Les Scott and his namesake Wt Off Gerry Scott went over on the night of 1/2 May and bagged another train. The following night four pilots went out, including Kuttelwascher, but saw nothing but a motorboat. On the night of 4/5 May, the *Baedeker* raiders hit Exeter very severely. It was a bright moonlit night with very little cloud – ideal for bombing and intruding. Five pilots set off, led by Mac (now flying his repaired JX-Q), who headed for Rennes and Dinard. He described the operation in an Air Ministry Bulletin:

"I went to one aerodrome from which the Hun raid this country but there was nothing doing, so I pushed off to another about ten miles away. Three huge black bombers were circling round at about 2,000 feet. I chose the nearest, followed him for two minutes at 200mph and, as he was going in to touch down, I lined him up beautifully in my sights. When he was just right I pressed the button. I remember seeing the rings round the exhausts glowing beautifully as my four cannon let him have it. A one-second burst was enough – there was a shower of flashes, the engine fell out and the whole place lit up like daylight. I turned and watched the bomber fall straight down and burn on the ground. There was a pillar of dense black smoke lit with a cheery pink glow on the underside. It looked good. But I'd no time to watch and turned away to see another, a He111 [sic], coming straight at me. A one-second burst from my cannon set his port engine on fire. Bunches of sparks, bits of tin and other oddments came flying off and it looked good, too. I gave it another burst for luck at the other engine and then formatted on him as he went into a shallow dive. I kept about 100 yards away and watched the Heinkel flying along, flames leaping back from it. As it got lower, the trees and bushes were lit up. It hit the ground and spread forward, like an unopened fan, picked out in bits of flame where the burning wreckage spread. I was really bucked. I circled round to look for the third Hun but couldn't find him. There was nothing else to do there so I cracked off home after about six times round. But the night's work wasn't done, for on the way back I saw a train – the long trail of smoke condenses in the cold air. I went down to make sure it was a goods train and then gave it a two-second burst. Little explosive twinkles, like fireworks, sparkled about the engine and it came to a stop emitting clouds of steam. The column rose 500 feet and I gave the engine a final burst for luck and then turned for home. My squadron has 'bagged' eight definitely destroyed, some more probably destroyed and seventeen trains since the last moon – that's almost quits for my arm."

Mac's victims were in fact two Ju88s from KuFlGr506, both of which crashed near Dinard. From Fw Robert Bogel's Ju88A-4 (WrkNr.1528) only the gunner was able to bale out, while Lt z.See Roman Wallner (observer) and Obgfr Johann Biebl perished with the pilot. There was also one survivor from Uffz Josef Palmer's Ju88D-4 (WrkNr.1154), Uffz Karl Schorn, who was wounded but managed to bale out before the aircraft crashed. The observer, Lt.z.See Ernst Tramp, and gunner, Uffz Richard Staub, were killed together with the pilot. Meanwhile, Kuttelwascher had had to turn back after engine trouble over the Channel and none of the other three pilots saw a thing.

Next night, 5/6 May, as the moon was waning, Kuttelwascher went one better than Mac, who took off at 2320, heading once again for Rennes, Dinard and Caen. Mac ran into heavy cloud and saw no activity except flak. However, both Sgt Dennis and Flt Lt Scott saw aircraft landing at Boos, but failed to get into attacking positions in time, while Sgt John Campbell managed to hit a tanker lorry near Dreux as well as two trains, disabling both. Kuttelwascher had also taken off at 2320 and headed for Evreux and then for St André. The airfield was suddenly lit up as six Heinkels returned to their base after a raid on Cowes. They were off guard and caught completely by surprise. Within four minutes, three of them were destroyed by the Czech pilot and, at 0205, he returned to Tangmere to report this achievement to his colleagues. It was to be the most outstanding intruder operation carried out by any pilot of No.1 Squadron and Mac paid tribute to him in a subsequent radio broadcast.

The squadron's success elicited another congratulatory telegram from Sir Trafford Leigh-Mallory at No.11 Group: 'Heartiest congratulations on your splendid show last night.' There were rewards for both pilots; Mac was awarded the DSO (see Appendix III) and Kuttelwascher the DFC for his eight victories. Mac wrote to mother on 16 May:

"Just a line to let you know that Monkton are due for yet another half-holiday, as I have just been given a DSO. I'll be getting quite conceited soon!"

On 18 May, Mac made a broadcast just before the 9pm News on the BBC. In it, he gave his impression of what intruding was like:

"I'm afraid the dangers and hazards of flying on night offensive patrols have been rather exaggerated. Certainly the average intruder pilot is not the cat-eyed, carrot-eating killer that the press sometimes makes him out to be. Most of us night fighters are too fond of our mornings in bed to go flying around in the daytime. Personally, sleeping in the sun appeals to me infinitely more than chasing Me109s at 30,000 feet. Give me a moonlight night and my old Hurricane and you can have your Spitfires and dawn readiness. We've no formation flying to worry about, and no bombers to escort. In fact, nothing to do but amuse ourselves once we've crossed the French coast. I must admit that those miles of Channel with only one engine brings mixed thoughts and one can't help listening to every beat of the old Merlin engine as the English coast disappears in the darkness. I always get a feeling of relief and excitement as I cross the French coast and turn on the reflector sight, knowing that anything I see then, I can take a crack at. We have to keep our eyes skinned the whole time, and occasionally glance at the compass and clock. As the minutes go by and we approach the Hun aerodrome, we look eagerly for the flarepaths. More often than not we are disappointed."

The flarepath is switched off as soon as we arrive and up come the searchlights and flak. But if you're lucky it's a piece of cake.

Well, when your petrol and ammunition are nearly gone you are faced with the old Channel again. If you've got something, you leave the enemy territory with a sort of guilty conscience – not for what you've done – that's great fun. But somehow you feel they've got it in for you and that every one's going to shoot at you. It's a sort of nervous reaction, I suppose. The whole thing seems too easy to be true. Ten to one there's no Hun within shooting distance and the ground defences are quiet. That makes it all the worse, and I generally weave about till I'm half way back across the Channel. If you've done nothing, of course, you don't get this feeling as you're still looking for something at which to empty your ammunition. Out over the Channel you can hear your ground station calling the other aircraft of the squadron and you count the minutes and look eagerly for the coast. Often it seems to take so long coming back that you feel sure the compass is wrong and were it not for the North Star I might not be here today. At last, in the distance, you see the flashing beacon and soon you are taxiing in to your dispersal point. I dread the look of disappointment on my mechanic's face if my guns are unfired. But if the rubber covers have been shot off, I've scarcely time to stop my engine before I am surrounded by the boys asking what luck I've had. Then comes the best part of the whole trip – a cup of tea and a really good line-shooting session!

Since 1 April, the squadron has destroyed eleven aircraft for certain and probably three more. The lion's share of this total goes to my Czech Flight Commander Kuttelwascher. He's a first-class pilot and has the most uncanny gift of knowing which aerodromes the Huns are going back to. He'll look at the map and say, 'I'll go there tonight', possibly to some unobtrusive aerodrome. Sure enough, even if the others see no activity, he certainly will. One night we agreed to visit a certain aerodrome, but five minutes before we took off, 'Old Kuttel' changed his mind and went to another. I got to my aerodrome to find it covered with fog, while he calmly knocked down three!"

Mac's brother Gordon, now operational once again, commented on both these events in a letter home on 22 May:

"Yesterday I flew down to Tangmere from Wittering with two other chaps from this Flight. Unfortunately, Jay was not there. He had gone to the Isle of Wight to see some boats or ships or something. It's pretty wizard that he has got the DSO. I heard the last part of his line over the wireless. I didn't think he sounded nervous, only a spot more 'Oxfordish' than usual."

Fame was coming to Mac in other ways, too, as he informed mother on 23 May:

> "I have just had my portrait done by Sir Eric Kennington and I think that even you will agree that he has made an excellent job of it. Certainly everyone here likes it. I am glad you enjoyed the line on the radio. They gave me £2 12s 6d for the effort, so I think it was worth it!"

Sir Eric was an official Air Ministry artist and several of his wartime portraits, including his one of Mac, were exhibited at the National Gallery in London in October. The portrait also appeared in the *Illustrated London News* along with that of Flt Lt Kuttelwascher. Both pilots were finding their names frequently mentioned in the newspapers as the number of their victories mounted.

Bad weather set in during the middle of May, preventing further intruder operations. But it did not stop a grand dance at Merston to celebrate the thirtieth anniversary of No.1 Squadron. The pilots could feel justly proud of their achievements so far during the war, having been credited with some 230 enemy aircraft shot down, which surpassed the 200-odd claimed during the First World War.

With the new moon period approaching at the end of May and the beginning of June, operations began to be stepped up once again. The target area was switched from Brittany and Normandy further north and into Belgium and Holland. It proved a good move. On the night of 29 May, six sorties were flown and ten more trains were added to the tally. Next night a further three operations were carried out and eight more locomotives were destroyed. The last night of the month was an historic one for Bomber Command, which carried out the first 'One-Thousand' bomber raid against a single target, Cologne. It far outstripped anything the Luftwaffe had sent over during its *Baedeker* Blitz.

The intruders were out also, two pilots operating from Manston, while Mac took off in JX-Q from Tangmere against aerodromes and railway lines to the north and north-east of Paris. Airborne at 0055, he crossed the Channel at 500 feet and the French coast over Le Crotoy at 2,000 feet. While investigating an illuminated decoy airfield just south of Le Crotoy, his Hurricane was caught briefly in searchlights. There were no signs of activity at the first airfield he visited, Glisy, although he was greeted by searchlights and fairly accurate flak. Dropping down to 500 feet, he continued to Péronne, where the engine of a goods train was attacked, just south of the town. It ground to a halt amidst clouds of steam. Flying on to his main target of Juvincourt, he saw no activity, but he did see what he took to be another well-lit dummy airfield four miles to the east. After orbiting the area for a quarter of an hour, he flew back along the railway line from Reims to Soissons, damaging the engines of three goods trains he came across. It is a testimony to his eyesight that in the case of one attack, the smoke from the funnel which usually assisted the pilot's aim, was suddenly cut off after his first attack and he had to continue just with the aid of the glow from the firebox. He flew home via Abbeville, where he encountered some very inaccurate searchlights and flak, and landed at West Malling near Rochester at 0300.

André Jubelin related an amusing anecdote concerning Mac during the course of an intruder sortie over the hunting grounds of northern France:

"Mac left the Vire to look for Pincon Hill. A few minutes later he could see the moonlight reflected from the waters of the Orne. From the direction of Argentan a machine-gun flung a cherry-coloured garland on his tail. It fell short like a lasso. The windings of the river already told him that Ecouché was near. So, over the hill and dale, dodging occasionally, the Hurricane reached its game reserve. Mac had become an expert in this nameless geography. On a black night, to make doubly sure, he would seek out the Perche Pools. But this evening the Squadron Leader went straight for the [River] Iton, to see if 'Fanny' was there.

The pilots thought Fanny's lamp as wonderful as that of Aladdin. During the six months that they had been coming to examine the great German aerodrome at Saint-André-de-l'Eure, the intruders had always found that single faithful light agleam. It was invariably at the same spot, close to Breteuil, where the Iton and the railway border were an oval of shadow. On the first two occasions both Mac and Bennett had described the light. A little later, one morning when Wilkins was returning at low level, about daybreak, he had recognised the isolated point of brilliance caused by a providential forgetfulness every night upon our way, almost within arm's length of the big bombers' airfield. He spun the following yarn: 'It was almost daylight. I saw, through the window, a most beautiful girl, half dressed. She was pushing open the shutters to get a little fresh air.' No one believed this story. But people fancied all sorts of things. Someone baptised that imaginary girl 'Fanny'. After that she became a friend. The intruder off to St. André-de-l'Eure said, 'I'm going to visit Fanny,' and others bound for more distant places promised to go out of their way to give her a call. 'Fanny's probably just a bedridden old man, who suffers from insomnia,' I said to the Squadron Leader one day. But the latter did not care for this remark. He preferred to

keep the legend going. 'When I come back late I can see her in the
dawn with her fair hair and her brassière', he said, making the usual
gesture with his thumbs."

The night of 1/2 June saw both Mac and Flt Lt Kuttelwascher in action.
Mac (JX-Q) flew to Evreux, St André and Bretigny. The only thing he
hit was a bird at 3,000 feet! Kuttelwascher enjoyed better success on
his trip to Evreux by 'bagging' two trains and damaging another E-
boat, but, for the first time, it was some of the other pilots who began
to discover that instinct for finding enemy aircraft which so far had
been the prerogative of the CO and flight commander. Wt Off Gerry
Scott, a Canadian, claimed to have damaged a Ju88 as it landed at St
Trond in Belgium, while Sgt Pearson did better by actually destroying
a Ju88 over the Dutch airfield of Gilze-Rijen. The night's work was
rounded off by Plt Off Des Perrin and Sgt S.P. Dennis RAAF claiming
a boat each, and Sgt J.F. Higham destroying another train. The next
night saw more attacks launched against targets in the Low Countries.
Mac, flying from Manston, visited the airfield at Gilze-Rijen and then
flew on to Eindhoven, but had no luck. This night, however, it was the
airfields at St Trond and Venlo which provided targets. Plt Off Harry
Connolly damaged a Ju88 over St Trond and Canadian Flt Sgt George
English, after attacking a goods train near Venlo, went on to shoot
down a Do217. Sadly, English was killed in a flying accident later that
same day. On the night of 3/4 June, the squadron was to provide six
aircraft for a 'Fighter Night' patrol over Canterbury. This type of
operation involved individual fighter pilots looking for German
bombers flying above AA range. The previous night, the squadron had
done a similar patrol, but the Germans had hit Ipswich rather than
Canterbury. This night, though, they were back over Canterbury and, at
0325, Kuttelwascher sighted a Do217 and shot it down into the sea. It
was the Czech's first victory for almost a month. Mac wrote of this to
mother in a brief progress report:

"I have been over either France or Holland for the last three nights,
greatly enjoying myself. Three nights ago I went to an aerodrome
just near Reims and could see many of my old haunts in the
moonlight. I actually blew up four railway engines on the railway
line we used to go to Paris on! Holland is now the 44th country
I have flown over since war was declared. Kuttelwascher got another
Hun last night."

On the night of 3/4 June, Mac (JX-Q) was the first away at 0100. He
checked out the airfields at Evreux, St André and Dreux, but found
nothing. He was about to give up and go home when it struck him that
this was exactly the sort of place to which Kuttelwascher would come

sooner or later. So he turned back. It was a good decision. Returning to St André, he found it lit up by lines of different coloured lights across a white line of lights. The adrenalin must have pumped though his veins as he saw about fifteen Do217s orbiting at 1,000 feet as they prepared to land. They were part of the raiding force from Fliegerkorps IX that had attacked Poole and were continually switching their navigation lights on and off, which made them perfect targets. Mac arrived just as one Dornier was coming in to land, so he followed it, closing to 200 yards. Just as the enemy aircraft approached the runway at about 100 feet, he gave it a one-second burst from dead astern. Its nose was seen to go down immediately, and it crashed in a shower of sparks just short of the aerodrome.

At that moment six searchlights illuminated the Hurricane and flak opened up. Mac took evasive action by diving away to one side and was lost in the darkness. Now he could pick out a second target. He saw there were still about ten Dorniers circling. He selected the nearest one and followed it at a height of 500 feet as it went down the line of lights. From some 200 yards astern, he gave this aircraft a two-second burst. He saw his cannon fire hit, but he was once more picked up by the searchlights and then by flak. He had to break away and so lost sight of the damaged Dornier as he climbed back up to 2,000 feet. There, as luck would have it, he found another enemy aircraft with its navigation lights on. As he closed in on it, the lights were switched off, but were quickly switched on again. Mac opened fire with three one-second bursts from 200 yards range and saw sparks beginning to fly from its port engine. Then, after a few seconds, there was a bright red flash from the ground by the side of the aerodrome. Two down and a third damaged – and there were still many targets. Mac's appetite had been thoroughly wetted by this time and he picked up a fourth Dornier at 1,000 feet. It was coming in to land and he followed it down to the runway. As it was crossing the boundary, he fired from dead astern at about 200 yards range. He saw his fire hit the fuselage, but after three shells had been fired from each cannon, his ammunition was exhausted, so he turned for Tangmere, arriving back at 0350.

An hour after Mac had left St André for home, Flt Lt Kuttelwascher arrived on the scene, just as he had predicted! The German pilots must have felt cursed that night, for the Czech proceeded to shoot down a He111 and a Do217 as well as damaging another Dornier, but a second Czech pilot, Wt Off Josef Dygryn DFM failed to return. Kuttelwascher saw a fighter being shot down by flak over Le Havre as he was returning from his sortie. It may well have been his fellow-countryman. No one else had any luck that night. German records show that two Do217E-4s from KG2 were shot down on returning from the raid on

Poole, Uffz Gerhard Wagner's U5+LL (5392) of 3 Staffel crashing about three miles south-west of Evreux with the loss of all members of the crew (the others were Fw Wilhelm Oberwohr, Uffz Josef Maier and Obfw Anton Lamm), while Fw Hans Koch's U5+NR (5331) of 7 Staffel crashed near Coutances, about 40 miles south of Cherbourg; the latter was probably Kuttelwascher's victim. One member of the crew managed to bale out, but the other three were killed. A third Do217, from II Gruppe, crash-landed at Evreux while another, from III Gruppe, was badly damaged at St André.

The night's tally of four destroyed and three damaged provoked another stream of congratulatory telegrams. There was one from Sir Archibald Sinclair, Secretary of State for Air, and another from Sir Arthur Harris of Bomber Command, which put this particular set of intruding missions into context. It said:

'The exceptionally light casualties during the Cologne and Essen raids was undoubtedly in large measure due to the very effective intruding and special fighter arrangements made to cover the operations. I should be obliged if you would convey to the crews concerned the thanks of the bomber crews for the very efficient protection provided.'

Apparently the Germans had diverted much of their night-fighter effort to cope with the intruders and so there were few night fighters to deal with the British bombers. The telegram may have puzzled the pilots of No.1 Squadron, for they saw very little sign of any German night fighters at any time. There was a special message, too, from Air Vice-Marshal Karel Janousek of the Air Ministry Czech Inspectorate:

'Heartfelt congratulations on your squadron's last night's great success. Good luck in the future hunting to you and 'Old Kut'.'

The newspapers had another field day, too. The *Daily Express* hailed the two pilots as 'The Killers Who Stalk By Night' and 'The Two Terrors Who Stalk In The Dark'.

Mac wrote, on 6 June, to his brother Hugh, who was in North Africa with the 8th Army:

"I mustn't make you jealous, old boy, but life's simply wizard at the moment. As you probably know I've got a rather good little night-fighting outfit and the boys are putting up a simply terrific show. During the last two months we've shot down more Huns than any other squadron in the British Isles."

Unbeknown to Mac, he had in fact enjoyed his last success with No.1 Squadron. Before the end of the month he was to fly five more intruder missions, but the only excitement was on 26 June when he got lost flying over Holland. Before crossing the coast, on his outward journey, his map had blown overboard and he returned by flying over Antwerp and Ostend at 0 feet! Plt Off Des Perrin achieved a first for the squadron when he intruded into German skies, reaching Düsseldorf, but without any result. That same night, one of the squadron's most experienced pilots, Wt Off Gerry Scott, was lost over Holland. Another casualty was André Jubelin, although he survived a wheels-up crash-landing at Tangmere after having been slightly wounded by return fire from shipping he had attacked off the French coast:

"The heavy Hurricane, without bouncing, ploughed up the tarmac with its half-crashed frame for some distance, then turned right, made a leap into the grass and stopped. My harness had held. I was safe. Mac was the first to leap on the wing, into the midst of the flames licking the duralumin. His leather arm plunged into the cockpit, the iron hooks groping for me. Someone behind him shouted: 'Gently! Give him chance to undo his straps!' I jumped down into the grass with Mac. We walked off together for a few paces. The firemen were unrolling their rubber hoses and looking for the few dangerous places. A final tongue of flame ran under the edge of the wing, flickered along the ground and went out. The Squadron Leader thumped me on the back. 'A bloody good show, old scout!' I didn't answer. I hadn't yet taken off my sticky mask. Mac did not know I was wounded."

Flt Lt Kuttelwascher, meantime, continued his run of successes. When the next full moon period came towards the end of June, he shot down a Ju88 over his favourite haunt of St André and damaged another. On the 27th, he was awarded a well-earned Bar to his DFC. He had won both decorations in four weeks. Two nights later he destroyed a Do217 at Rennes and an E-boat off Barfleur, as well as damaging another. That same night, the squadron returned to train-busting when Plt Off Corbett and Sgt Higham attacked five goods trains between Rouen and Paris, and between Arras and Loos respectively, and brought the squadron's total to well over fifty trains destroyed. Mac flew his final intruder mission that same night over Brittany, but the 10/10 cloud meant he could see nothing over the target area at Dinard. Instead he patrolled north of Cherbourg for half an hour. He sighted what he took to be a twin-engined German aircraft flying on a reciprocal course at 1,500 feet and gave chase for a couple of minutes before it flew out of sight.

Overall in June, the squadron had flown in excess of 1,008 operational hours, which was a monthly record. There was a grand finale to come on 2 July, when the last intruder missions were flown on a night of heavy electrical storms. Mac had no luck, having chased in vain a Ju88 some 45 miles south of Selsey Bill. Sgt Higham and Plt Off Perrin were also out of luck, but Sgt Campbell claimed to have damaged a Do217 over St Lô as well as knocking out three trains – the last of the squadron's tally. Campbell had proved to be the real train-busting expert, having destroyed twice as many (21) as anyone else in the squadron. Sgt Pearson also claimed a Do217 near Carteret, having failed to find his original target at Dinard. However, it was Flt Lt Kuttelwascher who, taking off at 0210, had the last word. Another Dornier was destroyed north of Dinard airfield and a second was damaged, while a third was destroyed as it came in to land at the airfield itself. Kuttelwascher landed back at Tangmere at 0445, with his final total of kills now standing at fifteen. Mac's tally was now thirteen.

The *Daily Telegraph* summed up the effects of train-busting like this:

'The continuous attack carried out by the RAF on German communications has inflicted heavy damage on locomotives. During the last four months the Germans have been forced to rely more and more on canal barges and coastal shipping for the transport of vital war material in Western Europe. This blitz has had two main aspects: attacks on trains and tracks, and the heavier bombing assaults on such railway centres as Cologne, whose lines and marshalling yards were expressly laid out for the strategic purpose of supplying German armies in the West. The attacks on trains began when Sqn Ldr J.A.F. MacLachlan, the one-armed pilot who led Fighter Command's top-scoring Hurricane squadron on intruder operations, asked to be allowed to lead the squadron on special night 'engine-shooting sorties' over the great railway system between Paris and the northern coast of France. Flying alone up the Seine from Rouen one night in April he dived to 200 feet to attack two goods trains. Both engines blew up amid clouds of steam and came to a standstill. Before Sqn Ldr MacLachlan reached his base, his squadron was already out over France on its first specific train-wrecking expedition, and another successful intruder plan had begun. That first night, the cannon Hurricane squadron attacked 23 trains. Engines were badly damaged, some being blown up; trucks carrying inflammable war material were set ablaze. The following night, practically all mail traffic on the Nord system appeared to have stopped. Only one train could be found. Since then other fighter squadrons have taken a hand in attacks on railway engines in various parts of occupied territory, and the strain on Hitler's supply system has become increasingly acute . . .'

During the last three weeks of June 1942, No.1 Squadron had been joined at Tangmere by No.43 Squadron, which had flown down from Acklington. They now swapped places, with No.43 taking over the intruding role, while, on 8 July, No.1 went for a rest at RAF Acklington in Yorkshire. According to Jubelin, Mac had announced their imminent departure thus:

> "Chaps, we're being put out to grass for a time. I hope it won't be long. When we arrive [at Acklington], I want us to come down like thunder and lightning. Dive on the daisies in three lines, then fountain and fan out with a slow roll; land by sections at thirty-second intervals."

Jubelin remembered their arrival at Acklington very well:

> "It is the custom, when a famous squadron like our own arrives at a new base, to do some weird stunts. Rolling at a height of sixty feet is forbidden, it is true. But no one would dare to criticise anything done by MacLachlan. As usual, I was to be the other member of his section. 'Old Ju, you'll touch down under my wing.' We flew without incident through the sunny afternoon, from the picturesque Kentish countryside over the Yorkshire moors till at last we arrived in Northumberland. Our new aerodrome was an immense meadow, streaked with magnificent runways of asphalt. It lay in a plain surrounded by wooded hills. After doing our aerobatics on arrival, the squadron broke up. Mac and I prepared to land first. I thought the west wind must be blowing pretty hard, judging from the rigidity of the windsock, which scarcely flapped at all against its pole. After circling the airfield, Mac flew a good way past the runway in service. I was wondering why when I saw him going into a glide. The wireless informed me: 'Old Ju, I've missed it. Let's come in on a glide. All right with you?' 'OK.' I understood perfectly well what he wanted to do. He had overshot the runway by mistake. He was going to compensate for that by a feat, which would be difficult at low speed in such a heavy aircraft.
>
> It was the first time we had been here and a large crowd of spectators was waiting for the arrival of No.1 Squadron. It would have looked silly to circle the airfield again, and if we succeeded in making the spectators believe that we were going to land in a tight glide they'd think us real blackbirds! We duly glided. But as I was practically touching Mac's aircraft, I got into his slipstream and, though doing the same speed, dropped slightly faster than he did. I hung on desperately, but could not prevent my left wing touching my leader's fuselage. I tried very gently to get clear. But the wing wouldn't budge. I know I shall be told that the thing is an

impossibility. All the same, improbable as it may appear, I managed to keep formation till we reached the ground. The oddest thing about it was that, though Mac did feel a few abnormal bumps during the process, he was very far from suspecting the truth. When, after switching off his engine, he jumped out of his machine and saw the strange position that mine had got into, he at first could not believe his eyes. Then he dashed at me and seized me in his arms. No one, at that distance, had seen the accident. In the eyes of the spectators we seemed all the time to have been deliberately doing close aerobatics, on which they duly congratulated us. Mac would not rest till he had had a photograph taken of the damage to his plane."

Mac did not mention this incident in his latest letter home:

"The squadron has been moved to Acklington. Little did I think when I came here as an acting pilot officer four years ago, that I should ever return with a squadron of my own. It's really a very well run camp and the rest will do us all good."

It was a time for a change as well as a rest. Flt Lt Kuttelwascher was posted to No.23 Squadron to fly Mosquitoes, and Mac was informed of his imminent posting to No. 59 OTU at Crosby-on-Eden, where he was to be a supernumerary Chief Flying Instructor, while No.1 Squadron was to be re-equipped with Typhoons to replace its aged Hurricanes. Before departing, Mac naturally managed to get in a couple of flights in one of the powerful new fighters (R7851), the first three having been delivered a few days earlier. Accompanying him on one flight was Jubelin:

"Mac decided to come with me on a cross-country run in our new ships. We took off early, breakfasted at Montrose, lunched at Inverness, dined in Londonderry, [they also had cream cakes at Andres on the Isle of Man!] and landed in pitch darkness just after eleven o'clock. At each aerodrome we visited, a circle of experts admired our Typhoons. Mac's enthusiasm made me do things that, if I had been alone, I should have thought perfectly crazy. To touch down at night, without calling for runway flares, in that new, ultra-fast machine, after having got into it the day before for the first time, was a piece of recklessness characteristic of him, but I found it, for my part, a bit overdone."

The Frenchman added:

"He left this morning. I made an utter ass of myself by crying. Immediately after his departure Murray and Scott [the flight commanders] most tactfully came and asked me to take charge of training. They don't know I'm soon off to Russia."

There was to be one final link with No.1 Squadron when Mac was given a special honour by the Czech Government in exile. On 11 August, he and Wg Cdr Max Aitken DSO DFC, son of Lord Beaverbrook and commander of No.68 Squadron, another night-fighter unit, together with Flt Lt Karel Kuttelwascher DFC were decorated by Dr Edvard Beneš, President of Czechoslovakia, with the Czech Military Cross (also referred to as the War Cross). For Kuttelwascher, it was his fourth such decoration. The two British officers were also presented with Czech pilots' 'wings', which Mac wore on his tunic from then onwards.

Within days of arriving at Crosby-on-Eden, Mac found himself in one of the OTU's Typhoons, in which he performed aerobatics before putting it into a power dive and clocking 504mph! And before getting down to the task in hand, he took advantage of the unit's variety of aircraft to gain experience on other types, including a Beaufighter, Rapide, Magister, Henley, and Master in addition to meeting an old friend, a Battle trainer. On 3 August, he flew Hurricane MF-82 over to Northern Ireland where, at Newtownards airfield – south of Belfast – he renewed acquaintance with Bam Bamberger from Malta days, who was now in charge of a Fighter Gunnery Training Flight based there:

"Mac flew into Newtownards for a quick visit, to tell me he was taking over a new squadron and exploring the possibilities of my joining his unit. Regrettably, as I had not yet even been six months in my gunnery appointment, a move was unacceptable to Air HQ Northern Ireland."

It would seem that Mac was a jump ahead of himself, although life as a flying instructor did not appeal to him and he angled for something better. He hinted at an idea in his letter to his brother Hugh back in June:

"I am hoping to fly over to the States this winter and have a look round. I'm supposed to be writing a book but haven't got very far with it."

Something more to his liking did come up – no doubt having pulled a few strings – as mentioned in a letter to mother on 22 August:

"Now at last I have got the job I wanted and am posted supernumerary to the Air Fighting Development Unit at Duxford. The work here should be very interesting as it is mainly experimental and test flying and we have quite a few different types of aircraft. We have got a wing commander in charge of the outfit, and there are two other squadron leaders beside myself. They all seem to be very good types. Before I came here I did a lot of very interesting trips including a visit to Stornoway in the Hebrides, Belfast, Inverness, Gloucester and many shorter trips. My flying logbook is really getting quite interesting."

It was an interesting flying job, for after arriving on 20 August, he flew fifteen different types of aircraft in eleven days. An example of what he got up to can be found in the logbook entries for 23 August. Four pilots from AFDU went over to Bourn in Cambridgeshire to carry out co-operation with No.15 Squadron equipped with Stirlings. They flew over in an Oxford. Mac acted as 2nd Pilot to Sqn Ldr Swailes, also an AFDU pilot, in a Stirling as they practised fighter-evasion tactics. Mac then took up a Spitfire VA to carry out attacks, which the Stirling had to try and evade. He then flew back to Duxford in another type of Spitfire: a Mk.IIA. From Duxford he flew a Stinson Reliant (W7980) with one passenger on board to Great Sampford in Essex and returned once more to Duxford. There he flew a Bell P-39 Airacobra fighter, which No.601 Squadron had been using at Duxford when they were stationed there earlier in the year. The RAF had been disappointed with the Airacobra and had sent most of their remaining aircraft to Russia. A second new type was added to his list when he then flew a Spitfire IX and put it through its paces by doing aerobatics and flying it to Great Sampford. So ended a typical day in the life of an AFDU supernumerary.

While Mac had been out of action, his brother Gordon had been back in action – and successfully, too. In the letter telling mother of his posting to Duxford, Mac also gave her this news:

"I don't know if Baked has told you he damaged a Focke-Wulf 190 over Dieppe – very good show I think. I must say I'm very glad I wasn't on that show – it must have been like the Battle of Britain all over again."

Gordon now commanded A Flight of No.616 Squadron based at Great Sampford and the two brothers were to see a lot of each other over the next few months. On 26 August, they flew together down to Shoreham where they both had their first experience of flying a Walrus flying boat. On 7 September Mac records that his brother is now a flight lieutenant, "I shall have to watch out or he'll be beating me." Someone else was being mentioned in letters home – a steady girlfriend. He told mother about her on 30 August:

"I have been down at Ford near Tangmere for the last few days, doing some night flying trials on the Typhoon. Muriel and I spent yesterday at her brother's house near Maidenhead and had a marvellous time bathing in the Thames etc. Her brother took the enclosed photo . . . I'd love to bring her down for a weekend. You'd like her. I'm terribly fond of her, mother – she's a wizard type."

Obviously in her reply, mother had voiced some concern:

"Mother, darling, don't worry about Muriel. I'm far too young to get married. I'm just very fond of her, that's all. She's going into the WAAFs next month, which will be rather a pity. Still, I think she'll easily get a commission."

Hectic activity at Duxford continued. On 3 September, Mac affiliated with an American B-17 squadron at Chelverston, chasing them in a Spitfire. Unfortunately, he put up a 'minor black' when landing, tipping the Spitfire (AF-T) onto its nose. His next logbook entry for the 4th is a fascinating one: 'Typhoon IB (PR-3): Escorting Heinkel 111, Junkers 88 and Me110 to Atcham and return.' These German aircraft belonged to No.1426 (Enemy Aircraft) Flight, which was sometimes referred to as the 'RAFwaffe' by the press. The flight comprised captured German aircraft (and later Italian), painted in RAF colours, which toured the country, having first been tested and evaluated by the experts at the AFDU. Mac had himself flown as a passenger in the Heinkel (AW177, formerly 1H+EN of 5/KG26 which had force-landed in Scotland in February 1940) with Flt Lt Kinder as the pilot. He also later flew the Ju88A (HM509, formerly M2+MK of Küs106, which had force-landed at RAF Chivenor in November 1941). On 6 September, Mac went to Langley for a preview of the new Hawker Tempest, but he was not allowed to fly it. Perhaps the authorities were not too keen on Mac's low-flying exploits, for his next job was carrying out high flying in a Spitfire VI (BR289). Specifically, he had to test the aircraft's new pressure hood. To mother he recalled in a letter the exhilaration of flying at this height:

"I have been doing some high-flying trials today and was nearly eight miles high! I could actually see the French coast from over Cambridge."

On the 16th he went down to Yeovil and Chard to tour the Westland aircraft factories there and encourage the workforce, or as he put it, 'Duxford to Yeovil to shoot a line to factory workers'. Further affiliation exercises with the Stirlings of No.218 Squadron, more pressure hood tests, a new set of rolling tests on a Spitfire VB (AF-O) with square wing-tips, and visits to Acklington filled up the logbook for the rest of September and early October. But then what he had voiced as a hope in the letter to his brother in June came to pass. On 4 October, he wrote:

"My posting to the States has at last come through and I am due to leave in about a week. I am going to go round various American fighter and training units, flying and lecturing. It should be extremely interesting."

CHAPTER X

AN AMERICAN INTERLUDE

Mac sailed on board the *Queen Elizabeth*, which was serving as a troopship 'for the duration', departing from Liverpool for Canada and arriving on 17 October at Halifax, Nova Scotia. He travelled on to Montreal from where he wrote home on 24 October:

"I expect that by now you have got my cable so know that I have arrived safely. We had a wizard trip across, landing at the same port as Gordon did. I have just spent the night in Montreal and am going on to New York tonight. They are giving me a simply wizard time here. Two press reporters came on the boat to see me and when we arrived here yesterday, I was met at the station by photographers and all the rest. I was given a free dinner at the best club in town and treated like a local hero. I'll send you some of the press nonsense when it appears. The food here, and on the boat, is simply incredible. Butter and eggs *ad lib* – and the most terrific steaks etc. I think I'm going to like it here!"

From New York he went to Washington where, on 28 October, he received his orders from the RAF Delegation:

'Operational Liaison Duties: It has been thought that the British cadets under training in schools of the US Army Air Force are, on graduation, so lacking in RAF General Service and flying knowledge that they must be at a disadvantage when they reach the Operational Training Unit. For this reason three RAF officers have been established to liaise with the schools and teach British pupils what they are to expect in the service and on operations on their return to the UK. You are to fill the fighter pilot post.

You will be attached to the Headquarters of the Southeast Army Air Forces Training Center at Maxwell Field, Montgomery, Alabama. You will be based on Eglin Field and attached as necessary to the US Army Air Forces Advanced Flying Schools at Dothan and

Selma, other attachments to Orlando and other US Army Air Forces stations, and also to British Flying Training Schools may be arranged by this HQ. At these schools you will not have any executive position, but should put yourself completely in the hands of the US Commanding Officer. You should co-operate fully with the training staff in taking lectures and flying as they may require of you. You should mix with the cadets enough to understand their difficulties, to explain the Service to them and to ensure that their morale and discipline are of a high order.

Besides teaching British cadets about the RAF, you should let the various US authorities gain all they can from your operational experience and you should advise on training methods and requirements in the light of such experience. It is most important that you should co-operate whole-heartedly with the Americans without being critical of them. It is important that the Commanding General should consider you an asset and not a liability to his Training Center.'

With those instructions ringing in his ears, Mac flew in a DC-3 from Washington to Atlanta on 30 October. The Curtiss AT9 trainer, which he flew for the first time the next day, was the fiftieth type of aircraft he had flown. He followed his orders and was having a 'wizard' time, as he wrote to his old friend Karel Kuttelwascher in November:

"Just a line to let you know I'm still going strong and shooting an even bigger line than usual! I'm having a simply wizard time over here. I only wish you and the rest of the boys were here with me. I'm stationed at the American equivalent of the AFDU at Duxford and can fly any type of aircraft I want. I have already got in eleven different types here including the P-47 Thunderbolt and P-38 Lightning. I have to go to Washington fairly often and have had some simply wizard parties with Grp Capt Hess [the Czech Air Attaché, and former Battle of Britain pilot]. He's been damn good to me – he treats me as if I were a son: by God we get pissed! Do drop me a line and let me know what you're doing and what things are like at home. These Yanks don't know there's a war on, but they're damn kind and hospitable. I have a Mohawk of my own which I fly round in and give lectures and teach the boys aerobatics and odd things."

The US press took to him and he enjoyed headlines like, '13 Planes Credited to One-Armed RAF Flyer Who Holds Four Valor Medals at 23' and 'Brilliant RAF Ace Here Blushes Over Heroism' – and, no doubt, over the fulsomeness of some of the reporting. 'A pink-cheeked, fair-haired young man with an empty left sleeve was a visitor in Atlanta during a furlough in the United States, where he is enjoying (1) the

food, (2) the well-dressed women, and (3) an enforced rest from one of
the most hectically brilliant flying careers of World War II.'

When Mac wrote home from Selma in Alabama it was obvious that
he was enjoying it all and that his family would envy his situation in
the middle of a wartime winter:

"I'm having a simply marvellous time out here. After a lot of
wangling, I have managed to get my own aeroplane and sometimes
fly as much as 1,000 miles in a day. I have just spent a weekend up
in Washington where I stayed with some wealthy Americans. Some
of the girls out here are terrific! You've no idea. I seem to meet so
many people I can't keep up with them all. At the moment I am back
in Alabama. It's almost too warm to wear a tunic and the sunshine is
lovely. Tomorrow I am going down to Orlando in Florida and the
next day I have to go to Gulviston near Palm Beach. Next week
I hope to fly across to California to visit a gunnery school near Los
Angeles. I hope to spend a couple of days in Hollywood, so watch
the local scandal columns. I might marry a film star yet. My job here
consists mainly of visiting the different fighter-training units and
squadrons and giving lectures and flying with the pilots. It is all most
interesting. I'm getting quite well-known here already and have had
terrific write-ups all over the country. I have also broadcast twice,
and have been asked to do it a third time."

One of his visits was to the US Army Air Corps base at Clewiston
where embryonic RAF and Commonwealth pilots were receiving their
flying training. One young British pilot on whom Mac made a great
impression was Cadet Pilot Colin Downes (see pages 11-12).

Mac also visited Craig Field at Selma in Alabama, where Cadet
Pilot Alan Thomsett was undertaking flying training:

"Mac arrived to spend a few days at the airfield. First of all, he
lectured to the RAF and USAAC Cadets shortly before they were to
receive their 'wings'. The whole tenor of his talk was grim with the
likelihood of death for many of his listeners, and illustrated the real
savagery of war. This done, he then disappeared by air without
advising anyone of his intentions, not even his American hosts. It
was felt there was a good party somewhere, possibly in Washington.
When he returned, he and the Chief USAAC Instructor staged a
mock dogfight over the airfield for the benefit of the pupil cadet
pilots. Mac [flying a P-36 Mohawk] completely out-manouvred and
out-fought the American [in an AT6A Texan] to the delight of the
RAF Cadets. Prior to landing, he opened the cockpit canopy, flew
low down the runway with his one good arm held up, clear of all

controls, at the same time executing a slow roll. Certainly an extraordinary man and pilot."

Christmas was spent in Washington although being up north had its disadvantages:

"I'm just on my way back from Washington where I spent Christmas with the sister of the American Ambassador to Sweden. She has three sons and a daughter, so we all had great fun. I wish Muriel was over here. I miss her very much sometimes. I have been 'weathered-in' at Richmond for the last three days and this morning I took off only to find that my battery was flat and that I couldn't retract my wheels, let alone work my radio or change the pitch on my airscrew. Now I'm here for a fourth night and am getting pretty fed up."

With the New Year, he found himself attached to 1st Gunnery Group at Eglin Field in Florida. He was making a very good impression and had earned himself added recognition as this letter from the Southern Bell Telephone & Telegraph Company in Atlanta bears out:

"So many of our people have commented with great enthusiasm about your talk to them Monday that I could not refrain from letting you know how much it was appreciated. Everyone present came away with a new respect for England and the RAF. All of us felt as if we had had a close-up of war as it is fought today and achieved a new realisation of our responsibility to the men who are doing the fighting."

Hal S. Dumas. President

Mac was getting into his stride lecturing and was enjoying this aspect of his work. But the old urge to fly operationally was beginning to be felt. His final letter home from America was on 18 January:

"I am still enjoying myself immensely and shall be sorry in many ways when I have to come home. I've now flown practically every type of American fighter, including the Lightning, Thunderbolt, Kittyhawk, Tomahawk, Mohawk and several others. This week I am trying to organise a trip to California, Texas and Arizona, giving lectures as I go. I actually enjoy lecturing as I don't feel at all self-conscious now. I am beginning to feel the old longing to get another squadron and go on ops again. Everything is so peaceful over here, you'd never know there was a war on. The workers go on strike and everyone shoots a line about rationing, but so far it's made very little difference. Most of these Yanks are extremely hospitable. The war will certainly bring our two countries closer together and let us see each other's point of view."

It was in February that James at last got his trip 'out West', flying his Mohawk from Florida to Arkansas, through Oklahoma to Dallas in Texas. On 18 February, while flying from Fort Stockton to El Paso, he had to force-land in the desert, having run out of fuel. He refilled his tanks from an oil pipeline! At Mesa in Arizona, he put on an aerobatic display for the pupils of the flying school there on their graduation day, and then flew on to California. He enjoyed three days there and met the stars in Hollywood, being photographed with Orson Welles and Joan Fontaine. Mac benefited from the contacts he made in America. For example, Mr H.G.Turner of the Southern Bell Telephone Company and his family had entertained Mac when he stayed in Atlanta. They proceeded to send the MacLachlan family presents of chocolate and clothes such as could not be obtained in wartime Britain.

On 9 March, Mac set off home; not by sea this time, but by air. He flew all the way. First to Canada in a Lodestar (CF-TDE), where he spent eight days with Ferry Command in Montreal flying B-25 Mitchells – on one occasion under a railway bridge as he flew it back from Quebec! From Montreal he flew to Greenland on the first leg of his journey home, piloting an RAF Mitchell (FR170). En route, he was asked to carry out a search for a missing Hudson, which had crashed onto a frozen lake. One man was seen on the River Hamilton. The Mitchell landed at Goose Bay before flying on to Bluie West in Greenland. The next day Mac and his crew set out for Reykjavik in Iceland, bad weather delaying the final leg, but eventually, on 3 April, they safely reached Prestwick.

Between arriving home and his next posting, Mac visited old friends and old haunts: to Duxford to see the AFDU contingent there, to Lympne where No.1 Squadron was now stationed, to Ibsley to see his brother Gordon, and to Hunsdon to see the night-fighter ace Sqn Ldr John Cunningham. Mac may have wanted another squadron, but this was denied him. Instead, on 15 April, he was posted back to the Air Fighting Development Unit, which was now stationed at RAF Wittering.

CHAPTER XI

THE END OF THE BEGINNING – BUT REALLY JUST THE BEGINNING OF THINGS . . .

Mac rejoined the Air Fighting Development Unit on 15 April and was attached for flying duties. He had only been with them for four days and had just attended a conference at Farnborough with the CO, Wg Cdr E.S. Smith AFC, concerning the Hawker Typhoon, when the family was hit by a tragedy. He wrote to mother on 19 April:

> "I have just heard from Muriel that Baked is missing. I expect that by now you have had official notification. I am going down to Ibsley [No.616 Squadron's base] as soon as possible to find out the details and see what chance there is of him being OK. I will look after his things and come and see you as soon as possible. I don't know any details, but I should imagine there is a fair chance of him being picked up, as both the German and our own Air Sea Rescue services are pretty good. I know you won't let it get you down too much, mother darling."

They heard nothing and it became obvious that Gordon was not just missing, but probably dead. In fact, on the afternoon of 16 April he had been shot down over Brest, while escorting USAF B-24 bombers over the French port. The squadron became involved in a combat with FW190s from 1 Staffel of JG2, Uffz Erich Henning claiming a Spitfire at 1345, about 20 miles north of Brest, followed a minute later by Hptm Jürgen Heppe claiming a second just south-west of Plouguerneau. The latter was probably Gordon's aircraft (BS245), which was seen to go down, but no one had seen him bale out. No.616 Squadron lost not only its longest serving pilot in this action (Gordon), but also its CO, Sqn Ldr Pip Lefevre DFC, who survived, evaded capture and eventually returned to the UK via Gibraltar. However, Gordon was killed; his body was recovered by the Germans and was buried at Plouguerneau on the north coast of Brittany, 15 miles from Brest. This gave Mac another cause for seeking revenge and another reason to hit back at the Luftwaffe.

It was on 19 April that Mac began trials on the Mustang IA fighter (FD442), acquired by the AFDU for evaluation. Increasingly, it became the aircraft of his choice. Powered by an Allison V engine, it could reach a ceiling of 32,000 feet and a speed of 390mph, though Mac claimed to have reached only 375mph. However, it was believed to be the fastest low-level fighter at that time. It was armed with four 20 mm cannon, so it matched the 'punch' of his old Hurricane II but was much faster. Occasionally, he flew the Mustang X (AM203), which was powered by a Rolls-Royce Merlin engine. From time to time he was affiliated to squadrons equipped with Mustangs – Nos.2 and 4, both Army Co-operation units – and practiced dogfights with their pilots. Increasingly however, just testing the aircraft began to pall. Mac yearned for action and he devised a tactic for using these powerful aircraft. He proposed to penetrate the German fighter defence belt and get into those areas where Allied fighters had not been seen before in broad daylight and at low altitude. He went to great pains to perfect low-level navigation by hours of practice flying around England at treetop height.

In the meantime, he paid a visit to his old school for the grand finale of a local 'Wings For Victory' week. The village had aimed to reach a total of £5,000, which would have been enough to buy a Spitfire. Monkton Combe School pledged £1,000 of this total. Those who attended remember very clearly the visit of this almost god-like hero-figure. The school magazine described the events of 29 May as follows:

'A large number of parents and friends were here by twelve o'clock when Squadron Leader MacLachlan DFC opened the proceedings. In his speech he stressed the fact that whenever our armies had not been victorious in this war it was solely because they had not possessed adequate air support. He said that the RAF now had crews to fly the planes, and it was up to us to give them planes to fly. His words were obviously taken to heart, for the selling centre was busy the whole day, and indeed, there was often a long queue of people waiting to invest their money . . . Mr Anderton arranged an exhibition of RAF instruments in the old hall; this included a rubber dinghy which Squadron Leader MacLachlan demonstrated on the swimming pool . . . At the end of the day we were thrilled to hear that we had even exceeded £5,000 and had reached a total of £6,000.'

The article failed to mention that on the previous evening an Oxford

(BG549), piloted by Mac, had 'beaten up' Monkton Combe!

After much pestering of the authorities, a reluctant Fighter Command gave Mac permission to carry out a solo 'Ranger' operation over Occupied France in the Mustang (FD442), and, on 4 June, he took off from RAF Lympne in Kent, heading for Beauvais and Orleans. It was not a great success as his logbook records: 'Met two FW190s behind Le Tréport, evaded them, lost myself, and returned owing to unsuitable weather.'

Rearward vision was limited by the Mustang's construction and to have carried on into France with German fighters being able to approach him without being seen would have been courting disaster. On returning to Wittering, Mac began to work on camouflaging the Mustang, and had it painted a dark green to blend with the French countryside. On 8 June, he attempted another Ranger sortie but had to turn back owing to fog. He needed help and encouragement and discussed the problems with recently arrived fellow-AFDU pilot Flt Lt Geoffrey Page; he was another recovering from the scars of battle, having been shot down in flames during the Battle of Britain, suffering severe burns to his face and hands. He, like Mac, had determined on a mission of vengeance – one German for every operation he had had to undergo on his hands and face. Page was keen to have a go himself, which delighted Mac:

> "So you think it's a good idea too, eh? Thank God someone else thinks so. Nothing but opposition from everyone ever since I started. Two Mustangs! That's the answer to it. Must get another aircraft, but come and look at the maps first."

Having gained permission to expand the idea, a second Mustang (AM107) was made available and they began to practice together. Page wrote:

> "Hours of practice flying had to be devoted to split-second teamwork at zero feet. A standard had to be reached so that each of us knew automatically how the other would react under different circumstances. Mac found that his one arm was fully occupied flying the aeroplane and navigating without adding the push buttons and transmitting switch of a VHF radio set. After . . . training and planning we at last felt we were ready to undertake our unique task. It now remained for the right weather conditions to prevail over the route. Flying as we would be, just skimming over the rippling corn in the French fields, any prey that might be around would be flying above us. To assist in spotting the quarry, a complete cloud layer at about 3,000 feet was desirable; this helped to silhouette the enemy aircraft even at great distances. The visibility must be good for

obvious reasons and little or no wind blowing. A strong wind would add navigational difficulties and probably bumpy conditions, causing added fatigue on what was already a tiring enough flight. Putting a toothbrush, razor and stout pair of walking shoes (it was a long walk home from where we were going) into our aircraft, we took off on 27 June for Lympne airfield on the south coast. There we would remain until news came through that our weather requirements were fulfilled. It was also necessary to arrange for the Typhoon fighter-bombers to carry out their diversionary procedures."

Mac had already seen to this and had requested No.1 Squadron to assist. As a result, four Typhoons were tasked to carry out this operation. On 29 June, weather conditions were suitable. Page recalled that at 0855 he was told that his aircraft was ready:

"A voice behind me suddenly called, 'All set?' My tense nerves jumped in surprise. Turning, I found Mac grinning at me. His warm personality had a cheering effect on my depressed spirits, and temporarily I cheered up. 'Let's get cracking.' Saying this, he juggled with the claw-like mechanism that was attached to the end of his artificial left arm. 'Fine bloody pair we are,' I thought, 'going off to tackle the enemy with only one good hand between the two of us."

They headed for the Luftwaffe night-fighter airfields south of Paris. Five miles from the French coast the Typhoons turned north and carried out a diversionary attack on shipping off Boulogne, while the two Mustangs crossed the coast at Criel and flew to Beauvais, then turned south and crossed the Seine on a course for Rambouillet. Over a wood just to the north-west of that town, they sighted three training aircraft at 2,000 feet in line abreast. Page continued:

"All of a sudden there they were! Three enemy aircraft flying in close formation, 1,500 feet above and ten miles ahead. Apart from the initial involuntary gasp of astonishment and delight at seeing the culmination of weeks of hard work and planning, there was little time to appreciate the beauties and the grimness of the moment . . . A crackle of gunfire ripped out over the peaceful woods beneath and the port aircraft burst into flames from Mac's withering blast. Fascinated, I watched our dying enemy fly along in a flaming mass of steel, wood and fabric, and dive in a seemingly slow and dignified manner into a house on the edge of the ageless forest.

Then the game of fox and geese was on with a vengeance as we endeavoured to destroy the remaining two aircraft before the enemy fighters took off to intercept our raid. Soon we were able to send them on the same journey that their companion had taken a few minutes previously, and we continued on our way southward and further away from home. Literally moments later we sighted another aircraft and Mac's unleashed Mustang leaped into the attack with his four cannons spitting fire. Strikes appeared over the unfortunate victim and he dived steeply to earth [near Limours]. It was my privilege to finish him off on the way down and the wreckage was strewn over a large field."

Although originally thought to have been Henschel 126s, their victims were in fact FW56As from JG105, a Fighter Training Gruppe. Two were totally destroyed with the loss of both pilots, Gfr [Corporal] Walter Seliger in aircraft 'No.51' (WkNr.1868) and Gfr Kurt Prager in 'No.8' (WrkNr.2438); a third aircraft (WrkNr.907) crashed and was written off; with the pilot, Gfr Alois Erdl, wounded. The fourth machine, flown by Gfr Gotz-Gerd Kuhn, was able to land safely, although damaged. Page's account continued:

"Onwards we flew to Bretigny where greater satisfaction awaited our blood lust. German night fighters [*sic*] were carrying out their final checks . . . Two of them were preparing to land on their base as we closed in behind . . ."

Mac takes up the story:

"We had the luck to see two Ju88s going in to land. One actually had its wheels down as we both went in to attack. I hit it and Flt Lt Page finished it off. It landed all right but not in the way the Hun crew had expected. Then I turned my attention immediately to the second Ju88 which was about 100 feet up; in a matter of seconds it had also crashed onto the airfield . . ."

According to Mac's report, the first Ju88 he attacked had what he thought was the number '78' painted on the tail (but was probably '18') and was an aircraft from IV/KG6, a training unit. The other aircraft was also from IV/KG6, and it crashed near Bretigny, killing Uffz Karl Brocks and Gfr Gerhard Zimmermann. Page added:

"Needless to say, every flak gun around the airfield had witnessed the fate of their countrymen and all hell was let loose as we weaved our way across the centre of the airfield. But it was our day and we slipped through the stream of innocent looking orange balls that rose lazily from the ground in our direction. Joining up together we set course northwards for England."

They crossed the enemy coast about ten miles south-west of Dieppe and the English coast between Brighton and Newhaven at about 1,000 feet. They landed at Tangmere at 1125. The attacks were recorded on the camera-guns of the Mustangs and they made impressive photo-graphs in the newspapers, which again had their imaginations caught by the success of the two pilots. Mac wrote home soon afterwards:

> "Just a note to let you know my day ops are safely over and old Baked is more or less avenged – though he was worth more than the ten Germans I killed yesterday. The whole trip worked perfectly – an answer to many prayers, I'm sure. You have no doubt seen the account in to-day's papers, so I will not bother to repeat the story. I got 3¹/₂ destroyed, three of them were on fire and no one baled out. I think I shall get a bar to my DSO, but don't tell anyone in case I don't. I hope to get home soon."

In point of fact, for their achievement on this mission, Mac was given a second Bar to his DFC (see Appendix III) and Page was awarded the DFC.

It was inevitable that they would try once again. They waited impatiently for the weather conditions to allow them to fly their next mission. In the meantime, Mac looked up his former No.88 Squadron air gunner, Flg Off Les Davies, who was now piloting Mosquito night fighters with 96 Squadron based at West Malling:

> "Mac arrived at West Malling in his black and dark green Mustang and asked me to join him and Flt Lt Geoffrey Page in a low-flying unit. I said I would be delighted but Mac was killed shortly after."

On 15 July, Mac and Geoff Page flew down to Tangmere, which was to be their base of operations. Page describes what happened on this Ranger, flown on 18 July:

> "At 1400 hrs we once again set out with a Typhoon escort, but crossing in over the French coast near Dieppe, Mac must have collected some machine gun fire. His aircraft climbed steeply from our treetop height, and at 1000 ft his canopy opened. He presumably changed his mind about baling out, for the aircraft proceeded in a glide towards a small field. His approach speed was too fast, and the Mustang (FD442) first touched the ground three-quarters of the way across the field, with retracted wheels. Still moving rapidly, it ploughed into an orchard shedding its wings before it came to rest as a battered, dust-clouded wreck. I orbited the crash several times at a low height, but no sign of life emerged from the wreckage. For an instant I contemplated trying to land in the field to come to Mac's aid, but judgement ruled out the possibility of landing, wheels down, in such a confined area. Reluctantly I dived at the scene of the crash to register some camera-gun photographs, and heartbrokenly headed for home."

The Operations Record Book provides a few more details:

> '. . . black smoke was seen [by Flt Lt Page] to be coming from Sqn
> Ldr MacLachlan's engine . . . he then attempted to crash-land in a
> small field near a wood . . . the aircraft overshot the field and entered
> a wood, tearing both wings and tail off. Flt Lt Page did not see Sqn
> Ldr MacLachlan get out. He states that the cockpit appeared to be
> badly damaged. No enemy aircraft were observed, so the accident
> may have been due to small arms fire or to technical failure.'

Small-arms fire seems to have been the reason for the crash of the
Mustang at La Croix Godey in Normandy. Mac did survive the crash,
but the rumours that he managed to get out of the cockpit, evade
capture and join the Resistance before being captured by the Gestapo
and shot, are untrue. The official version is that the crash resulted in
severe head injuries, and that Mac was taken to Field Hospital No.711
at Pont-l'Évêque with a fractured skull. On 31 July, he died as a result
of those head injuries and was buried in Grave 4, Zone 7 at Pont-
l'Évêque Communal Cemetery. French civilian Monsieur Huet and his
son attended the funeral, which was conducted by a German priest.
They took a photograph of the grave, covered with flowers placed there
by French civilians. A wooden plaque was also put on the grave, with
the words 'He died that France might live', but this was quickly
removed.

Mac's grave is still there, tended by the Commonwealth War Graves
Commission, along with the graves of two parachutists and another
airman. On the tombstone are the words:

In proud and loving memory of our dear Jay.
Death is swallowed up in victory.

It was the end for the Happy Warrior, but really just the beginning of
things . . .

174

APPENDIX I

RADIO BROADCAST
BY NBC'S ROBERT ST JOHN, 23 JULY 1943

Last Friday I ran across this little item on the News Ticker: 'London, July 22nd. Squadron Leader J.A.F. MacLachlan, RAF pilot, was reported today to be missing.' That was all. I threw it into the waste basket. And then I suddenly realized – I suddenly thought – Why, that's Mac! One-armed Mac! My old friend Mac MacLachlan! I met him over in London last year. He's only 23-years-old [*sic*] but he's a giant of a young fellow – six feet three in his stocking feet, with blonde hair and blue eyes and a closely-cropped little moustache. But the one thing you notice about him is his eagerness. His fresh, vibrant interest in life.

He took part in that greatest air battle of all history – the Battle of Britain – a battle which tested the nerves and guts of those youngsters in the RAF as no aerial combat since has ever done. Then, they sent Mac down to Malta to help defend that atom of the Mediterranean. In those days, the odds were all against the boys of the RAF. The enemy had superiority in the sky over Malta. The British fliers flew and flew and flew until they actually went to sleep at their controls. It was in the Battle of Malta that Mac "came a cropper", as he says. Nazi bullets shot-away most of his left arm. He was in a hospital for a long time. Lying flat on your back on a bed, day after day, is bad enough for anyone, but for a boy in his early twenties . . . restless . . . impatient . . . eager for battle, for a boy who's been jousting with death in the sky for months and months. Well, it was just about too much for Mac to stand. And all the while he was obsessed with that black thought, that now his flying days were over. But he made a vow, lying there in a hospital bed, that he would get back into the air again.

And so he set to on an invention, a robot hand with some mechanical fingers, with which he'd be able to work on controls. And so he did finally get back into a cockpit again, back into the sky, back into action. Back at an English air base Mac met up with a young Czech flier – slender, fair-haired Karel Kuttelwascher – Old Kut, as the boys called him. The two of them worked out a new technique in fighting with planes. Then, it was something entirely new. Today it's an accepted part of RAF operations and it has a name

– night intruder fighting. It was Mac and Old Kut who originated the technique. They'd stand-by, at their airdrome, somewhere in England, all night, waiting for coastal watchers to flash them [sic] the word that the Luftwaffe was on its way across the Channel to give Britain another night bombing. As soon as they heard the Nazi planes were over Britain, Mac and Old Kut would jump into their fighters, and streak off for Europe. They became experts at guessing (from the general direction the Germans had come) what French airports they were based on. In the dark of the night, they'd hover over the enemy base, waiting for that moment when the roar of the German bombers would split the air and drown-out the noise of their single engines. And then – lights would go on, down on the enemy airfield, flare-path lights, to guide the Nazi bombers to a landing.

That was the big moment. The German fliers would be off their guard. Their bomb racks were empty. They might also be all out of ammunition for their guns. Their night's mission was over. They were home now, about to land on their own airports. In another few minutes they'd be drinking mugs of beer. They were off their guard, relaxed, unprepared to do combat with two little British Hurricanes, which would suddenly swoop down from the clouds, with the cannon and machine-guns roaring. Mac and Old Kut got dozens [sic] of big enemy bombers by their new technique – stalking enemy planes – night intruder fighting. Mac did quite well with his robot-arm, with the mechanical fingers. He was equally as good as Old Kut. They were rivals. I remember how, day after day, their box-score would appear in the London papers. The British people followed the box-score with as much relish as we might the score of an especially exciting World Series baseball competition. Headline-writers nicknamed them "The Killers Who Stalk by Night."

And then Mac became a pioneer in a new aerial technique – the shooting-up of railroad trains in enemy occupied Europe. He started playing that game one night when he guessed wrong on which airport the Nazis were using that night. He stooged around in the dark until he was almost out of fuel, and had to start home. But he hated to go back with all that unused ammunition. He knew what the boys in the groundcrews would say, when they looked and saw that the covers they'd put over the muzzles of his guns hadn't been shot-off. And so, on the way home, he kept a sharp lookout for the smoke and the sparks from railroad locomotives. Each time he spotted a train he went into a dive and blasted at the engine and cars with his cannon and machine-guns. Generally, the locomotives blew up and the trains were de-railed.

I'll never forget the time the BBC finally, after days and days of begging, got Mac to agree to come to London and do a broadcast for them. He was supposed to tell about his experiences – he was supposed to tell all about shooting up trains and shooting down enemy bombers. We thought it was going to be an exciting broadcast of personal experiences. Mac began something like this: "There really isn't anything to this intruding. If you're lucky – it's a piece of cake. My squadron has blown up 17 locomotives for certain and in the last few weeks we've shot down 11 enemy bombers. Of course, the lion's share of this total goes to my Czech Flight Commander Kuttelwascher. . . ." On and on he went, talking with boyish enthusiasm about the exploits of his pal, Old Kut, but with hardly a word about his own equally-daring and reckless battles in the sky. That was Mac – Mac the mere boy of a flier.

Once I got Mac in a really talkative mood and asked him about the dangers and hazards of that night offensive work. I asked him how he saw in the pitch-dark. Well, here's his answer, as well as I can remember it. He laughed. His boyish blue eyes twinkled and then he said: "I'm afraid the dangers and hazards of the job have been, well, rather a little exaggerated. We intruder pilots are not the cat-eyed, carrot-eating killers some people make us out to be. I don't eat any more carrots than anyone else, even if they are supposed to help you see at night. It's just this . . . most of us night-fighters are lazy. We're too fond of our mornings in bed to want to go flying around in the daytime. Personally, sleeping in the sun appeals to me infinitely more than chasing ME109s at 30,000 feet. Give me a moonlight night and my old Hurricane, and you can have your Spitfires and the dawn patrol. We have no formation flying to worry about and no bomber escorts. In fact, we have nothing to do but to amuse ourselves, once we've crossed the French coast. Of course we do have to keep our eyes peeled the whole time. And we have to glance occasionally at the compass and the clock. I get a big thrill out of pressing the button-trigger and seeing a cluster of flashes appear on the enemy bomber – and then a spurt of dark red flame – and then the whole thing seems to fold-up and fall out of the sky, burning beautifully." Boys like Mac seem to get a certain weird, poetic pleasure out of their work. He wasn't the first pilot who used adjectives out of literature to describe what he called "the sheer beauty" of dipping down in the moonlight, spotting the white plume of smoke from a railroad train against the dark back-drop of the sky, giving the train a few short bursts from cannon and machine-guns, watching pin-points of crimson quickly turn into globes of deep red and then a whole sheet of flame envelop the whole train.

Well, anyway, not long ago they gave one-armed Mac a Mustang – one of those lightning-fast American strafing planes. He took it and went off to Paris. In ten minutes he [sic] shot down six Nazi planes. But he didn't come home from the next trip and now the British Air Ministry has put out a one-sentence announcement – Squadron Leader James Archibald Findlay MacLachlan is reported missing in action. He got revenge for the way they shot off his arm. But now, well there's always a hope that Mac got to earth safely. He may be in a prison camp, or . . . it's more likely . . . that he may be in hiding, somewhere around Paris, waiting for the day when Allied troops will storm the French capital and he can take part in the battle. That is the saga of one-armed Mac, hero of the Royal Air Force.

APPENDIX II

COMBAT CLAIMS

No.88 Squadron, France 1940

13 June 1940	Battle L5393	2 Bf109s claimed 'possibly' damaged

No.73 Squadron, England 1940

7 October 1940	Hurricane V6676	Bf109 damaged

No.261 Squadron, Malta 1941

9 January 1941	Hurricane V7474	2 Mc200s
19 January 1941	Hurricane V7546	2 Ju87s, CR42 probable
	Hurricane V7545	Z506B, Ju87
8-9 February 1941 (night)	Hurricane V7671	He111, Ju88

No.1 Squadron, England 1942

26-27 April 1942 (night)	Hurricane BE215/JX-I	Do217, Do217 damaged
4-5 May 1942 (night)	Hurricane BD983/JX-Q	2 Ju88s
3-4 June 1942	Hurricane BD983/JX-Q	2 Do217s, 2 Do217s damaged

AFDU, England 1943

29 June 1943	Mustang FD442	2 FW56As, Ju88, plus Ju88 shared

Total: $16^{1}/_{2}$ aircraft destroyed, 1 probable, 4 damaged, 2 possibly damaged, 9 locomotives damaged/destroyed, 1 tug damaged.

APPENDIX III

AWARDS

AWARD OF DFC – No.88 SQUADRON
Gazetted 16 July 1940 – No Citation

AWARD OF THE BAR TO THE DFC – No.261 SQUADRON
Gazetted 11 February 1941

During intensive operations one day in January 1941 this officer destroyed four and possibly five enemy aircraft. Ten days previously he destroyed two enemy aircraft, one of which he had pursued for many miles out to sea. Flight Lieutenant MacLachlan has set a fine example of courage, initiative and leadership.

AWARD OF THE DSO – No.1 SQUADRON
Gazetted 29 May 1942

During the early part of the war, this officer served in the Middle East where he destroyed eight enemy aircraft. Following an injury, his left arm was amputated, but, within a few weeks, he was flying again. Since his return to England, Squadron Leader MacLachlan has trained intensively in night flying operations and has achieved much success. One night in April 1942, he shot down a Dornier 217 over northern France and damaged another near an enemy aerodrome. One night in May 1942, near Dinard, he destroyed a Dornier 217 and a few minutes later he shot down a Heinkel 111. The latter burst into flames on impact with the ground, causing a fire which could be observed from a distance of ten miles. Squadron Leader MacLachlan has attacked goods trains, trucks and barges with damaging effect. He is a gallant and skilful pilot whose example is an inspiration to all pilots.

AWARD OF SECOND BAR TO DFC
(and of DFC to Flt Lt A.G. Page) – AFDU
Gazetted 30 July 1943

Recently, these officers in the course of an operation over enemy occupied territory, shot down six enemy aircraft, three of which were destroyed by Squadron Leader MacLachlan and two by Flight Lieutenant Page, while the other was destroyed jointly. The operation, which was planned by Squadron Leader MacLachlan, was brilliantly executed and the successes were worthily earned.

AWARD OF THE CZECH MILITARY CROSS –
No.1 SQUADRON
Announced 30 July 1942

I write this to inform you that our Ministry of National Defence has the intention of submitting to the President of the Czech Republic, the Czech Military Cross 1939 to be conferred upon S/L J.A.F. MacLachlan DSO DFC.

NB: The authors were not only privileged to see the collection of medals but to actually handle them – a moving and poignant experience.

APPENDIX IV

FROM THE LOGBOOK

A selection of entries to be read across the page.

YEAR 1941		AIRCRAFT		PILOT, OR 1ST PILOT	2ND PILOT, PUPIL OR PASSENGER	DUTY (INCLUDING RESULTS AND REMARK
MONTH	DATE	Type	No.			
—	—	—	—	—	—	—— TOTALS BROUGHT FORWA
UARY	8	HURRICANE	V 7474	SELF	SOLO	SCRAMBLE AND PATROL "HOT X AT 10,000 FT. NO INTERCEPT
	9	"	"	"	"	SCRAMBLE TO 22,000 FT. SHOT DOWN TWO "MACCHI 200s". ON OVER ST PAUL'S BAY, AND ONE 25 MILES N. OF NAATA. BOTH WERE CONFIRMED.

	19	HURRICANE	V 7540	"	SOLO	SCRAMBLE AND PATROL "HOT DOG" AT 12,000 FT. SHOT DO TWO JU 87s (ONE IN FLAMES AND GOT ONE POSSIBLE C.R. 4 MY AIRCRAFT WAS HIT SEVERE TIMES BY MACHINE GUN FIRE
"	"	"	V 7545	"	"	SCRAMBLE AND PATROL SEA T MILES N. OF CYCLONE. SHOT DOW ONE CANT Z 600 B IN FLAMES.
"	"	"	"	"	"	SCRAMBLE AND PATROL OVER S 15 MILES N.E. OF "HOT-DOG". N INTERCEPTION.

GRAND TOTAL [Cols. (1) to (10)]

......812...... Hrs. ....25...... Mins.

TOTALS CARRIED FORWAR

YEAR 1941		AIRCRAFT		PILOT, OR 1ST PILOT	2ND PILOT, PUPIL OR PASSENGER	DUTY (INCLUDING RESULTS AND REMAR
MONTH	DATE	Type	No.			
—	—	—	—	—	—	—— TOTALS BROUGHT FORWA
NUARY	19	HURRICANE	V 7545	SELF	SOLO	SCRAMBLE AND PATROL "HOT-D AT 17,000 FT. SHOT DOWN ONE JU 88 WHICH CRASHED IN SEA 100 YDS OFF ZONKOR POINT. O OF CREW BAILED OUT.

SINGLE-ENGINE AIRCRAFT				MULTI-ENGINE AIRCRAFT						PASS-ENGER	INSTR/CLOUD FLYING [incl. in cols. (1) to (10)]	
DAY		NIGHT		DAY			NIGHT					
	PILOT	DUAL	PILOT	DUAL	1ST PILOT	2ND PILOT	DUAL	1ST PILOT	2ND PILOT		DUAL	PILOT
(1)	(2)	(3)	(4)	(5)	(6)	(7)	(8)	(9)	(10)	(11)	(12)	(13)
25	669·50 ·30	1·25	55·35	·45		23·50				93·25	11·15	4·00
			MACCHI 200 Ⓦ CONFIRMED.									
	·45		MACCHI 200 Ⓦ CONFIRMED.									

				Ju 87 ☒ CONFIRMED								
					Sᵍᵗ KELSEY SHOT DOWN.							
	·30			Ju 87 ☒ CONFIRMED								
	·30		CANT Z506B Ⓦ CONFIRMED									
	·15		CR 42 Ⓦ POSSIBLE									
·25 (1)	677·45 (2)	1·25 (3)	55·35 (4)	·45 (5)	(6)	23·50 (7)	(8)	(9)	(10)	93·25 (11)	11·15 (12)	4·00 (13)

SINGLE-ENGINE AIRCRAFT				MULTI-ENGINE AIRCRAFT						PASS-ENGER	INSTR/CLOUD FLYING [incl. in cols. (1) to (10)]	
DAY		NIGHT		DAY			NIGHT					
	PILOT	DUAL	PILOT	DUAL	1ST PILOT	2ND PILOT	DUAL	1ST PILOT	2ND PILOT		DUAL	PILOT
(1)	(2)	(3)	(4)	(5)	(6)	(7)	(8)	(9)	(10)	(11)	(12)	(13)
25	677·45	1·25	55·35	·45		23·50				93·25	11·15	4·00
	·25		Ju 88 ☒ CONFIRMED.									

		Type	No.		Pilot, or 1st Pilot	2nd Pilot, Pupil or Passenger	Duty (Including Results and Rema...)
"	"	MAGISTER	N5428	"		P.O. ELIOT	FROM TA-KALI TO LUCA.
"	"	"	"	"		"	FROM LUCA TO TA-KALI. LOW FLYING TO GOZO &c.
"	6	HURRICANE	V7102	"		SOLO	SCRAMBLE TO CLOUD BASE. NO INTERCEPTION.
"	7	"	V7671	"		"	NIGHT SCRAMBLE TO 17,000 FT. SHOT DOWN ONE JU 88 IN SEA 10 MILES SOUTH OF FILFLA I°. CONFIRMED BY M.R.

GRAND TOTAL [Cols. (1) to (10)]

...920...Hrs.......5.......Mins.

TOTALS CARRIED FORWA...

YEAR 1941		AIRCRAFT		PILOT, OR	2ND PILOT, PUPIL	DUTY
MONTH	DATE	Type	No.	1ST PILOT	OR PASSENGER	(INCLUDING RESULTS AND REMA...)
—	—	—	—	—	—	— TOTALS BROUGHT FORW...
FEBRUARY	8	HURRICANE	V7671	SELF	SOLO	NIGHT SCRAMBLE TO 16,00... SHOT DOWN ONE JU 88 IN SEA 2 MILES NORTH OF ... HARBOUR. CONFIRMED BY PO...

YEAR 1941		AIRCRAFT		PILOT, OR	2ND PILOT, PUPIL	DUTY
MONTH	DATE	Type	No.	1ST PILOT	OR PASSENGER	(INCLUDING RESULTS AND REM...)
—	—	—	—	—	—	— TOTALS BROUGHT FOR...
FEBRUARY	15	HURRICANE	P3330	SELF	SOLO	ENGINE TEST AND AEROBAT...
"	"	"	V7331	"	"	ENGINE TEST AND SCRAMBLE LANDED OWING TO OXYGEN FAIL...
"	16	"		"	"	SCRAMBLE AND PATROL AT 20,000 FT. WHILE ATTACKING ME 109 I WAS MYSELF SHOT IN THE LEFT ARM, AND HAD T... BAIL OUT. LANDED IN FIELD N... ZIETUN.

O.C. "A" FLIGHT   P/O

O.C. 261 SQUADRON.   S/LDR

SUMMARY FOR FEB:

261 SQDN   HURRICANE

·10												
·10												
·50												
·15												
Ju 88	1·30	卐	CONFIRMED									
25	687·25	1·25	57·50	·45		23·00					93·40	11·15	4·00
(1)	(2)	(3)	(4)	(5)	(6)	(7)	(8)	(9)	(10)	(11)	(12)	(13)

SINGLE-ENGINE AIRCRAFT			MULTI-ENGINE AIRCRAFT						PASS-ENGER	INSTR/CLOUD FLYING [incl. in cols. (1) to (10)]	
DAY	NIGHT		DAY			NIGHT					
PILOT	DUAL	PILOT	DUAL	1st PILOT	2nd PILOT	DUAL	1st PILOT	2nd PILOT		DUAL	PILOT
(2)	(3)	(4)	(5)	(6)	(7)	(8)	(9)	(10)	(11)	(12)	(13)
687·25	1·25	57·50	·45		23·00				93·40	11·15	4·00
Ju 88	1·15	卐	CONFIRMED.								

SINGLE-ENGINE AIRCRAFT			MULTI-ENGINE AIRCRAFT						PASS-ENGER	INSTR/CLOUD FLYING [incl. in cols. (1) to (10)]	
DAY	NIGHT		DAY			NIGHT					
PILOT	DUAL	PILOT	DUAL	1st PILOT	2nd PILOT	DUAL	1st PILOT	2nd PILOT		DUAL	PILOT
(2)	(3)	(4)	(5)	(6)	(7)	(8)	(9)	(10)	(11)	(12)	(13)
688·15	1·25	61·55	·45		23·00				93·40	11·15	4·00
·20											
·25											
·40	AND	7	MINUITS	BY	PARACHUTE.				🪂		
4·20		4·10									

"	"	"	"	"		"	WANSFORD TO SUTTON BRIDGE
"	"	"	"	"		"	SUTTON BRIDGE TO TANGMERE.
"	"	"	"	"		"	INTRUDER TO BRETIGNY, S.ᵗ ANDR
							AND EVEREUX. SHOT DOWN ONE 1
							AND DAMAGED ANOTHER. BOTH H
							JUST TAKEN OFF FROM EVEREUX

GRAND TOTAL [Cols. (1) to (10)]
...1235... Hrs ...25... Mins.

TOTALS CARRIED FORWA

30	"	"	"	"		"	INTRUDER TO EVEREUX, DREUX,
							ROUAN. BLEW UP TWO RAILWAY
							ENGINES AND SET FIRE TO TUG O
							SEINE.
"	"	"	"	"		"	TO NORTHOLT.

							NORTHOLT TO ABINGDON.
"	"	"	"	"		"	ABINGDON TO TANGMERE (PISSED
							A COOT)
"	2	"	"	"		"	TO OATLAND'S HILL
"	"	"	"	"		"	OATLAND'S HILL TO M.WALLOP
							AND RETURN.
"	"	MUSTANG I	AG.383	"		"	OATLAND'S HILL TO TANGMERE
							RETURN, ALSO AEROBATICS.
"	"	HURRICANE IIC	JX-1	"		"	OATLAND'S HILL TO TANGMERE
							ENGINE CUT SW. OF WORTHY D
							SO FORCED LANDED. KITE TURN
							UPSIDE DOWN & I WAS DUG OU
"	"	PROCTOR	R.N.	"		NAUTIC	WORTHY DOWN TO TANGMERE.
"	3	MASTER I	JX-Q	"		P.O. CHOWN.	TO WORTHY DOWN
"	"	"	"	"		"	WORTHY DOWN TO TANGMERE.

GRAND TOTAL [Cols. (1) to (10)]
...1250... Hrs ...20... Mins.

TOTALS CARRIED FORWAR

·15												
·50												
Do 217ᴇ	3·00	✹	CONFIRMED									
Do 217ᴇ		✹	DAMAGED.									
53·25	938·55	1·25	134·40	1·25	11·35	94·50				197·50	11·50	4·00
(1)	(2)	(3)	(4)	(5)	(6)	(7)	(8)	(9)	(10)	(11)	(12)	(13)

			🚂 DAMAGED.								
		3·00	🚂 DAMAGED.								
			⛴ DAMAGED.								
·25		·									

·20											
·20											
·50											
·15											
			🚗 SHAKEY DO!								
·20											
·20											
·20											
5 945·25	1·25	143·05	1·25	12·00	94·50				197·50	11·50	
(2)	(3)	(4)	(5)	(6)	(7)	(8)	(9)	(10)	(11)	(12)	

	4					INTRUDER TO RENNES AND DINA SHOT DOWN ONE Do 217 AND O HE III, BOTH IN FLAMES. ATTACK RAILWAY ENGINE WHICH BLEW UP. TO HENDON.

						INTRUDER TO JUVINCOURT. A/ BUT NO E/A SEEN. BLEW UP F RAILWAY ENGINES BETWEEN RI AND SOISSONS. FLEW BACK 1000 FT IN 9/10 SHIT. LANDED W. WEST MALLING TO TANGMERE.
	31					
						NIGHT FLYING TEST.
			J. MacLachlan Lt.			SUMMARY FOR MAY. HURRICANE 1942 MUSTANG No 1 SQUADRON. MOSQUITO TANGMERE. PROCTOR

GRAND TOTAL [Cols. (1) to (10)]

1289 Hrs 40 Mins.   TOTALS CARRIED FORWA

4						INTRUDER TO EVREUX, St ANDRÉ, S DREUX. SHOT DOWN TWO Do.217s & DAMAGED TWO OTHERS. INTENSE FLAK AND SEARCHLIGHTS. SAW OVER 20 HUNS WITH NAV LIGHTS ON.
5						NIGHT FLYING TEST
6	HURRICANE I	JX-L				TO READING.

GRAND TOTAL [Cols. (1) to (10)]

1302 Hrs 25 Mins.   TOTALS CARRIED FORWARD

YEAR 1943		AIRCRAFT		PILOT, OR 1ST PILOT	2ND PILOT, PUPIL OR PASSENGER	DUTY (INCLUDING RESULTS AND REM
MONTH	DATE	Type	No.			
—	—	—	—	—	—	TOTALS BROUGHT FORW
JUNE	29	MUSTANG IA	FD 442	SELF	SOLO	DAY RANGER PATROL TO B S.W. PARIS, & BRETIGNY. SHO 2 Hs 126's NEAR RAMBOU (ONE IN FLAMES). F/LT PAGE

He III 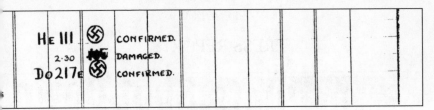 CONFIRMED.
2.30   DAMAGED.
Do 217E   CONFIRMED.

3.00   DAMAGED
  DAMAGED
  DAMAGED
  DAMAGED
.30
.25

966.10	1.25	159.55	1.25	12.30	94.60				197.50	11.50	6.00

Do 217E   DESTROYED
Do 217E 2.50   DAMAGED.
Do 217E   DESTROYED
Do 217E   DAMAGED.
.10
.20

969.15	1.26	169.35	1.25	12.30	94.50				197.50	11.50	4.00
(2)	(3)	(4)	(5)	(6)	(7)	(8)	(9)	(10)	(11)	(12)	(13)

SINGLE-ENGINE AIRCRAFT										FLYING (incl. in cols. (1) to (10))	
DAY		NIGHT		DAY			NIGHT			PASS-ENGER	
										DUAL	PILOT
DUAL	PILOT	DUAL	PILOT	DUAL	1ST PILOT	2ND PILOT	DUAL	1ST PILOT	2ND PILOT		
(1)	(2)	(3)	(4)	(5)	(6)	(7)	(8)	(9)	(10)	(11)	(12)	(13)
25	1376.15	1.25	187.00	1.25	84.05	97.40		2.05		226.25	11.00	8.15

Hs 126   DESTROYED
2.15   Hs 126   DESTROYED
Ju 88   DESTROYED

APPENDIX V

PRESS REPORTS

wo Pilots Shot Down Six in Ten Minutes

ONE HAS ONE ARM, THE OTHER JUST OUT AFTER 18 MONTHS IN HOSPITAL

TWO Fighter Command pilots yesterday morning shot down six enemy aircraft in ten minutes in three combats a few miles from Paris.

The pilots were one-armed Squadron-Ldr. J. A. F. MacLachlan, D.S.O., D.F.C. and Bar, the intruder ace, and Flt.-Lieut A. G. Page, who was shot down in the Battle of Britain in August, 1940, and badly burned, particularly about the hand.

For MacLachlan it was his first operational sortie since he returned from special duties in the United States. For Page it was his first operational flight after some

Page 2.—DAILY SKETCH, WEDNESDAY, APRIL 29, 1942

Squadron - Leader

One-armed DFC Gets New Hand–and Nazi

'Daily Sketch' Reporter DAVID HOLLOWAY

THERE were cheers in a little Putney factory yesterday when the managing director, Mr. Hugh Steeper, rushed out of his office and shouted, "'One-armed Jimmy's' done it."

For weeks the staff had worked to make an artificial arm and hand for Squadron-Leader J. F. D. Jimmy MacLachlan, D.F.C. and Bar, the ace Hurrica' pilot, so that he could have "another crack" at the Hun.

Now Jimmy has proved that he can fly and fight with one arm as

FAMOUS A FIGHTER

So'tonian Report Prisoner

The announcement dur[.] week-end that Squadron James A. F. MacLachlan, D.F.C., and two bars, the Southampton one-armed ace, who was reported mi[.] July, is a prisoner of war ceived with gratification many friends in the town.

"It had previously been that he was probably kill[.] his Mustang crashed into [.]ter being shot down

One - armed Squadron-Leader MacLachlan in hi[.] plane.

One-armed pilot kept his promise

HIT BY SHELL—BALED OUT—LOST ARM

So'ton R.A.F. Fighter Pilot Back in Fray!

BRITAIN'S one-armed fighter pilot, Flight-Lieut. James Archibald Findlay MacLachlan, D.F.C. and bar, is a Southampton man.

He is one of the four sons of Mrs. MacLachlan, of 53, Shaftesbury avenue, Highfield, who is now living with her sister at Hayward's Heath, Sussex.

Another son is also an R.A.F. pilot, one is in the Army in the Middle East, and the youngest is at school.

James MacLachlan, who is 24, attended King Edward VI School, Southampton, from 1928 to 1931. He was commissioned in the R.A.F. in 1937.

About six months ago, while in air combat over Malta, he was hit by a German cannon shell, which splintered his left arm. He baled out and landed safely.

His arm was so badly injured that it had to be amputated. It

Flight-Lieut. MacLachlan has shot down 12 enemy aircraft—six in the Battle of Britain last year, and six in raids n Malta. Four of his second batch of victims were destroyed in one day.

ESCAPES IN FRANCE

When war broke out he went to France with a bomber squadron of the Advanced Air Striking Force. He was twice shot down in operations in France.

One-Armed Pilot Strikes Again

SQUADRON-LEADER J. A. F. MACLACHLAN, the one-armed pilot, who led Fighter Command's top-scoring Hurricane Squadron on intruder operations, is blasting Nazi railway transport between Paris and the northern coast of France.

In Paris, flying alone up the Seine from Rouen

INDEX